Building a Better World with Our Information

The Future of Personal Information Management, Part 3

Synthesis Lectures on Information Concepts, Retrieval, and Services

Editor

Gary Marchionini, *University of North Carolina, Chapel Hill*

Synthesis Lectures on Information Concepts, Retrieval, and Services publishes short books on topics pertaining to information science and applications of technology to information discovery, production, distribution, and management. Potential topics include: data models, indexing theory and algorithms, classification, information architecture, information economics, privacy and identity, scholarly communication, bibliometrics and webometrics, personal information management, human information behavior, digital libraries, archives and preservation, cultural informatics, information retrieval evaluation, data fusion, relevance feedback, recommendation systems, question answering, natural language processing for retrieval, text summarization, multimedia retrieval, multilingual retrieval, and exploratory search.

Building a Better World with Our Information: The Future of Personal Information Management, Part 3
William Jones

Information Communication
Feicheng Ma

Social Media and Library Services
Lorri Mon

Analysis and Visualization of Citation Networks
Dangzhi Zhao and Andreas Strotmann

The Taxobook: Applications, Implementation, and Integration in Search: Part 3
Marjorie M.K. Hlava

The Taxobook: Principles and Practices of Building Taxonomies: Part 2
Marjorie M.K. Hlava

Measuring User Engagement
Mounia Lalmas, Heather O'Brien, and Elad Yom-Tov

Building a Better World with Our Information: The Future of Personal Information Management, Part 3
William Jones

ISBN: 978-3-031-01167-2 print
ISBN: 978-3-031-02295-1 ebook
ISBN: 978-3-031-03423-7 epub

DOI 10.1007/978-3-031-02295-1

A Publication in the Springer series
SYNTHESIS LECTURES ON INFORMATION CONCEPTS, RETRIEVAL, AND SERVICES #42
Series Editor: Gary Marchionini, University of North Carolina, Chapel Hill

Series ISSN 1947-945X Print 1947-9468 Electronic

Building a Better World with Our Information

The Future of Personal Information Management, Part 3

William Jones
University of Washington

SYNTHESIS LECTURES ON INFORMATION CONCEPTS, RETRIEVAL, AND SERVICES #42

ABSTRACT

Personal Information Management (PIM) is *the art of getting things done in our lives through information*. How do we—can we better—manage our information at home, at school, at work, at play and "@large" in a global community? How do we use information not only to know but also to represent, communicate and effect useful change in the world around us?

In the study of PIM, does the search for practical methods with practical impact lead to methods that are "massive open on-line"? Can the ancient practice of storytelling help us better to weave our fragmented information together? In the practice of PIM, how can our information best serve as "near knowledge"—close at hand and, through our information tools, serving in practical ways to extend the knowledge that's "in the head"? If attempts to multitask lead to ineffective, even dangerous, instances of task switching and divided attention, can better PIM help us to realize, instead, opportunities for "multi-goaling" where the same time and effort accomplishes not just one but several goals?

These and other questions are addressed in this third and final book to conclude the series on "The Future of Personal Information Management."

Part 1, "Our Information, Always and Forever," covered the fundamentals of PIM and then explored the seismic shift, already well underway, towards a world where our information is always at hand (thanks to our devices) and "forever" on the web.

Part 2, "Transforming Technologies to Manage Our Information," provided a more focused look at technologies for managing information. The opening chapter discussed "natural interface" technologies of input/output to free us from keyboard, screen and mouse. Successive chapters then explored technologies to save, search and structure our information. A concluding chapter introduced the possibility that we may see dramatic reductions in the "clerical tax" we pay as we work with our information.

Now in **Part 3, "Building a Better World with Our Information,"** focus shifts to the practical present and to the near future. Part 3 is in three chapters:

- **Group information management and the social fabric in PIM.** How do we preserve and promote our PIM practices as we interact with others at home, at work, at play and in wider, even global, communities? (Chapter 10).

- **Designing for PIM** in the development of tools and in the selection of teachable (learnable) "better practices" of PIM. (Chapter 11).

- **To each of us, our own** concludes with an exploration of the ways each of us, individually, can develop better practices for the management of our information in service of the lives we wish to live and towards a better world we all must share. (Chapter 12).

KEYWORDS

PIM, personal information management, information overload, information fragmentation, HCI, human-computer interaction, cognitive science, keeping found things found

For Oliver

Contents

Preface

This is Part 3, *Building a Better World with Our Information*, the final book in a series, "The Future of Personal Information Management". The series has been several years in the making.

Part 1 (2012), with its theme, "Our Information, Always and Forever," laid a foundation for the treatment of personal information management (PIM) in four chapters:

> **Chapter 1.** A new age of information. What PIM is (and isn't). A short history of PIM and its relationship to other fields. Metaphors that work well and not so well for the discussion of PIM. Our information "flows" as a liquid in communication to and from others. But increasingly it persists, as a "solid" on the Web. A home. We need roads to and from our home. But also walls…

> **Chapter 2.** The basics of PIM. The six senses in which information is personal combine to form a personal space of information (PSI). PIM is about minute-by-minute tactical decisions of keeping and finding. PIM also needs to be about longer-term meta-level strategies for maintaining and organizing, managing privacy and information flow, measuring and evaluating, and making sense of and using personal information.

> **Chapter 3.** Our information, always at hand. Through mobile devices, our physical and digital worlds meet—and sometimes collide. We're always connected but always on call. How to avoid the dangers of multitasking "busyness"? How to really get "real" things done and, in the process, how to preserve precious memories for a lifetime and beyond?

> **Chapter 4.** Our information, forever on the Web. Reading, writing, and making things happen on the Web. From vertical, monolithic, "do-everything" applications that fragment personal information to horizontal, PIM activity applications that work together toward a common unity of personal information. Going "Neolithic": How to live with, through, and on the Web. Our information on the web may outlive us, standing in reflection of and legacy for our lives.

Part 2, 2013, with its theme, "Transforming Technologies to Manage Our Information," explored basic enabling technologies of PIM in five chapters:

➢ **Chapter 5.** Technologies of input and output. Technologies in support of gesture, touch, voice, and even eye movements combine to support a more natural user interface (NUI). Technologies of output include glasses and "watch" watches. Output will also increasingly be animated with options to "zoom." Technologies combine to support a radically immersive experience of information in which the physical and digital combine in ways that will transform or experience of reality for good and bad.

➢ **Chapter 6.** Technologies to save our information. We can opt for "life logs" to record our experiences with increasing fidelity. What will we use these logs for? And what isn't recorded that should be?

➢ **Chapter 7.** Technologies to search our information. The potential for personalized search is enormous and mostly yet to be realized. Persistent searches, situated in our information landscape, will allow us to maintain a diversity of projects and areas of interest without a need to continually switch from one to another to handle incoming information.

➢ **Chapter 8.** Technologies to structure our information. Structure is key if we are to keep, find, and make effective use of our information. But how best to structure? And how best to share structured information—between the applications we use, with other people, and also with ourselves over time? What lessons can we draw from the failures and successes in web-based efforts to share structure?

➢ **Chapter 9.** PIM transformed and transforming: Stories from the past, present, and future. Part 2 concludes with comparison between Licklider's world of information in 1957 and our own world of information today. And then we consider what the world of information is likely to look like in 2057. Licklider estimated that he spent 85% of his "thinking time" in activities that were clerical and mechanical and might (someday) be delegated to the computer. What percentage of our own time is spent with the clerical and mechanical? What about in 2057?

Now in this final Part 3 of the series, with its theme, "Building a Better World with Our Information," focus shifts from the foundational (Part 1) and the technical (Part 2) to more practical concerns in three chapters:

➢ **Chapter 10.** Group information management and the social fabric of PIM. We don't (and shouldn't) manage our information in isolation. Group information management (GIM)—especially the kind practiced informally in households and smaller project teams—goes hand in glove with good PIM. The chapter considers information for its value to represent, as the thing communicated and, especially, as the means to know. The chapter considers PIM in several social situations: @home, @school, @work, @play, and at "@large".

> **Chapter 11.** PIM by design. What considerations apply to the design of tools in support of PIM. What about better practices of PIM to be shared in programs of training and teaching PIM? What methods work best? What bigger challenges and opportunities of PIM must we keep in mind?

> **Chapter 12.** To each of us, our own. This final chapter is a "songs of experience" counterpart to Chapter 11. Just as we must each be a student of our own practice of PIM, we must also be a designer of this practice. This concluding chapter looks at considerations, methods, and challenges and opportunities of PIM as we design our own Practices of PIM.

CAVEATS AND DISCLAIMERS

References to scholarly articles of direct relevance to personal information management (PIM) are grouped together into a bibliography at the end of this book (Part 3).

Web references and references for non-PIM background reading are often included directly in footnotes.

I include no references to information you can easily find on the Web. Instead of references, I sometimes include suggested search terms.

I am an unabashed citer of Wikipedia (http://www.wikipedia.org/) articles when these are reasonably clear, complete and objectively written. The interested reader should use these articles not as a final destination but as a springboard (through references cited) for further study of a given topic. You the reader may discover—especially if you are expert on the topic of a Wikipedia article (whether or not cited here)—that the article is inaccurate or incomplete. If so, you should change it. Wikipedia and the like are an essential part of the world-wide, web-enabled dialog we must have to realize the power and potential in our information.

Part 3, "Building a Better World with Our Information," takes a turn toward the practical in coverage of the social fabric of PIM and PIM by design both in tools and in individual Practices of PIM.

Even so, as with Parts 1 and Part 2, Part 3 is not a step-by-step "how to" manual. The aim instead is to provide guidelines, considerations, methods of inquiry, and a sense for larger challenges and opportunities of PIM. Equipped with these, it is hoped that readers, whether developers, instructors, or end users, are better able to meet their own special circumstances.

Acknowledgments

I thank…

…John Levy for his helpful comments throughout this series and especially for his detailed comments on Part 3.

… Max Van Kleek, Richard Neiman, Robert Capra, and Anne Diekema for their good comments on selected chapters in Part 3.

…Kaitlin Light Costello and Anita Crescenzi for discussions and research pointers.

…Robert Capra, Anne Diekema, Jesse David Dinneen, and Manuel A Perez-Quinones for conversations, research pointers, and the companionship as we worked to update ELIS and Wikipedia articles on PIM.

… Jonathan Grudin for his help and ready willingness to engage in extended email conversations relating in particular to the history of HCI and cognitive modeling. My email conversations with Jonathan nicely illustrate the power of dialog, extended over time and space in a digital age, to shape thought and facilitate its expression,

…Gary Marchionini for his excellent leadership as editor of the "Synthesis Lectures on Information Concepts, Retrieval, and Services" lecture series in which all three parts of *The Future of Personal Information Management* appear.

…Diane Cerra for her assistance in getting this book and also Parts 1 and 2, to press. Were it not for Diane's consistently good nature and steady encouragement, I would likely have abandoned this project along the way.

…my wife, Maria, for her detailed comments on this book and for putting up with me as I struggled to complete this book and the other two in the series.

CHAPTER   10

Group Information Management and the Social Fabric of PIM

10.1   WE ARE NOT ALONE

As we manage our information to manage our lives, we do not act alone. To paraphrase Aristotle, people are by nature social animals.[1] We know this to be true for each of us reading these words here and now wherever and whenever "here" and "now" may be—true even if we find ourselves reading by firelight in some isolated cave. Reading is a social activity. Reading completes an act of communication, with varying degrees of success, begun by a writer possibly many thousands of miles and many thousands of years away from "here and now." Aristotle "speaks" to us from an ancient Greece of the fourth century BCE.

Information and communication are much intertwined. Indeed, in the spirit of Shannon's work[2] information might be said to owe its very existence to an ability to communicate. Toward better, more purposeful support for the communication of information, a whole field of practical research and development, *information and communication technology*, or ICT, has arisen.[3] Communication between people, in turn—whether in oral, written, or visual forms, whether through books, emails, texts, tweets, or "Snaps"[4]—is a social activity.

As a practical matter, the social is embedded in our Practices[5] of PIM[6] as when, for example, we depend upon a spouse for help in keeping, maintaining, and organizing and later finding information relating to home and family. Perhaps one member of the household takes responsibility for

---

[1]   "Man is by nature a political animal" (http://en.wikiquote.org/wiki/Aristotle), i.e., a member of the polis (city, community).

[2]   Shannon, 1948.

[3]   For more information on ICT, see, for example, Brynjolfsson and Hitt, 2000; Cline, 2014; Garvey, 1979; Vaishnavi and Kuechler, 2015, or, for additional references, http://en.wikipedia.org/wiki/Information_and_communications_technology, or for earlier thinking in this direction see Simon, 1971.

[4]   http://en.wikipedia.org/wiki/Snapchat.

[5]   In relation to PIM, it is useful to use "practice" in two different senses: 1. *Practice* (with a capital "P") refers to the sum total of all techniques, methods, tactics, strategies, and other activities of information management that a person uses in support of and as enabled by the information (content and structure), information channels, and tools in their personal spaces of information (PSIs). 2. *practice* (with a small "p") refers to a technique or method of PIM that was initially selected by the person to accomplish some purpose and is now a part of the person's PIM repertoire. For example, the use of "self-appointments" in a calendar to manage and remind of tasks and to-dos is a practice of task management.

[6]   Capra and Teevan, 2012.

financial information while another member manages medical information for family members. Similarly, we might depend upon a colleague or team member at work to manage information relating to one aspect of a project and to inform us of important developments as warranted.[7] We get reminders concerning important meetings and deadlines—often in an incidental way as when an email closes with "see you at the review."

Conversely, the needs of individuals and their individual practices of PIM must be considered if efforts at group collaboration—whether at home, at school, or at work—are to succeed. Individuals working in a company or other organization, for example, may need to have their own private space for "working drafts" (e.g., for reports, specifications, engineering drawings) prior to sharing these with other members of the team.[8] A document management system that doesn't take this into account is likely to fail or, worse, be subverted in ways that compromise security (as when, for example, an employee keeps company documents on a personal laptop). More generally, systems of computer-supported cooperative work may fail outright or at least underperform if the costs of use by each individual involved are not compensated for by benefits directly accruing to the individual (and not just to selected members such as a manager or the larger group overall).[9]

10.1.1 WHO IS THE GROUP?

Group Information Management (GIM, usually pronounced with a soft "G") has been written about elsewhere[10] in the context of PIM. The study of GIM, in turn, has clear relevance to the study of *Computer Supported Collaborative Work* (CSCW).[11] As a useful way to relate acronyms we can say that GIM is to CSCW as PIM is to HCI (human-computer interaction). Concerns of PIM substantially overlap with but are not fully subsumed by concerns of HCI. Indeed some of the more influential papers on PIM over the years have been published in HCI journals and conference proceedings.[12]

However, the "I" in PIM is, of course, for information—how can we as individuals (the "P"), better manage (the "M") our information (in all six senses as described in Chapter 2, Part 1[13]) regardless of the form it takes—papers and books, digital documents and emails, or even the letter

---

[7] Many managers manage their information in this manner, for example, through their administrative assistants and their staff (see Auster and Choo, 1994; Danis et al., 2005; Farhoomand and Drury, 2002; Jones and Thomas, 1997; Jones et al., 2002; Katzer and Fletcher, 1992; Mintzberg, 1973).

[8] Hicks et al., 2008.

[9] Grudin, 1988.

[10] Erickson, 2006; Lutters et al., 2007. See also http://en.wikipedia.org/wiki/Group_information_management.

[11] Grudin, 1994; Schmidt and Simonee, 1996. See also http://en.wikipedia.org/wiki/Computer-supported_cooperative_work.

[12] For example, *ACM Transactions on Computer-Human Interaction* (TOCHI) (http://dl.acm.org/citation.cfm?id=J756) and CHI (http://www.sigchi.org/conferences).

[13] The future of personal information management, Part I: our information, always and forever (Jones, 2012).

magnets on a refrigerator in the kitchen. The "I" in HCI stands for "interaction" as this relates to the "C"—computers.

A similar distinction can be made with respect to GIM and CSCW. Lutters et al.[14] write that the study of GIM involves "practice and the study of the individual actions performed to support group activity." We might amend this somewhat to say that GIM involves the practice and study of information management activities by the individual as performed to support group activity. GIM certainly involves information but doesn't necessarily involve computers.

As we shall explore in examples throughout the chapters of Part 3 in this "The Future of Personal Information Management" series, a focus first on information and second on enabling tools of management (computer-based and otherwise) can make all the difference. But first, a caveat concerning the "G" in GIM. The transition from PIM to GIM may seem logical, even obvious. But we must question whether the "group" is an entity that can manage its information in the same way that a person tries to manage her/his information.

In legal contexts it may be useful to treat a corporation as an entity—a "person"—in its own right. A corporation or other organization may have policies, procedures, habits, history, and routines that further give it a collective identity as an entity in its own right. But in many situations, there really is no group entity operating on its own behalf to manage information toward a realization of goals and a fulfillment of roles. Rather, there is a collection of individuals. Members of a group may hold in common some goals—more or less—but apparent agreement is often illusory.[15] Members may apportion group roles (e.g., treasurer, secretary, president, etc.) but ultimately members are individuals operating on their own behalf and collaborating in the group only so long as it serves their purpose to do so.

The challenges presented by and to the individual in group situations has been the subject of numerous studies. Although a collaborative "divide and conquer" approach as described above for households and workplace teams can reduce the burdens of PIM, the opposite is frequently the case when people seek to share information collections. People may vary greatly in their approaches especially to keeping, maintaining, and organizing information.[16] Working together through these issues often requires a delicate negotiation process.[17] Folders, for example, don't simply effect an organization of information but also a way of categorizing the information and of viewing the work involved.[18] The people working as a group must agree to and articulate conventions for the creation and naming of files and folders—and in ways that group members can consistently, sustainably follow over time.[19]

---

[14] Lutters et al., 2007.
[15] See, for example, Orlikowski, 1992 for a case study revealing the differing goals of individuals in a group.
[16] Berlin et al., 1993. See also Fourie, 2012.
[17] Capra et al., 2014; Wulf, 1997.
[18] Jones et al., 2005b.
[19] Mark and Prinz, 1997.

Some users may customize shared information spaces to meet their own needs, but at the cost of decreasing the intelligibility of that space for others.[20] These challenges later affect re-finding information in shared spaces, where attempts to retrieve information from a shared collection are more likely to fail than when retrieving from a personal information collection (PIC) that is not shared.[21] Many problems in the sharing of information are rooted in the richness of our natural languages and a diversity of ways we not only express ourselves but also think about the world around us.[22]

Over the years, tools explicitly designed to aid in GIM have had a decidedly mixed track record for reasons that belie the "G" in GIM, i.e., members of the group act as individuals and according to the perceived benefits that accrue to them as individuals. When faced with the challenges (e.g., learning curves, occasional lack of transparency or flexibility in use) of applications and services that are designed explicitly to support group work, people may prefer more familiar methods of collaboration that make ad hoc use of existing tools.

For example, given drawbacks—real or perceived—in the use of web services that support a shared use of folders,[23] people working in a group may opt to share information instead through the use of e-mail attachments.[24] Email of course has its own problems,[25] but these are at least "familiar." Resistance to change and to the adoption of new tools intended to support the "group" is sometimes sufficiently strong that people may avoid these tools even when their use receives strong institutional support.[26]

10.1.2 IT'S ABOUT THE INFORMATION…

Distinctions above between PIM and HCI (and between GIM and CSCW) bring us again back to some very basic questions. What is PIM really? And how might things be different—better—for a focus on PIM as a field of inquiry? As already noted above, PIM and HCI overlap with HCI conferences and journals frequently serving as an outlet for PIM publications. Aren't matters then already well in hand? If the phrase "personal information management" had never been coined[27]… if efforts had never been made toward PIM as a field of inquiry with a self-identified community

---

[20] Dourish et al., 1999.
[21] Bergman et al., 2014.
[22] Furnas et al., 1987.
[23] Bergman et al., 2014; Marshall and Tang, 2012.
[24] Capra et al., 2010.
[25] For a discussion of problems with email overload see, for example, Bellotti et al., 2005; Dabbish and Kraut, 2006; Fisher et al., 2006; Whittaker and Sidner, 1996. For a longer discussion of email in the context of other modes of communication see Chapter 10 in the book *Keeping Found Things Found: The Study and Practice of Personal Information Management* (Jones, 2007).
[26] Johnson et al., 2009.
[27] Lansdale, 1988.

of researchers… wouldn't the same issues related to PIM still be addressed and in much the same way as now? How does a focus on PIM make things different?

These questions were raised at the very outset of this "The Future of Personal Information" series, in Chapter 1 of Part 1.[28] It was noted, for example, the modern discussion on the power and potential of information management at a personal level, especially as supported by modern technology, began with Bush's "As we may think" article[29] and that seminal work on PIM was completed years before there was a so-called field of PIM, some of it completed even before the phrase had been coined.[30]

Chapter 1 (especially as depicted in Figure 1.2) also noted the essential triangle between people, information, and technology—the "P," "I," and "M," as it were, in "PIM" (and the "G," "I," and "M" in "GIM"). The human element is explicitly called forth in both HCI ("human") and PIM ("personal"). The obvious, even simple-minded, some might say, difference is between "computer" in the one and "information" in other. This makes all the difference.

The definition of PIM again from Chapter 1:

> ***Personal Information Management (PIM)*** *refers to both the practice and study of the activities a person performs in order to locate or create, store, organize, maintain, modify, retrieve, use and distribute information in each of its many forms (in various paper forms, in electronic documents, in email messages, in conventional Web pages, in blogs, in wikis, etc.) as needed to meet life's many goals (everyday and long-term, work-related and not) and to fulfill life's many roles and responsibilities (as parent, spouse, friend, employee, member of community, etc.).*[31]

Or more succinctly: *PIM is the art of getting things done in our lives through information.*

As Chapter 1 noted, we can't consider information without also considering our ways of managing our information as enabled by our tools and technology, computer-based and otherwise (e.g., the Post-it® Notes that are so often seen around the edges of a computer display). People report, for example, having a different experience when viewing "the same" information on a computer screen vs. the display of a palmtop device such as a smartphone vs. in a paper printout. We may notice differences in digital forms as when more mistakes in a draft document are noticed in its PDF vs. Microsoft Word form.[32] Likewise, there are clear differences in affordance between

---

[28] Jones, 2012.

[29] Bush, 1945.

[30] Work by Malone (1983) for example precedes Lansdale's use of the phrase (Lansdale, 1988). Other PIM-related work precedes its inception as a field of inquiry (in 2004/2005) by a decade or more (e.g., Barreau and Nardi, 1995; Kwasnik, 1989; Marchionini, 1995).

[31] Jones, 2012, Chapter 1.

[32] For self-reported, self-observed preference, even among millennial students, for paper forms of information for reading coupled with pen for writing see, for example, Mizrachi, 2013; Mizrachi and Bates, 2013.

notes taken with paper and pen vs. online and possibly even differences in the experience of and memory for doing so.

A proper understanding for information need and use must, therefore, include an assessment of the tools (applications, devices, Web services, etc.) available for experiencing and working with the information. But the converse holds with even greater force. Our use of computer applications and gadgets should not be an end in itself. We can't properly consider tools and technologies—nor even well-intentioned efforts to improve the usability of these—without also considering the point for doing so. And this point—their purpose—is informational. Write a document, read a blog post, send an email, give a presentation—it's all about the information…

Back at the CHI 2006 conference, I organized (together with Peter Pirolli) a panel discussion, titled "'It's About the Information, Stupid!' Why We Need a Separate Field of Human-information Interaction"[33] on the pivotal importance of information. We wrote: "Trends toward a ubiquity of computing, an increasing transparency of user interfaces and the overall integration of computing technologies into our everyday lives may push computers into the background as a basic service—like electricity or heating. If our computers disappear we are left with our information" (p. 66).

As a participant on the panel, Stu Card, a pioneer in the application of human factors principles to HCI,[34] wrote in his panel position statement: "In fact, with global networks, one could say information has been liberated to its own pure sphere." Further, a focus on information should involve several themes including *"Device independence*. User interaction focuses on information abstractions rather than device controls" and *"Representation*: Re-representation of information is a key to interpreting it"; (p. 66). Let's consider each theme in turn.

Device interchangeability will be used here in place of device independence as a more achievable, and still desirable, feature for our information. As Card writes, our information online (e.g., on the Web) has already been "liberated" from dependency on a given device for storage and use. Our information no longer need be confined to a single desktop computer, a paper filing cabinet, or a laptop. Today, we can see the same web page or read our emails alternately from a palmtop device (e.g., a smartphone or small tablet), a laptop, or a desktop computer. Some of us now get this information from what I, back in 2007, playfully dubbed a "watch watch"[35] such as the Apple Watch[36] or from special eyewear such as Google Glass.[37] But device interchangeability stops short of device independence. We see (or hear) the information but our experiences of this information may be distinctly different depending upon the device through which it is presented.

---

[33]   Jones et al., 2006b. The reference is a riff of the successful campaign slogan used by Bill Clinton to defeat George H. W. Bush in the 1992 presdential election; http://en.wikipedia.org/wiki/It%27s_the_economy,_stupid.

[34]   Card et al., 1983.

[35]   Jones, 2007, Chapter 12.

[36]   https://www.apple.com/watch/.

[37]   See http://en.wikipedia.org/wiki/Google_Glass and https://www.google.com/glass/start/.

Re-representation might seem like a curious phrase but we do it all the time. We rephrase and elaborate upon the information provided. We attempt to form useful associations between the newly provided information and the "given" knowledge already in our heads. We draw implications. "If you text me that you're running 15 minutes late then maybe I have time to tank up the car first…" An effective way to insure that people have understood our instructions, for example, is to ask that they repeat these, i.e., to paraphrase or "re-represent" (in their own words) the information provided.

The initial *representation* of the information we receive also matters a great deal especially since we may have limited time to re-represent in ways that make sense to us. The "same" information that is easily understood in one format may be gibberish in another. To take an obvious example, we may follow a page of assembly instructions in English but not the Spanish version presented on the flipside (or vice versa). Or we may struggle and curse as we seek to follow the "language-free" illustrations in the assembly of IKEA furniture.[38]

Norman, in Chapter 3, "The power of representation," of his book, "Things that Make Us Smart,"[39] provides a number of a compelling examples for the importance of representation in the communication of information. Included in these is an example drawn from the work of Day[40] involving a comparison of different formats for the representation of instructions to take a set of six prescribed medicines each at differing intervals through the day (e.g., "3 times a day," "before meals and at bedtime," "once a day," etc.). A patient given instructions as a simple list—one line per medicine—reported considerable difficulty in determining which medicine to take when. The "same" information presented in a matrix (with one row per medicine and a column each for "breakfast," "lunch," "dinner," "bedtime") was much easier to follow.

Note that "same" is placed in quotations marks above since, in the spirit of Shannon's work equating information to the reduction of uncertainty, we can question whether the information in different representations is the same. It might be "only a matter of time" before the patient can glean the same information from the simple listing of instructions for taking medicines as from the comparable matrix representation of these instructions. But living is all "a matter of time." Moreover, representations that place excessive strain on working memory may simply not inform no matter the amount of time we spend. (See, for example, the rules for "15" also described in Chapter 3 of Norman's book as an alternate representation for the rules of Tic-tac-toe).

Tufte, in the book *The Visual Display of Quantitative Information*, provides numerous examples for the communicative power of a good representation. Most famous is Charles Joseph Minard's graphical depiction of Napoleon's ill-fated invasion of Russia. A line superimposed upon

---

[38]   Better in many cases, to provide both text (in a language we understand) and accompanying illustrations. See, for example, Larkin and Simon, 1987.

[39]   Norman, 1993.

[40]   Day, 1988.

a map of Eastern Europe represents the advance and subsequent retreat of the *Grande Armée*; line width represents the size of the army, starting with over 600 thousand men and in retreat dwindling to a fraction of this number as the army finally crosses the Russian border.

In my book *Keeping Found Things Found: The Study and Practice of Personal Information Management*, I explore the evolution in Mendeleev's depiction of essential qualities of the chemical elements from a set of fragmented notes to a tabular representation quite akin to the periodic table we all study today in our first course in chemistry.

Later in this chapter, we consider another tabular representation, which is structurally similar to the periodic table, and that most of us use, in one form or another, everyday: the calendar. In a manner directly comparable to the ordering of chemical elements by increasing atomic number, a simple calendar orders the days of the month by increasing day, starting in the upper left hand corner, going to the right, returning, and one row down, to the left with the start of a new week. In the periodic table, elements in the same column have similar behavior (i.e., same valence and similar readiness to combine with other elements). Likewise, the columns in a calendar group the days of the month so that Mondays fall in one column, all Tuesdays in another, and so on. Many events tend to recur on the same day every week and the calendar's format makes this repetition of behavior easier to see and to plan for.

As the calendar illustrates, a good representation of information, as enabled by the right tools, can be especially important in group situations, especially those requiring not only effective communication but also coordination of individual activities, schedules, and constraints.

It's about the information. Information is the thing that we work with and understand through our tools but that can be transformed, copied, and exchanged to have existence independent of any given device or software application (albeit with experiences and affordances that can vary with form and the tools at hand). Changes in the representation of information can mean enormous differences in ease of comprehension and impact.

Information is the thing, but not an end in itself. It's not like happiness—the more the better. Sometimes quite the opposite. Information is a means to an end. Information is to represent, to communicate, and to know. The social aspects of each of these is now considered in turn.

10.1.3 INFORMATION TO REPRESENT (AND FIVE OTHER "R"S AS WELL)

In Chapter 6 of Part 2 in this series,[41] technologies of information storage (and capture) were considered for their potential to support a high-fidelity record of our life experiences (i.e., P5, the fifth sense in which information is personal).

Sellen and Whittaker[42] provide a skeptical but insightful analysis of so-called *lifelogging* systems aiming toward "total capture" of information for life experiences. What might we do with this information? Sellen and Whittaker identify what they term the "five Rs" (paraphrased slightly here to convert from gerund to active verb). With information we might better:

- *recollect* so that we could recall, for example, the name of the person we talked to at a party last night or the instructions we received from our supervisor during a drop-in meeting;

- *reminisce* (as a special case of recollecting) in order to re-live past experiences (especially the good ones);

- *retrieve* specific items such as our car keys or forms of digital information such as an email, document, or web page. (We might, for example, want "the web page I saw on my iPhone while watching my daughter play softball.") Information can also be "reflexive" in its support for its own retrieval as when, for example, the content of an email supports its retrieval later in a full-text search;

- *reflect* upon past events including our interactions with other people. Could we have been more understanding? Less argumentative? In correlating our activities with physical measures, we might reflect upon situations that tend to make our heart rate or blood pressure go up (or down). At what times of the day are we at our best for completing tough tasks or making difficult decisions? Does the second cup of coffee make us more or less productive? Are we getting good sleep at night? Does it matter what we ate for dinner? When?[43] and,

- *remember* our intentions. Did we remember to pick up the milk? Did we take our medication? Throughout the day or even as we awake at night, we form intentions to do something in the future. A review of a recording of intention formation might help us to remember and then fulfill the intention.

Call these five potential benefits of any information item or indeed of any object with informational value. Certainly three of these (to support our ability to retrieve items, reflect upon the

---

[41] Jones, 2013.

[42] Sellen and Whittaker, 2010.

[43] The ability to capture and correlate not only external events but also internal physical state relates to *personal informatics* about which more in Chapter 12.

past, and remember our intentions to take future action) apply more generally to the information we share in social settings and not just to information as a record of what we "do and see" or otherwise experience (P5).

For instance, our calendar may remind us of an appointment or an important to-do even if our memory for the formation of this intention is absent. The information a friend provides—in the form of an oral story concerning an unpleasant "road rage" altercation—may prompt us to reflect upon our own occasionally aggressive behavior in traffic and to resolve to exercise more restraint in the future. The instructions we encounter on a friend's Facebook page can help us to retrieve a schedule of events for a film club.

Moreover, our minds are highly associative so that nearly any experience, not just recordings of past experiences, may cause us to recollect, reflect, or reminisce. A smell, a sound, a song hummed by someone nearby, the picture on a billboard as we drive by, these and many other forms of information can also provide each of the benefits listed above. The same event can provide several. John, stuck in rush hour traffic, hears a favorite song while "flipping" from one radio station to the next. The song helps him to *recollect* his wife's birthday dinner party from last year. He *reminisces* as he *reflects* upon the passage of time and he *remembers his intention* to start planning for this year since her next birthday is just around the corner. The song, mediated by a chain of associations triggered, might even evoke the memory of having purchased a gift for her already and lead to its *retrieval* from a hiding spot he might otherwise have forgotten about.

To "Five Rs" can be added a sixth benefit. And, in keeping with the sixth activity of PIM—making sense of and using information—and the sixth sense in which information is personal—information that is potentially relevant to us, this benefit of information is the broadest and can be seen to permeate the others: We can use information items and information-bearing objects to *represent*.

The picture taken of a whiteboard after a meeting can help the participants to recollect the meeting. But sent to others who were not at the meeting, the picture, especially as accompanied by a verbal description, can represent the understanding that was achieved.

Information to represent. Of course. Information is *all* about representing. This was discussed in Chapter 1 of this series. Information represents worlds removed from us in space and time that we can't experience directly. Information represents future situations to be sought or avoided. Information has particular power in social situations.

The "R"s, especially the uses people make of information to accomplish the "sixth R"—to represent matters at a remove of time and location, for self and others—will frequently figure into the review of social situations of PIM in the next section.

Note that "represent" as the "sixth R" is not only broader and more general than the others (after all, what does not "represent" in one way or another?) but also places us in a different role as the sender (provider, creator) of information rather than the receiver of this information. We take a picture, write a memo, draw a sketch, or write a whole book as a way to represent. The representation is then used in subsequent communications with others and with ourselves.

In the previous section, we considered examples where differences in the representation of information (e.g., structured in a matrix vs. lines of text) can make for significant differences in a person's ability to understand, remember, and draw the right conclusions. The current discussion concerning the use of information to represent might be considered a slight inversion of that message. But the two closely relate.

The "right" representation of information depends upon what the information is meant to represent. What to represent in turn depends upon what we wish to know and what we wish for others to know.

Our representation also depends upon the selected mode of communication. We wish to represent the outcome of a daughter's soccer game to our spouse. This representation is likely to be distinctly different depending upon whether the outcome is sent as a text message, an email, or with a picture with accompanying text in Snapchat.

Information at a distance to represent what the recipient can't apprehend directly depends upon, indeed is defined by, the mode of communication.

An attempted communication can fail. Sometimes information sent arrives too late or in the wrong form or not at all. And sometimes intentions of sender and receiver don't match or even oppose. We move then to a look at PIM considerations in the social communication of information.

10.1.4 INFORMATION TO COMMUNICATE

Information is the stuff of personal communication. The communication metaphor is applied more broadly in everyday language as when, for example, John in deciding whether to take a rain jacket with him to work looks out the window and asks, "what is the weather trying to tell me?" Approaches involving assessments of information value and the effectiveness of communication are now widespread from biology (e.g., protein synthesis, genetics) to physics.[44]

It is a simplification, but a useful one, to say that knowledge is information in action.[45] The communication metaphor invites another useful simplification: *Information is data in motion.*[46]

In social interactions, we might also say that information is data sent or received with intention. Participants in a study by Zins[47] often defined information in relation to data and knowledge with reference to expressions of intention. For example, information is "the intentional

---

[44]   For an accounting of information theoretic approaches to physics, see, for example, Mézard and Montanari, 2009 or the more accessible Gleick, 2012. Or if time is short, try the following chapter-by-chapter summary first: Graham, 2013.

[45]   O'Dell and Essaides, 1998, p. 5.

[46]   Expression first used in Jones, 2010.

[47]   Zins, 2007. And information is "data arranged or interpreted…to provide meaning" (p. 486).

composition of data by a sender with the goal of modifying the knowledge state of an interpreter or receiver" (p. 485).

But intentions needn't match. Nor does successful communication mean that intentions of sender and recipient were equally met. Tom, snooping with ear to closed door, hears his manager on the other side talk of an impending layoff. Tom's intention is to receive information concerning the layoff but it certainly isn't the manager's intention to provide this information. The creator of a website may intend to impress prospective employers but if the website is badly designed that intention may not be realized. The negative impression prospective employers form can be considered information unintentionally communicated by the website creator.

In a human context, failures of interpersonal communication may be technical in nature as when we "break up" in a cell phone call. But many failures to communicate are usefully regarded, instead, as failures of information management.

The messenger never reaches Romeo with the news that Juliet isn't really dead but rather in a deathlike coma from which she will awake. But really? Only one messenger? No redundancy? No verification (i.e., by the friar who promised Juliet he would dispatch the messenger)? With better information management we might have had a comedy rather than a tragedy.[48]

At least intentions—of Romeo, Juliet, Friar Laurence, and, presumably, the messenger— were good. Consider another of Shakespeare's plays, *Othello*, in which Iago, as the villain, does not intend to "inform" but rather to deceive. Othello, fooled by Iago's treachery, smothers his beloved Desdemona convinced she has committed adultery and only learning—too late!—of her innocence.[49] But really? No vetting and cross-checking of Iago as a source of information? No independent validation?

It might be said—with tongue only slightly in cheek—that Juliet and Friar Laurence as senders of information and Othello as a receiver of information are better seen not as the tragic victims of communication failure but rather as perpetrators of egregious mistakes of information management, the kind of mistakes we would expect a student—certainly by graduate school and with only the rudiments of training in information literacy—to avoid. Alas training in information literacy is still not widespread even at the collegiate level.[50]

We each, as the heroes of our own stories and in our daily interactions with a wide range of characters, practice social kinds of information management at a personal level, i.e., we practice social PIM. As receivers of information, we decide which emails to open, which meetings to attend, and even which routes to take as when, for example, we go one way rather than another through the corridors of a workplace in the hopes of "running into" someone with whom we want to speak. In

---

[48] See http://en.wikipedia.org/wiki/Romeo_and_Juliet, for a synopsis of the play *Romeo and Juliet* or for full text, see http://en.wikipedia.org/wiki/Book:Romeo_and_Juliet.

[49] See http://en.wikipedia.org/wiki/Othello for a synopsis of *Othello*, or for full text see http://read.libripass.com/william_shakespeare-othello.htm.

[50] For more on the state of information literacy in our schools see Eisenberg et al., 2004.

deciding what to believe, we consider basic matters of *provenance*: Who provides the information? When? Where and under what circumstances?

Similarly as information senders, we may apply intricate models for the flow of information and for the habits, preferences, and current states of knowledge of our intended recipients. When sending an email, for example, we decide whom to place on the to: line, whom to place on the cc: line, whom to place on the bcc: line, and whom to leave out altogether. We may send a text message instead knowing that the recipient obsessively checks and responds to texts but only checks email occasionally. Or we may walk down to someone's office to deliver bad news in person. We even practice a kind of social PIM with ourselves as, for example, when we archive a document or caption and save a photograph directed to ourselves—as best we can ever know these—some years into the future.[51]

Information as a remove from direct, person-to-person interaction is increasingly the stuff of interpersonal communication. Information communicated is toward an end that people should know (or think they know) and should be moved to take action.

10.1.5 INFORMATION TO KNOW

Information is traditionally presented as the thing to take people from data—raw sensation, unprocessed bits—to knowledge. This pivotal role for information is reflected in our definitions and our understanding of the terms "data," "information," and "knowledge." In the survey mentioned earlier by Zins, 57 experts in the broad area of information science from 16 separate countries were asked to define each term.

The result? Definitions for "data" and "information," though distinct, frequently overlapped. Likewise, definitions for "information" and "knowledge" overlapped. For no expert was there evidence for an overlap between the terms "data" and "knowledge."

Some excerpts: "**Knowledge** is 'no-thing' (contrary to 'information-as-thing'…)" (p. 481). "**Knowledge** is that which is known, and it exists in the mind of the knower" (p. 481). "The verb 'inform' normally is used in the sense to communicate (i.e., to report, relate, or tell) and comes from the Latin verb *informare*, which meant to shape (form) an idea" (p. 481).

In a phone conversation, Mary *informs* John that she must work late at the office and so won't be home until 10 pm or later. John may repeat this information nearly verbatim during the conversation as a kind of confirmation as in, "OK. So I'll expect you sometime after 10 pm." But the proof that John really *knows* that Mary will return late from the office is in the application of this information. We can all think of occasions where we were informed of something but didn't

---

[51]   Considerations of social PIM, i.e., of deciding what to communicate with whom, when and how, relate closely to notions of a theory of mind. For a nice write up see http://en.wikipedia.org/wiki/Theory_of_mind or well-cited academic classics such as Baron-Cohen et al., 1985; Perner, 1991; Premack and Woodruff, 1978.

still make the appropriate connections. John, partly by habit, puts a setting for Mary at the table for dinner at 7 pm and then says, "Of course! Mary won't be home for dinner."

Testing is all about the differences between information and knowledge. Students receive a great deal of information in a course but how well do they really know the material? There can be degrees of knowing as manifest in differences in test scores. Most students answer the easier questions. Only the better students answer the questions requiring broader, less obvious application of the course information. Even better tests of course knowledge await the students after graduation in jobs where they may be called upon to apply all that they have learned so far, through their courses and elsewhere too.

The relationship between information and knowledge is pithily expressed by O'Dell and Grayson[52]: "Knowledge is information in action" (p. 5).

There is an understandable temptation to want to deal with knowledge directly. Wouldn't it be nice, for example, if we could "mind meld" to directly ingest knowledge into our heads? This would be so much faster than the more laborious process of encoding and apprehending new information via our senses and then "making sense" of this information through our efforts to understand the information more deeply, forming as we do, new knowledge in our heads connected to existing knowledge. Alas, there is no such thing as a mind meld nor is knowledge a "thing" we can directly stick into our heads. In this, knowledge differs from information.

Information, even in digital forms, is a thing[53] to be managed and manipulated (albeit as mediated by our tools). Elsewhere I argue[54] that all our efforts to render knowledge in forms to be managed directly yield instead information. We don't, can't, "capture" knowledge. Efforts at *knowledge elicitation* produce information—whether in the form of a paper book or a digital set of if-then rules for an expert system. The converse of activities of knowledge elicitation then are activities of *knowledge instillation* which is, somewhat playfully, contrasted with "knowledge installation"—we might wish we could "install" knowledge (e.g., to speak French or program in JavaScript) the way we install new applications on a computer but the actual process is much slower, involving practice, repetition, elaboration, and integration of new knowledge with older knowledge.

The study of knowledge management is then properly understood to be about improving, e.g., through tools, techniques, and training, efforts at knowledge elicitation and knowledge instillation. How, for example, can an organization better elicit the expertise and lessons learned of a senior engineer who is about to retire? How, in turn, can the knowledge elicited, and necessarily rendered as information in one form or another, be transferred to others, i.e., through which activities of knowledge instillation?

---

[52] O'Dell and Essaides, 1998.
[53] Buckland, 1991.
[54] Jones, 2010.

On the personal level of personal knowledge management (PKM), how can people as individuals take stock of what they know or don't know already (i.e., assessment through testing and knowledge elicitation)? People might do this, for example, to determine whether or not to apply for a job or to ask for a raise and to determine what additional knowledge to acquire first. Knowledge is then acquired with the aid of tools and techniques for knowledge instillation or, more simply, learning.

Knowledge is everywhere within us but nowhere in particular. Knowledge is distributed. Knowledge is internal. Larger assemblies of organisms, organizations of people, and whole societies can also be seen to embody knowledge. In his careful study of navigational activities on a carrier ship, for example, Hutchins[55] described an organic process in which different abilities and responsibilities were distributed among the crew in a redundant fashion. This overlap in responsibilities and training procedures gave the ship as a whole an ability to repair and recover from losses in individual personnel.

The distributed nature of knowledge, cognitive processing, and the ability to respond intelligently to circumstances has given rise to psychological theories of *socially distributed cognition*.[56]

Hollan et al.[57] identify three kinds of distributed cognition:

1. *Cognitive processes may be distributed across the members of a social group.*

2. *Cognitive processes may involve coordination between internal and external (material or environmental) structure.*

3. *Processes may be distributed through time in such a way that the products of earlier events can transform the nature of later events* (p. 176).

Taking a perspective of socially distributed cognition, they argue, then makes apparent three fundamental questions about social interactions in relation to knowledge and cognition:

1. *How are the cognitive processes we normally associate with an individual mind implemented in a group of individuals?*

2. *How do the cognitive properties of groups differ from the cognitive properties of the people who act in those groups?*

3. *How are the cognitive properties of individual minds affected by participation in group activities?* (p. 177)

---

[55] Hutchins, 1994.

[56] Hollan et al., 2000, Hutchins, 1994; Hutchins, 1995. **See also** http://en.wikipedia.org/wiki/Socially_distributed_cognition.

[57] Hollan et al., 2000.

From a practical PIM perspective, we can regard our social interactions with other people to be a key part of our personal space of information or PSI. Recall that a person's PSI was defined in Chapter 2 of this series[58] to be an aggregate of all personal information—in all six senses in which information is personal (relates "to me")—and also tools and techniques used by a person to manage information.[59]

From Chapter 2:

> *A person's PSI might be visualized as a vast sea of personal information. If the "home waters" represent information under the person's control, then, farther out in the PSI, are waters of information that are shared, disputed or under exploration. This area includes information about the person, the use of which the person might like to control (or at least monitor) but which is currently under the control of others (credit agencies, tax authorities, insurance companies, etc.). At the periphery of a person's PSI are oceans of available information (on the Web, corporate intranets, public libraries, etc.), only the tiniest fractions of which the person explores in order to complete various tasks and projects and in order to fulfill various roles in the person's life* (p. 25).

and

> *Our own personal spaces of information (PSI) are large, mostly unexplored, with uncertain boundaries and big areas of overlap (with the PSIs of other people and organizations).*

> *But PIM is about extending our control, or at least our influence, out over this sea of personal information* (p. 25).

In his position statement for the panel, "It's about the information, stupid!,"[60] Card identified a key role for information in our daily interactions with it, namely, the "externalization of cognition": "Most significant cognition is too complicated to fit in the head" (p. 66).[61]

Kidd cautioned that organizations (and individuals, too, we can add) should not think that "storing information is an alternative to being informed by it."[62] But much that was once a matter of speculation[63] concerning the potential of our information and information tools to extend our memories has now already come to pass and with impact.

Studies show, for example, that in an age of fast, sophisticated search support providing quick easy access to information ("just 'Google' it") people are less likely to internalize and know the details of relevant information and more likely, instead to recall (know) where and how to access

---

[58] Jones, 2012.

[59] We might also call the PSI a personal information ecology (Davenport and Prusak, 1997). See also http://en.wikipedia.org/wiki/Information_ecology.

[60] Jones et al., 2006b.

[61] See also Marchionini, 2008.

[62] Kidd, 1994, p. 190.

[63] Jones, 1986a, 1986b; Lamming et al., 1994.

this information as needed.[64] I use "auto-complete" features of my email application where once I knew a person's email "by heart." I use features of my smartphone to "dial" the telephone numbers of friends and family where once I "knew" these numbers internally (even in "muscle memory") through their repeated manual entry.

Consider our information and our information channels—especially close at hand in our PSIs—to be a kind of *near knowledge*, i.e., information quickly converted into useful knowledge and into action (decisions, changes of state) via our tools and techniques of PIM.[65]

Sometimes knowledge is both in the head and also represented as near knowledge. Kalnikaite and Whittaker[66] describe the tradeoff people often face between "software and wetware," i.e., between external information that may be more accurate and more complete and internal knowledge that, though sometimes faster to access, may be incomplete and less accurate. As tools of information access and analysis continue to improve, we can expect the tipping point to continue to shift in favor of information and information channels (i.e., channels to others via email, Facebook, Twitter, etc.).

In our social interactions, information to know—information in action—moves in two directions:

1. We depend heavily upon our social interactions with others as a way to keep abreast of—to know about—important events and developments. "Word of mouth" is increasingly not delivered orally in direct person-to-person contact but rather at a remove through other modes of communication as tweets, texts, emails, Facebook posts, and so on. We act on this information as when, for example, we decide to see a movie, read a book, get a medical checkup, or attend a meeting as a consequence of information received through our social network.

2. We project outward to others, through emails, texts, phone calls, personal meetings, Facebook posts, etc. the information we want them to know. We do this sometimes only to build a relationship of exchange and reciprocity (i.e., they in turn provide us with useful information) but often with conscious intent to effect action on their part. The outward projection of information so that others know what to do (information in action) can take many forms ranging from a multi-page wiki tutorial to the detailed instructions in an email to a simple text to tell the recipient we're running late or to ask to "get milk" (while the recipient is already shopping at the grocery store).

---

[64] Sparrow et al., 2011.
[65] Barreau and Nardi (1995) classified the information people use into three categories according to "self-life" and relative accessibility. Information can be ephemeral, working, or archived. Using their scheme of classification, near knowledge is especially to be found in a person's ephemeral and working information.
[66] Kalnikaité and Whittaker, 2007.

Information in action. Information to know—so that we know what we need to know and how we should act (or react). Information so that others know and can better act in accordance with our common (or at least overlapping) interests.

Data, information, knowledge. There is a fourth element typically placed at the very top of the pyramid: Wisdom.[67] A proper discussion of wisdom and how it might be managed—indirectly—through the management of information is beyond the scope of this book and the abilities of its author. But the progression that already relates data, information, and knowledge invites a third simplification. If information is data in motion and knowledge is information in action then—why not?—*wisdom is knowledge in perspective.*

10.2   SOCIAL SITUATIONS OF PIM

Information is to represent—especially that which cannot be perceived and understood directly.

Information is to communicate between sender and recipient each according to their separate circumstances. Technologies of communication bridge large gaps separating sender and receiver for time and place and now also for other gaps such as preferred language (e.g., English vs. Korean) or method of delivery (aural vs. written).

Information is to know. Information is so that we know—what to do, how to act or react. Information is so that others "know"—and are more likely to do, act, react in accordance with our interests. Admit it! We are all at least a little Machiavellian in our uses of information to "win friends and influence people."[68]

But here we consider social situations of PIM where there is, or should be, at least some overlap in the interests of those involved as manifest in and supported through the ways information is shared and managed:

- **PIM @home.** Whether part of a traditional nuclear family or roommates thrown together by circumstance, the members of a household—unless dysfunctional—share interests as well as living space.

- **PIM @school.** Leaving aside the many documented failures of education, parent, teacher, and student share—or ought to share—a common interest that learning and a useful transfer of knowledge take place.

- **PIM @work.** Members of a company or other organization share, or ought to share, a common interest that the group succeed in its efforts. A sense of common interest should apply with even greater force to the members of a workplace team who must work closely toward successful completion of a project.

[67] See, for example, Rowley, 2007 or http://en.wikipedia.org/wiki/DIKW_Pyramid.
[68] http://en.wikipedia.org/wiki/How_to_Win_Friends_and_Influence_People.

And then two additional situations of PIM but with more limited coverage:

- **PIM @play.** "Play" is broadly defined. People come together in social situations both in real space and online, for shared interest (e.g., as members of a political advocacy group or members of a condominium association), common activity (e.g., hiking, sailing), companionship, or love.

- **PIM @large.** People flash their lights at an oncoming car to warn of a hidden highway patrolman around the corner. People share their hard-won expertise and their time, through the creation of Wikipedia articles. People share intimate details of their battles against cancer on sites such as "Patients like me."[69] People demonstrate real altruism in these and many other cases of information sharing "at large" and with complete strangers.

Shared interests don't, of course, mean complete overlap. The teacher may be burnt out and interested mostly in hanging on until retirement. The student may be more interested in "hanging out" with friends. At work, people may be more interested in getting the credit than doing the work. On first dates (an example of "@play") both people may exaggerate their accomplishments in order to impress. Still, in each case, there is some basis for a collaborative sharing and management of information. As party to one of these social situations, our own practices of PIM are surely impacted. We consider how as we explore each of these social situations of PIM in turn.

10.2.1 @HOME

Considerations of PIM @home apply to living arrangements that range widely to include people living as a family and as the long-time occupants of a single house to roommates coming together temporarily in a monthly rental and, even, to people who live alone or who are homeless. Considerations of PIM @home are multi-faceted and include:

➢ The physical environment of the home—including physical layout, surfaces (walls, shelves, refrigerator door), furniture, memorabilia, internet connectivity, etc.

➢ The social interactions among members of the household.

➢ The home as a nexus of connections to extended family members, friends, acquaintances, and caretakers who live outside the home but regularly return to the home either in reality or virtually as, for example, when video calls using a service like Skype are scheduled to occur when family members are at home.

Even in an age when information is digitized and Web-based, the home is still often the place where people manage the "sit down" work relating to matters of health (e.g., medical infor-

---

[69] http://www.patientslikeme.com/.

mation, bills, insurance, appointments) and wealth (e.g., review of credit card and checking account statements, investment portfolios, and real estate). Home is a place to plan for future family activities from tomorrow's softball game to next summer's rafting trip in Idaho. Home is a place to manage the memorabilia and the information items for past family events. Especially, home is a place to manage (and use) photographs.

Photographs, still mostly in paper form (e.g., printouts, or paperbacked, or as larger posters) are used in the home where they often serve different purposes in different rooms.[70] In shared spaces such as the kitchen, living room, or a rec room, photos can help to reinforce family bonds. Pictures of a family vacation or of a family gathering, for example, can aid in a kind of collective *reminiscing*. Also, photos in more public areas of a home can provide a kind of controlled communication of family values to invited guests. These photos also of course can have aesthetic appeal and can help to spark conversation.

Photos in public areas can be contrasted with photos in more private areas of a home, e.g., a bedroom or a home office, which function more in support of an *immersive reminiscence* according to Petrelli et al.[71] Also, intermediate spaces are semi-private, semi-public. I and some other guests were once given a tour of someone's home where he showed us what he called a "happy wall" of photos on the stairway from the ground floor of his house up to the more private area of bedrooms on the upper floor. The wall showed pictures of this person in numerous activities including as a pilot of a small aircraft and as the skipper of a sail boat. The placement of photos served the purpose—semi-private, semi-public. The photos were seen by this person every day as he ventured upstairs to his bedroom for the night. But, since guests were not likely to venture up the stairway except by invitation or as part of a tour, the photos remained semi-private. The photos reaffirmed for this person core values, e.g., competence, a love of the outdoors, etc., that were occasionally selectively shared with some of the guests.

What does the future hold? Digital picture frames are have been available for a long time now.[72] These will increase in size, aesthetic appeal, and viewing angle as they decrease in cost.

Digital photo frames that are attractive enough to take the place of conventional frames would seem to have many advantages. Each frame might cycle through a different set of pictures with different sets for different locations. One set might cycle through family vacation photos. A second set might cycle through classic works of art. A third might cycle through photos of relatives, family friends, and children who have left home for college or work, etc.[73] A fourth set—perhaps placed in the most frequented room of any house, the kitchen—might cycle through publicity photos of a destination for a planned vacation next summer. The pictures then help the family to learn

[70] Petrelli et al., 2014.
[71] Petrelli et al., 2014.
[72] Simply search on "digital picture frame" to see a large selection available for order online.
[73] Kirk and Sellen, 2010.

more about the destination and, by making the trip more real, more immediate, might aid in its planning. The picture of people rafting down a river, for example, might serve as a reminder to book places on a rafting expedition now while spaces are still available. Interaction with a digital picture frame and its photos can be two-way. Use a palmtop (i.e., smartphone), for example, to get more information about any photo in display, e.g., when it was taken, where, by whom, who is shown? Or use the palmtop to advance through the pictures in a frame. Or change from one set to another.

If issues of cost, quality, and technical feasibility are addressed, we are left with more basic questions of human-information interaction:

1. How often should pictures cycle in a given frame? Through what transitions?

2. How many frames on how many walls should be equipped to change in this manner? Does too much change produce a sense of unease and disorientation (perhaps only subliminal but still serious)?

3. Is it important to reserve some walls to have conventional frames with paintings and pictures that don't change?

Walls, side tables, the shelves of cabinets, bulletin boards, etc., are shared *attentional spaces*[74] in the home—surfaces that household members see and may notice (esp. if something visibly new is in the space) and so have incidental informational value—especially to represent and remind. The kitchen in the home is particularly communal as a space that all household members may routinely traverse several times in a typical day. And no surface in the kitchen is more visible than the front (and sides) of the refrigerator. The fridge provides especially visible surfaces to which to affix magnets, notes, photos, brochures, etc., with a variety of information functions. Items on a fridge can represent feelings of happiness or discontent (e.g., "please clean up your mess!"), remind of upcoming events, or support a collective reminiscence of past events.[75] Such "high value" attentional real estate! As fridges go to stainless steel there is already an emerging market for non-magnetic ways to affix information to the fridge surface.[76]

The home provides information not only on its walls, shelves, fridge, and other attentional surfaces[77] but also through computers (desktop, laptop, tablet, smartphones) that are often "parked" in the home and also through containers of paper-based information (e.g., filing cabinets and bookshelves).

---

[74] Jones, 2007, Chapter 4.

[75] Jedrzejowski, 2009; Swan, 2010; Swan and Taylor, 2005; Taylor et al., 2006; for more on "intelligent" refrigerators see Odlyzko, 1999; Rothensee, 2008.

[76] See, for example, http://www.mylulalu.com/blogs/news/8315864-humanizing-the-kitchen-again-and-making-stuff-that-sticks-to-stainless-fridges; and http://www.ebay.com/gds/Stainless-Steel-And-Refrigerator-Magnets-7-Solutions-/10000000009942958/g.html; or simply search on "post it notes for stainless steel refrigerator."

[77] Jones, 2007, Chapter 5.

Many other physical items in the home may also have strong informational value. Kirk and Sellen[78] note the power of a child's toy or the cog from a motorbike to support recollection, reminiscence, reflection, and often to represent something more—the importance of family, for example, or the more risk-taking attitudes of a younger self. In their study, people appeared to keep items not only to remember but also out of a sense of duty or even to "forget," i.e., items were too important to throw away but evocative of painful or embarrassing memories. The items were, therefore, kept stowed away in places where they would not likely be seen or otherwise experienced.

Another study of physical items in the home revealed the "ambiguous" value of household clutter as amorphous collections of items, some to be discarded or donated and others to be (someday) more properly organized into the home. Pending such a more proper treatment, there was a need for "safe" places to contain the clutter (e.g., in bowls and drawers).[79]

Shared calendars, in digital and physical forms (e.g., on a whiteboard or the paper calendar on a wall) are also an important locus of household coordination. Calendars are a means of information exchange among family members of all ages.[80]

Neustaedter et al.[81] outline a topology of calendars containing family activities as used by three different types of families where type is based upon the level of family involvement in the maintenance and use of calendars.

Calendars shared in the home—whether via online link or simply as a paper calendar visible on the wall or shelf of a well-trafficked space in the home (e.g., and most especially on the fridge door)—are an effective way to make time more visible and to share with members of a family or other household the succession of temporal events, passed and planned.

Information can help household members to share other goals, relating to better exercise, for example, or the better management of household finances, and to make more visible (or otherwise apparent) the collective progress toward the attainment of these goals. Information in various forms helps for example to engage the family in efforts to promote behaviors in support of weight reduction and obesity control.[82]

Information can also be used in support of reductions in household energy consumption, both as a worthy end in itself and also for the monetary savings. Further, information formatted by a calendar can potentially help household members to better understand the correlations between their activities and the variations in the consumption of electricity and energy used for heating. However, the calendar should present or provide access to sufficient information for household members to understand the correlations and the steps they might take to effect positive change.[83] It

[78] Kirk and Sellen, 2010.
[79] Swan et al., 2008.
[80] Kirk and Sellen, 2010.
[81] Neustaedter et al., 2009.
[82] Colineau and Paris, 2011.
[83] Neustaedter et al., 2013.

seems likely that finer-grained breakdowns of energy consumption by room or even specific appliances or as a function of doors and windows might also prove effective in promoting conservation.[84]

Considerations of PIM@home brings to the forefront the need to better connect the physical with the digital. How, for example, might physical objects provide access to digital information? Increasingly, for any given object in the home—kitchen appliance, multi-media device, and even for furniture or floors—we can expect to sense or photograph these to retrieve digital information concerning operation and maintenance. But the mapping between physical objects we can see, touch, and hold and digital information can be less direct. Ylirisku et al.,[85] for example, explore the use of physical tangle knots or strings that can be placed somewhere (in a bowl for example) and that provide access to resources on the Web.

Concerns of the digital and the physical and the need to better relate the two arise also with respect to questions of legacy. What is passed down from one generation to the next? What is lost in transition? I have a beautiful old brass school bell bequeathed to me while I was still a child by Leora, my first cousin, twice removed, now long since passed. The bell came with a hand-written note describing its use by another relative of mine in the 1800s in her role as teacher in a one-room school house in Wisconsin. The bell is still with me after at least seven moves. The note is long gone. I might wish that a similar physical object I someday bequeath might also include better support for curation. Pictures of an heirloom might be used, for example, to construct a "key" to connect to information "in the cloud" concerning the heirloom and its history.

A larger problem today as items, most notably pictures, are increasingly in digital form is how to properly curate these both for later use in our own lifetimes and as legacy to our family. How to imbue these items with more of the affordances of the physical? The photos I once got back as prints from the photo development store had some physical presence—even if only in a pile in a recess of my home office. There is nothing comparable today to remind me of the many thousands of digital photos I've taken.

Gulotta et al.[86] describe legacy as "the meaningful and complex way in which information, values, and possessions are passed on to others" (p. 1813). Included among the challenges highlighted by their studies concerning the curation of digital information are better support for selective archiving and better assurances that digital items can have the "longevity" of physical items. In support of the notion of selectivity in the archiving of items, digital and physical, is work by Petrelli et al.[87] They observe that "people are less interested in exhaustively digitally recording their past than in reconstructing it from carefully selected cues that are often physical objects."

---

[84] Guo et al., 2013.
[85] Ylirisku et al., 2013.
[86] Gulotta et al., 2014; Gulotta et al., 2013.
[87] Petrelli et al., 2009.

With respect to the curation of information items in support of recollection, reminiscence, and a longer-term representation (i.e., the legacy of family members after they die). Lindely[88] observes a need to make a distinction between "personal" memory and memory "for family." Physical items and also pictures (printed or digital) can be a powerfully evocative source of family memories supporting recollection, reminiscence. and reflection and providing a basis for collective story-telling by members of the family that may help to increase familial bonds.[89]

Holidays, such as Christmas or the Chinese New Year, are an especially opportune time to use storytelling as a means to reconnect with family and to interconnect information-bearing items, physical and digital. The same items are often retrieved year after year for decoration (e.g., ornaments, window displays, candles, etc.) and these can be richly evocative of family memories. A larger challenge is to capture the memories evoked and to interconnect with digital information items such as photos and video clips from past years, in ways that would prove useful to family members later—for entertainment value and to re-inforce familial bonds and values.[90] Family stories well-told, captured, and preserved (in audio and visual forms) can be a subsequent entertaining source not only of reminiscing but also a source of serendipitous discovery.[91] Stories that engage younger members of the family can, for example, represent and communicate intriguing, lesser-known facts about older members of the family.

As household information is increasingly digitized and homes are programmed for remote, online monitoring and control, new concerns of security, privacy and usability arise.[92] The adoption rate for "smart home" technology, beyond connectivity for entertainment and internet access, remains low. Barriers to adoption include expense, inflexibility, difficulty in managing overall, and especially in managing for and achieving effective security.[93] There is typically wide disparity between the supported controls of a system and the nuanced, multi-dimensional nature of controls people actually want, leading household members to opt for ad hoc access-control mechanisms which don't always work as desired.[94]

A consideration of PIM at home should allow for a diversity of households and domestic situations. An ethnographic study of 22 diverse families in the San Francisco Bay Area, for example, found systematic differences in the attitudes of parents toward the use of information technology as a function of socioeconomic class.[95] Yardi and Bruckman[96] note that "minorities are the fastest growing demographic in the U.S. and the poverty level in the U.S. is the highest it has been in

---

[88]   Lindley, 2012.
[89]   Jarusriboonchai and Väänänen-Vainio-Mattila, 2012.
[90]   Petrelli and Light, 2014; Petrelli et al., 2012.
[91]   Bentley and Chowdhury, 2010.
[92]   Denning et al., 2013.
[93]   Brush et al., 2011.
[94]   Mazurek et al., 2010.
[95]   Ames et al., 2011.
[96]   Yardi and Bruckman, 2012.

50 years." In their study, they observed important differences as a function of socio-economic and ethnic background including, for example, that families of low socioeconomic status were especially likely to share devices such as mobile phones and that teens in these families had more responsibility and also more independence in the use of information technology.

In line with previous discussion concerning socially distributed cognition, families are sometimes prime examples of cognitive systems and may come very close to functioning as an entity in activities of GIM. This can be especially true in families where one member has significant cognitive deficits. In a study of ten families, each with a family member suffering from amnesia, Wu et al.[97] report that families work "closely together as cognitive systems" in order to compensate for the memory deficits of one member of the family. The study revealed a need, in the design of assistive information technologies, for such features as increased redundancy and more methods to alert and to heighten awareness of status changes.

A discussion of PIM at home can also expand to include the needs of the homeless. In a study of homeless young people, aged 13–25, Woelfer and Hendry[98] found that information systems (e.g., as accessible through a community center or local library) were used in a variety of ways including to find employment and to construct online identities. In another study of homeless young people, aged 19–29, Woelfer and Hendry[99] found that personal belongings, digital and non-digital (including mobile phones, music players, and even wallets), were exchanged to form bonds to create and reciprocate goodwill with other homeless youth.

10.2.2 @SCHOOL

Socialization outside the home typically begins at school, starting in kindergarten continuing on through collegiate years when students may be living away from home for the first time in their lives but are still in a relatively structured, supportive environment.

I'm struck by the differences in practices of PIM that I notice between undergraduate and graduate students. My sample size is small and anecdotal but, in my observation, students working on advanced degrees seem much more inclined to take an active role in the management of their information, course-related and otherwise.

Graduate students may not have much choice. As a rule, the undergraduate courses I've taught or am otherwise familiar with are fairly structured with quizzes, tests, and assignments and definite due dates. Graduate-level courses are often more open-ended with students given considerably more leeway for independent study. By graduate school, students are also more likely to have other things to manage, possibly including a part-time job, a house or condo, a marriage, and maybe children, too.

[97] Wu et al., 2008.
[98] Woelfer and Hendry, 2010.
[99] Woelfer and Hendry, 2011.

As noted in Chapters 3 and 4,[100] technology has wrought huge changes in the ways we all practice PIM: Our information is always at hand through our mobile devices and forever on the Web.

Today's student population, from those in kindergarten to those working on advanced degrees at college, can all be considered "digital natives,"[101] i.e., students today grew up with the Web and in a world where ever-smarter cell phones and other devices (e.g., the iPod in its day) were commonplace.

To what extent then do students in their current practices of PIM reflect their youth and their circumstances as students and to what extent are their practices of PIM a product of the enormous changes that technology has brought to the ways of potentially practicing PIM?

In a study of 41 undergraduate students at UCLA, aged 18–22, Mizrachi and Bates[102] paint a picture of PIM practices that may seem familiar, even to those of us who (like me) are—at best—"digital immigrants." Notwithstanding the "digital native" sobriquet, for example, paper figured prominently into the students' practices of PIM. One student, for example, eschews the note-taking functions of her phone in favor of the use of a paper planner, which she indicated was faster and easier. Another student indicated that though he appreciated the convenience of online materials ("you can just click on it") he "definitely" got more out of the reading when on paper (p. 1598). Most students reported keeping a paper spiral notebook—one per course.

Some practices of PIM—such as taking notes using pen on hand—are much the same as practices I recall from when I was a college student back in the 70s. But other practices are distinctly modern and make use of tools and technology only recently available. For example, "Elaine often takes pictures of her professor's notes on the classroom whiteboard with her camera and then posts them on Facebook to share with her classmate 'friends'" (p. 1598). All students reported having a Facebook account. Facebook, though primarily used for social purposes, also had academic uses as the example above illustrates. In addition, students mentioned the use of Zynga,[103] Tumblr,[104] Twitter,[105] and Skype.[106] Course websites providing access to online readings, assignments, lecture presentations, etc., were also considered an essential tool for students in the study.

Mizrachi and Bates describe students as each working within their own "information ecologies" (what in this book series is referred to as a personal space of information or PSI). They nicely draw an analogy to the web spun by a spider—we can't understand the spider without considering

---

[100]   Jones, 2012.

[101]   The term was apparently coined by Prensky (2001); see also http://en.wikipedia.org/wiki/Digital_native.

[102]   Mizrachi and Bates, 2013; see also Hardof-Jaffe and Aladjem, 2014; Hardof-Jaffe, and Nachmias, 2011; Jacques and Fastrez, 2014.

[103]   With a mission to "connect the world through games" (https://zynga.com/).

[104]   https://www.tumblr.com/.

[105]   https://twitter.com/.

[106]   http://www.skype.com/en/.

its web. Call it an information ecology or a PSI, these overlap for students and, as the example of posting whiteboard pictures to Facebook illustrates, students work together in a kind of socially distributed cognition.

Mizrachi and Bates describe the external information environment as "essentially a scaffold, simplifying work with information intensive tasks by providing external reminders and by physically structuring the information in a way that supports internal mental manipulation and use ..." (p. 1591). Important objects in the students' immediate information environment (close at hand) include the desks of their dorm rooms and their backpacks. Information pulled from their backpacks to desktop or other surfaces is often ordered to place items representing the most time-critical tasks on top.

What about the other side of the exchange? What about teachers? Diekema and Olsen[107] conducted a study of PIM practices among elementary and secondary teachers. The teachers were found to depend heavily on the information they organize into personal information collections (what are termed PICs in this series) both in paper and digital forms. Information in PICs was mainly of three kinds:

> *(a) Information about and from students (e.g., grades, assignments), (b) information used for teaching (e.g., lesson plans, activities, pedagogy books, textbooks), and (c) administrative information (e.g., year plans, school schedules, phone directories)* p. 2268.

Close colleagues are an important additional source of information, followed by the Web. Somewhat surprising is their finding that teachers, like many of their students, prefer to use a general search service such as Google or Bing rather than to use the facilities of a school library.

Although teachers found it especially challenging to maintain dualistic systems of digital and physical information, going completely digital in their PSIs was seen as a remote possibility for the distant future. "Not until there are computers for each student in the classroom and all students have computers (or smart phones) and Internet access at home will the classroom have a chance to go paperless" (p. 2268).

Other interesting findings from their study include:

- Maintenance activities such as "spring cleaning" to re-organize and to toss duplicates and dated material are typically initiated by major events such as moving classrooms.

- Teachers are reluctant to throw out information including the information they "inherit" from other teachers (often left behind by other teachers during a classroom move).

- Teachers look for information to get ideas, to update outdated information, to find background information, to find teaching materials, and to customize instruction.

---

[107] Diekema and Olsen, 2014.

Parents are the third leg of the stool, so to speak, in considerations of PIM @school. Roshan et al.,[108] in a qualitative study of parents in financially depressed communities in the west side of Atlanta, identified issues which would seem to apply more generally to parents seeking to help and keep pace with their children as school instruction is increasingly mediated by e-learning technologies. Parents were, for example, observed to limit their use and their children's use of online services not only for concern about the appropriateness of content but also for concern about viruses and malware and the high cost of doing without or repairing devices once infected. The vetting of important online resources through trusted groups in the community was seen as one way to increase their adoption and use by parents. For parents in this economically depressed community, smartphones had especially broad adoption (more so than laptops, for example). Already here in "beta"[109] is support for the smartphone to connect to larger screens and various input devices.

Classroom teaching is expensive. Individual, one-on-one tutoring is more expensive still but with very strong benefits. Bloom[110] identified the now classic "2 sigma problem" by observing that students working individually with a qualified human tutor obtain average achievement levels that are two standard deviations higher than in a conventional (e.g., 30 student) classroom. How then to realize the clear benefits of one-on-one tutoring more economically? One sigma is apparently realized through "Mastery Learning" where students in a conventional classroom are given "feedback followed by corrective procedures and parallel formative tests to determine the extent to which the students have mastered the subject matter" (p. 4).

How then to realize the remaining "sigma"? Efforts over the years have tended to focus on the development of computer-based tutors.[111] However, this essentially A.I. (Artificial Intelligence) approach may never fully succeed in capturing the remaining difference between tutoring and classroom instruction for want of consideration for the social and emotional aspect to one-on-one tutoring. The good human tutor fosters a relationship with the student and a desire to please (to succeed).

Considerations of the human and the social figure prominently also into suggestions to "fix" MOOCs (Massive Open Online Courses) in the face of interim results pointing to abysmal rates of completion.[112] In one report, for example, are recommendations to "retain the human element," "foster focused collaboration," "provide ongoing feedback," and "blend" the online with more traditional face-to-face contact among students and with the instructors.[113]

---

[108]   Roshan et al., 2014.
[109]   http://www.winbeta.org/news/windows-10-phones-recap-release-date-interactive-tiles-continuum-and-more.
[110]   Bloom, 1984.
[111]   See, for example, Anderson and Skwarecki, 1986, or, more recently, Corbett, 2001; Polson and Richardson, 2013; Wenger, 2014.
[112]   See, for example, Konnikova, 2015.
[113]   Miller, 2014.

A study of e-learning involving the modeling of data from 345 individuals pointed strongly to the importance of course interaction and "social presence" as manifest in measures of overall course performance and satisfaction.[114] Social considerations also figure into the modeling done by Mohammadyari, and Singhof[115] of data on e-learning as a basis for training in a work environment (taken from a survey of accountants using e-learning as convenient way to complete training). However, social considerations are folded into a larger concept of *digital literacy*[116] that includes not only technical awareness but also "social and cognitive skills required in the digital environment" (p. 14).

Moving in the other direction are investigations into the enhancements of a traditional classroom learning experience through social media–enabled methods for sharing information and building a sense of community among students outside of class using, for example, Facebook groups (private and public).[117] One study in South Korea suggests that social media might enhance the learning experience even for students in elementary school. Fourth graders given the means for basic blogging (and the encouragement to blog) were more "engaged" than other fourth graders in a control group. Students also "collected more resources for their assignments...." and "also posted more annotations" during the six-week period of the study.[118] Across grades, we are only beginning to explore the possibilities for "disruptive" (but positive) innovation to be realized through integrations of e-learning technologies into the traditional classroom.[119]

As in other circumstances of PIM, information overload and, especially, information fragmentation are major problems for students, teachers, and parents, too, as they seek to manage (and cope with) school-related information. Whether schooling takes place at a distance, in a traditional classroom, via human tutor, computer tutor, or some combination of all, students, teachers, and parents face enormous quantities of information often widely scattered and in need of updating nearly as soon as it is posted. In addition, there is a continual need to add new information from many sources, including the student (completed assignments, questions on course material, and comments on each other's work), the teacher (lesson plans, lecture notes, assignment descriptions, etc.) and also, even the parents (who may wish for ways to be more involved). How best to integrate a large and growing amount of school-related information in ways that provide for good access but

---

[114] Johnson et al., 2008.

[115] Mohammadyari and Singh, 2015.

[116] For other examples of the global movement toward digital literacy with special focus on support for student learning see Otopah and Perpetua, 2013.

[117] Lamanauskas et al., n.d.; Pasek et al., 2009; Wang et al., 2014.

[118] Lee and Ik, 2014. However, in recognition for the class Hawthorne effect (see http://en.wikipedia.org/wiki/Hawthorne_effect) we might question whether students in the blogging condition weren't on their best behavior for the duration of the study. Stronger evidence would come from a study lasting over a longer period of time (even the whole academic year) and where observational methods were minimally apparent.

[119] See, for example, Christensen et al., 2008.

also for good privacy protections? This a big question for which current tools and techniques have only a partial answer.

Bruns and Humphreys[120] review school-related implications of a networked economy and increasingly networked means of production as manifest, for example, in classroom uses of Wikipedia, open source software projects, YouTube, wikis, blogs, and even computer games and the community of gamers who develop around a particular game as supported by a service such as Twitch.[121] Effective educational usage of such tools and services has four basic characteristics:

1. It is **community-based**;

2. But participants in this community occupy **fluid roles** with, for example, teachers also in the role of students (i.e., as they strive to keep pace with new developments not only in course content but also in tools and technologies for teaching);

3. The "artefacts" are always **unfinished** (e.g., the wiki for a course must continually expand to stay current); and

4. Wikis and other output of the collaboration (among students, teachers, and parents) is **communal property** but still the **individual merit** of contributors must be acknowledged (and, we might add, privacy concerns of the individual must be recognized).

Venkatesan et al.[122] note the importance of accommodating cultural differences and, we might add, individual differences when using Wikis and other social media in support of collaborative learning. For example, students may vary in their willingness to share work-in-progress with teachers and other students. Also important, they note, is to strike the right balance between synchronous modes of collaboration that allow for instant, interactive feedback and asynchronous modes that allow for more flexibility in participation and also reduce some of the social pressures that may impede open discussion.

10.2.3 @WORK

When I was in high school I worked with two high school friends, Ned and Ron, to restore a classic, old 1957 Chevrolet to working order. The car was parked in a side garage of Ned's parents' house. We worked several days each week in the garage over a period of three months to get the car in shape. Ned was a year older than Ron and I and knew a lot more about cars. He directed the efforts. Ned's directions were easier to follow for the shared context we had, including the history

[120]   Bruns and Humphreys, 2007, see also Poore, 2012.
[121]   http://www.twitch.tv/.
[122]   Venkatesan et al., 2014. **See also** Rick and Guzdial, 2006.

of our interactions together and the relative similarity of our backgrounds. (We all attended the same high school).

We also, more or less, shared the same situation. We could each "see" that, for example, the rebuilt water pump was only partly attached and that Ned would probably next need the wrench lying over to one side on a shelf in order to complete the installation of the water pump. It also helped that we liked and trusted each other. We didn't worry that one of us would make an unreasonable or dangerous request. The project was a success. The car ran. Maybe it still runs.

In many other cases of collaborative effort, the work done by different members of a group is scattered in space and time. Work relating to some collaborative efforts such as the Boeing 787 Dreamliner[123] is done globally and over a period of decades (from initial conception to a final decommissioning of the last plane). Even work which takes place roughly in the same place and in the same period of time, it is often too complicated for any one person to understand "at a glance." We then use information in various forms to *represent* the "current situation" and to provide a shared context including a history of actions taken and tasks completed, the current state of the project, and the work that remains.

From the PIM perspective of any individual involved in the larger effort, there is then a major challenge to use information effectively. The project's overall success depends upon the PIM effectiveness of the people involved. Conversely, an individual's success at work, perhaps even the individual's life (e.g., when work is dangerous and safety issues are paramount) will depend upon an ability to effectively manage information.

As in other exchanges, information used in communication with the larger workplace group is in two directions. How to receive the right information (at the right time and place…) to know what to do at work (and when, where, how)? How, in turn, to send/share the right information so that others (or yourself at a later point in time) know what to do at work (and when, where, how)?

Practices of PIM @work vary with roles and responsibilities of the individual and the nature of the work being done. Here we can only consider a sampling of the research into this variation of PIM practices at work, where this research itself covers only a smallest fraction of workplace situations.[124]

In a review of research into PIM practices of engineers, Hicks et al.[125] note the availability (and company support for use) of computer support for engineering, e.g., systems for support of product data management systems (PDM), product-life cycle management (PLM), and computer-aided design (CAD). Even so, "a large number of electronic files remain within an engineer's personal file space and directory structure" and "[i]t is the nature of engineering work that causes

---

[123] http://en.wikipedia.org/wiki/Boeing_787_Dreamliner.

[124] For one interesting breakdown of workplace activity patterns and associated uses of information tools, see Grudin, 2004.

[125] Hicks et al., 2008.

engineers to retain a significant amount of project information … in personal electronic files…." (p. 23:3). An engineer's personal information collections (PICs) include not only formal information (e.g., CAD models) but also informal information (e.g., personal notes and logbooks). Indeed, a study by Anderson et al.[126] found that 60% of aerospace scientists and engineers referred first to their PICs before consulting others in their department.

Jones et al.[127] review studies conducted over the years into the PIM practices of managers (especially mid-level managers). Managers depend upon others (e.g., direct reports, a personal assistant, their supervisor, and colleagues), traditionally through oral communication, for much of the information they receive. Managers expend relatively little time directly gathering information (e.g., from the corporate library, the corporate intranet, or the Web).

In their own study, taking place in 2001 and 2002, Jones et al. found that managers heavily relied upon email to gather and disseminate information. PIM practices of managers, especially with respect to finding, keeping, and organizing information, contrasted with analogous behaviors for researchers (at a university and in a software corporation) and information specialists (librarians) who reported and were observed to spend much more time directly researching on the Web for relevant information. Between the two groups, information specialists were more likely to invest effort to keep and organize "found" information (e.g., in bookmark folders).

Social media are more readily available now than at the turn of the new millennium. How have these impacted the PIM behaviors and job performance of people at work? Researchers conducting a recent survey of 1,799 people associated with the insurance industry in Greece concluded that social media "significantly and positively impact the employees' performance."[128] Over half the respondents indicated, for example, that they used social media in order to track developments in the market and with competitors. The survey did not, however, endeavor to differentiate between different forms of social media (e.g., blogs, wikis, and social networking services) as used in the work environment.

From a longitudinal study of social media use, Archambault and Grudin (2012)[129] report a "near-universal" (p. 9) adoption of Facebook and LinkedIn by employees at Microsoft though they acknowledge that, in contrast to workers in other companies and other industries, Microsoft employees are more likely to be early adopters and to face fewer company-imposed barriers to the use of social media. They note that the "principal work-related benefit of social networking software was in the easy, unobtrusive creation, maintenance, and strengthening of weak ties among colleagues" (p. 102). There was strong agreement among employees that social networking helped them to do their jobs more efficiently. A recruiter commented that "I can't recall how I did this job without

---

[126] Anderson et al., 2001.
[127] Jones et al., 2002.
[128] Leftheriotis and Giannakos, 2014, p. 140.
[129] See also Skeels and Grudin, 2009.

LinkedIn" (p. 7). Ferro[130] notes that services that mix the social with the strictly work-related "may engage employees more fully with the organization and with their work" (p. 165).

Nevertheless, social networking services such as Facebook and LinkedIn represent imperfect attempts to support the social networking needs of people. In particular, these and other services have not yet fully solved the problem of how to maintain boundaries between different groupings of "friends." When posting, for example, it is often important to segment work-related contacts from friends and family outside the workplace and, further, to segment contacts within a workplace (e.g., reports from colleagues).

Zhang et al.[131] note, for example, that notwithstanding access control features such as the option in Facebook to create multiple groups, few people use these features (or are comfortable doing so) and that "there is little segmentation of 'friends'." Instead, many people accomplish a partitioning of sorts by having different accounts with different services (e.g., Facebook for one set of contacts, LinkedIn for another). Archambault and Grudin[132] note that the ability to direct some posts selectively to work colleagues "emerged repeatedly" as a desired feature in interviews with users. Further they note that people "have limited bandwidth for creating and managing multiple groups" and that access control features (e.g., of Facebook) "...may never be simple enough to use effectively. And the question of data security would remain." (p. 7).

Leaving aside issues of boundaries and grouping, how do our tools and technologies of communication and coordination combine in support of work that is distributed in time and space? How close can workers come to the "garage" situation I described above? Olson and Olson[133] provide a nice analysis of technologies designed to support distance work (see especially Table 1, p. 33). Notwithstanding significant advances in technologies of communication and coordination over the past few decades (e.g., email, video conferencing, shared calendars, shared files, wikis, blogs, etc.) they identify several "stubborn" problems in distance work. People striving to work together while distributed in time and space must deal with the practical problem of differing time zones and then more basic issues of trust and the challenges of differing cultures. Most notably, there is the "out of sight, out of mind" problem that useful incidental contact is less frequent for people working at a distance from one another and communication must be more deliberate.

We have likely all encountered times where problems or issues arise for which a more interactive discussion via phone or even a face-to-face meeting may be a much more effective way to make progress (e.g., in preference to email discussions that spiral out of control). Research also suggests that different modes of communication may be associated with different "moods." Face-to-face interaction and Facebook use in the workplace are more commonly associated with positive

---

[130]   Ferro, 2012.
[131]   Zhang et al., 2014.
[132]   Archambault and Grudin, 2012.
[133]   Olson and Olson, 2014. **See also** Bjørn et al., 2014.

affect while email use is more commonly associated with negative affect, perhaps in large measure due to the interruptive nature of email and the demanding nature of email content (e.g., frequently involving in-depth discussion and challenging decisions).[134]

At least partly in recognition of the benefits of direct person-to-person contact, Yahoo not long ago rescinded its work-at-home policy.[135] Demanding physical presence (e.g., at Yahoo) is one thing. Blocking use of social media is another. Zhang et al. paraphrased one IT architect at a tech company as noting that company attempts to block employee worktime access to social networking sites are easily circumvented through the simple use of a smartphone.

Moreover, attempts to control or outright block social networking access may backfire, placing the companies at a competitive disadvantage. Evidence for the work-related benefits of social networks are increasing. For example, the query of a social network may often produce useful answers faster than the query of a search service.[136]

Workplace uses of social networking through services such as LinkedIn and Facebook are an overall success (albeit with a need for more transparency in support for privacy and selective sharing). Results are more mixed for what we might consider to be two extremes in social media:

1. At one extreme are microblogging services such as Twitter where posts ("tweets") are limited to 140 characters in length and last for only a short period of time.[137]

2. At the other end of the spectrum with respect to size and persistence are wikis where pages (articles) are meant to endure as targets for cross-referencing from other pages and where an article can go on for pages and pages—length limits are not rigid but rather a matter of style, reader attention span and article coherence.

Archambault and Grudin[138] report that Twitter profiles among Microsoft employees in 2011 increased by only 4% (to 40% from 36% in 2010) and daily use by a scant 1% (from 10% to 11%) noting that "At that pace, it will take a long time to reach existing LinkedIn and Facebook levels" (p. 8). Moreover, rates of abandonment for Twitter are relatively high compared with Facebook and LinkedIn. One employee noted that though he used Twitter outside of work to track trends, he saw "no place for it at work" (p. 8).

Zhao and Rosson[139] note that issues of access control and grouping (who? in what groups? see what?) arise with Twitter and other microblogging services just as they do for Facebook and LinkedIn. Again, one option exercised by some employees is to keep two separate Twitter accounts, e.g., one for work and one for social activities outside of work. Or people might use

[134]   Mark et al., 2014.
[135]   Miller and Rampell, 2013.
[136]   Morris et al., 2010.
[137]   http://ghostblogwriters.com/tweet-lifespan.
[138]   Archambault and Grudin, 2012. See also Zhang et al., 2010.
[139]   Zhao and Rosson, 2009.

Twitter for social activities while using another service at work, such as Yammer[140] with its built in protections for the enterprise. Archambault and Grudin speculate that the use of Twitter (or possibly of another microblogging service) could eventually increase more rapidly in companies as useful features are more widely known. Of particular potential power is the ability to search the stream of recent tweets.

Zhang et al.[141] report that the use of Yammer aids in helping users to stay "aware about what others are working on and making new connections" (p. 131). At the same time they note that users experienced considerable noise (irrelevant information) in the microblogging channel and that this in part may inhere to the nature of microblogging as a mode of communication. Across studies, issues of boundaries and separation between work-related and not have not yet been addressed and are likely to act as a drag on attempts to make social networking and microblogging "work" at work.

With respect to the use of wikis at work, some problems are apparent immediately; other problems become apparent only as the wiki grows in size to include more and more pages. Grudin and Poole[142] note that the openness of wikis can run counter to ingrained corporate attitudes or to rules to restrict access (e.g., denying access to vendors or temporary workers). The need to impose a more formal release process (e.g., of review and approval) may lead to the creation of a separate document management system, which overlaps in content and exists uneasily with the wiki. Other problems are apparent only later: "Contributors to team wikis mentioned time and again that seemingly arbitrary choices of how to organize information at the outset became suboptimal as a wiki grew in size and scope" (p. 5). Wikis are often not properly staffed by a human editor with sufficient time and authority to make difficult choices concerning what to edit, update, and delete.

The 5Rs + 1. Examples readily come to mind where information is used in the workplace in support of each of the "5Rs" discussed earlier in this chapter. A meeting summary possibly augmented by photos of the whiteboard and then sent as email or posted to an intranet website supports the **recollection** of the meeting and its outcome. Photos taken of a company picnic and similarly distributed support **reminiscences** that may help to preserve intended morale-building benefits of the event long after it has passed. Organizational websites support the **retrieval** of information. Systems of task management and time-tracking can help people to **remember intentions**.[143]

Prilla et al.[144] note that "**Reflection** is a common means to improve work: Every day, people think back to past work and—oftentimes in a group—try to find out whether they can improve it

---

[140] https://www.yammer.com/?ref=googlefy15h2semyammer. See also http://en.wikipedia.org/wiki/Yammer.

[141] Zhang et al., 2010.

[142] Grudin and Poole, 2010.

[143] There is considerable literature on task and time management that is beyond the scope of this already long chapter to review, but see, for example: Adamczyk and Bailey, 2004; Bellotti et al., 2004; Bellotti, et al., 2003; Bellotti et al., 2007; Bellotti and Thornton, 2006; Czerwinski et al., 2004; Danis et al., 2005; Gonzalez and Mark, 2004; Mark et al., 2005; Mark et al., 2008.

[144] Prilla et al., 2012. See also Høyrup, 2004; Marcu et al., 2014; Odom et al., 2012; Odom et al., 2014; Prilla and Renner, 2014; Schon, 1984.

or whether they can derive better practices from it" (p. 55). There are also efforts to use information to **represent** company values both for new and long-time employees. Thom-Santelli and Millen[145] describe the use of photographs within the organization as a way to support acculturation, i.e., "the process in which a newcomer makes sense of the culture that he or she has joined as a new employee" (p. 2088). Photos can be especially effective in creating stronger connections to and a more positive attitude toward geographically dispersed members of a team.[146]

10.2.4 @PLAY (INFORMAL, SOCIAL, SEXUAL)

With respect to the use of information and information technologies in support of social activity, one of the more innovative areas of exploration is in support of intimate relationships. Related is the notion that sex (in one way or another) is nearly always one of the first uses to which any new tool of communication and information exchange is put. A, by now, classic case in point is Second Life.[147] In the *Keeping Found Things Found* (KFTF) book[148] in a "Life Is Better Here" sidebar I presented a riddle of sorts drawn from a true story as relayed to me by an acquaintance:

> *Frank, who lives in Seattle, attends a business conference in Palo Alto on Thursday and Friday. On Thursday evening he and his wife, Susan, go to a popular night spot, Maxwell's, and dance the night away. On Friday evening, Frank wants to go back again. But his wife says, "Can't we go out for a change instead?"*

What's going on? Frank and Susan "got together" on Thursday evening courtesy of SecondLife.com. As I explained, Susan thought this was fun to do when she and Frank were in different cities. But now, on Friday evening, Frank is back in Seattle and Susan does not see the point of getting together in virtual space when they can get together in real space instead.

Of course Second Life is about more than simply "dating," whether with someone new or with a spouse or partner. Second Life, at least in the first years after its introduction in 2003, also had a lot of virtual sex.[149]

Search now using phrases such as "whatever happened to second life" and you will get different viewpoints concerning where Second Life is these days and how it is being used.[150] Our tools

---

[145]   Thom-Santelli and Millen, 2009.
[146]   Marlow and Dabbish, 2011, 2012.
[147]   Secondlife.com.
[148]   Jones, 2007, Chapter 2, "A personal space of information."
[149]   See http://www.alphr.com/features/354457/whatever-happened-to-second-life.
[150]   See http://www.theverge.com/2013/9/24/4698382/second-lifes-strange-second-life; https://chroniclevitae.com/news/456-what-ever-happened-to-second-life; https://modemworld.wordpress.com/2013/06/23/whatever-happened-to-second-life-doing-rather-nicely-tyvm/; https://gigaom.com/2013/06/23/second-life-turns-10-what-it-did-wrong-and-why-it-will-have-its-own-second-life/.

and technologies now provide other options for interaction at a distance, including video chat. Neustaedter and Greenberg[151] describe the motivations for a couple's use of video chat:

> Many couples live a portion of their lives in a long-distance relationship (LDR). This includes a large number of dating college students as well as couples who are geographically separated because of situational demands such as work (p. 753).

In their study,

> we have investigated how couples use video to "hang out" together and engage in activities over extended periods of time. Our results show that regardless of the relationship situation, video chat affords a unique opportunity for couples to share presence over distance, which in turn provides intimacy (p. 753).

However, "complete sexual intimacy is difficult to gain over a video channel because there is a lack of true physicality between partners" (p 761). Instead, study participants reported turning chat systems into "tools that connected two locations in a more permanent fashion…" to produce a "shared living experience":

> In this joint setting, partners pursued their independent activities, took part in shared activities, and conversed as needed. When conversing, the video added a crucial element of seeing the other person's face and facial expressions. When performing activities, having one's partner "around" created stronger feelings of connectedness (p. 761).

Shared activities even included sleep, with some participants reporting that they "would sometimes watch their partner fall asleep, or vice versa" (p. 759).

Intimacy between partners separated in physical space from one another can be preserved (or re-established) by other forms of continuous communication besides video, and with considerably lower rates of data transmission. In two studies, Janssen et al.[152] demonstrated, "using self-report and behavioral tracking in an immersive virtual environment, that heartbeat perception influences social behavior in a similar manner as traditional intimate signals such as gaze and interpersonal distance." But not just any heartbeat: "the stimulus must be attributed to the conversational partner in order to have influence."

Also, video messages, when created (with some help from a "digital media artist") to serve as a storybook of a relationship's meaningful experiences can promote greater intimacy by supporting reflection and serving as "snapshots" into a beloved's thoughts and feelings. Even an increase in the number of emoticons used in communications between partners can greatly increase each partner's

[151] Neustaedter and Greenberg (2012)
[152] Janssen et al., 2010.

perception of the relationship's intimacy particularly if emoticons are selected "by hand" for inclusion in a message rather than being generated automatically.[153]

Tools of communication and information exchange among the partners in a relationship is not all "wine and roses." For most partners, simple texting is likely a much more frequent means of communication at a distance. But texts are subject to misinterpretation and may exacerbate the perceived seriousness of previous face-to-face conflict.[154]

Another frequent means of communication is through Facebook and here too tensions can arise when a romantic partner is also a "friend." Drawing upon the results of their two-week observational study, Zhao et al.[155] note that romantic partners "engage in subtle negotiation around and appropriation of Facebook's features to accomplish both personal and relational goals." (p. 771). Study participants also allowed that things could become very difficult should partners decide to breakup since this may also mean a need to "unfriend" a former partner's friends. A breakup also produces a more general need for a special kind of curation of digital artifacts created during the relationship (e.g., photos, emails, videos, etc.).[156] How, for example, to dispose or hide artifacts without a careful review that might be upsetting and disturbing?

Overall though, tools of communication and information exchange—whether phone calls, texting, Facebook, or tools using more exotic methods such as those reviewed above—can help greatly to bridge gaps of time and distance for effects that are overall beneficial (especially in cases where the alternative is no communication for extended periods of time and a gradual weakening of emotional bonds). But the studies reviewed above also suggest that these tools or their successors are not, anytime soon, likely to provide a full substitute for face-to-face interaction. Whether friends at a social gathering, tennis partners on the court, or lovers together in bed, there is often no proper substitute for the pleasure of same-time, same-place, in-person interactions.

But then, in our hectic, over-scheduled, "multi-tasking" lives, we turn to tools of communication and information exchange for another purpose: not as substitute for face-to-face (F2F) but to plan F2F meetings. In some cases, this can be done through a simple exchange of email, or through Facebook or through a shared calendar. Many of us have several calendars, several email accounts, and possibly even several Facebook accounts, each for a different circumstance or a different set of friends.[157]

But in other cases, email simply doesn't work well, the Facebook mediated interaction doesn't insure agreement, and the complexities of a shared calendar preclude its use.

Consider the example of my poker group.

---

[153] Janssen et al., 2014.
[154] See for example, Scissors et al., 2014.
[155] Zhao et al., 2012.
[156] See, for example, Sas and Whittaker, 2013.
[157] See, for example, Thayer et al., 2012, 2013.

The group (consisting of eight middle-aged men) meets roughly once per month for pizza, beer, political discussion, and even a little poker. We meet on a Friday but finding the best Friday for us all or even any Friday when at least five of us can play can be very challenging. I have no idea how our parents might have made such a coordination prior to digital forms of communication. Possibly a great deal of time was spent on the phone with one person calling (and calling) to find the right date. Or possibly such a game was set for the "first Friday" of every month but then with the possibility that not enough people showed up on some Fridays to make a game.

Over a period of a decade or so, our own efforts to coordinate have followed, albeit ad hoc, a progression:

1. Emails sent back and forth sometimes over a period of several weeks of the prior month. Emails were of the form "I can make next Friday but not the Friday after that. I'm not sure about Friday of the 17th or 24th..." Constraints were difficult to track since emails were separated in time and sometimes by different threads (i.e., different subject lines).

2. In frustration, I devised a simple spreadsheet with upcoming Fridays listed as rows and each poker player listed by name in a column. For the cells in their column, people responded with "yes" ("I definitely can make it"), "no" ("I definitely can't make it"), or "maybe" ("I don't know yet").

3. Later another player added simple scoring for yes's, no's, and maybe's so that we could easily see which Friday was best by its additive score from each of our responses.

Progress. But people would sometimes forget to attach the spreadsheet in their responses. Or worse, they might attach the wrong one. We took the next step in our evolution toward more effective information management when...

4. Another member placed the spreadsheet online (using the Microsoft OneDrive service). We kept our format (rows for candidate Fridays, columns for each member) and our scoring system (otherwise, we might have used a Web service such as Doodle[158]) but now information—the aggregate depiction of everyone's availability—had a "place."

We're not done yet. People don't always update the shared spreadsheet to reflect changes in their social schedule. To save time (theirs not the time of other members of the group), people sometimes still communicate through email ("Oops! I forgot that my daughter's birthday is that Friday..."). Also, not everyone can easily find the spreadsheet in its cloud location. I myself would be in trouble without the auto-complete of the URL in my web browser (type in "poker" and viola:

---

[158] http://doodle.com/.

the long, complete URL appears). Absent handy access to the URL, some members again revert to simple email to "represent" their availability. What might be next steps in our efforts to coordinate through better information management?

One next step might be an integration so that our shared spreadsheet is synchronized with our individual calendars. We can dream. Solutions, as I write these words now do not, seem neither simple, nor robust, nor cross-platform. Sharing is somewhat easier[159] but steps are still involved and then someone must still form an aggregate availability from a review of separate calendars. An integration of calendars also presumes that privacy issues are properly addressed and that people's individual calendars are complete and current. Each is a big assumption.

A complementary next step would involve making the "location" of our online representation of availabilities more like a real place. We can typically get to a physical place by any of several means. We can get close, i.e., we can get into the general neighborhood of our destination then possibly ask for directions or wander around a bit in the hopes of recognizing part of the previous route. With each return to a physical place, our confidence of getting back again increases. Over time we may internalize a map-like ability to return by an alternate route if our preferred route is blocked.[160]

Not so for the online poker spreadsheet. If I should lose my auto-complete settings or decide to switch browsers (without importing these settings) I would be at a loss. There are fallbacks—I could search through emails to find the email providing the original link. But this secondary re-finding task has its own challenges. More striking to me: No matter how many times I return to the spreadsheet, I have no greater confidence in a subsequent return. I'm just as vulnerable to a loss of the "link" (e.g., as an auto-complete suggestion). A challenge of PIM, both in its study for the design of supporting tools (see Chapter 11) and in our individual "Practices of PIM" (see Chapter 12), is to support ways to make digital information, such as the poker spreadsheet, more "real" through additional paths to retrieval. For one additional path to the spreadsheet, for example, one of us in the poker group might create a Facebook group with each of us as a member and with a link to the spreadsheet.

But now consider a final irony as evidence for the value of taking a broader, informational perspective: No matter how sophisticated the means for an online sharing of schedules becomes, there are still situations where a simple physical or paper-based system will work better. If we were in our late teens rather than in middle age and all lived in the same college dormitory, for example, a simple whiteboard by the entrance to the dormitory might be just as effective. Or consider Figure 10.1 with its depiction of notes of "whereabouts and availability," one per person, for members of a

---

[159]   A search with ""sharing online calendars" on June 14, 2015, produces several options for the sharing of online calendars including, for example, http://www.wikihow.com/Share-Your-Google-Calendar. A search with "merging online calendars" produces options such as: https://discussions.apple.com/thread/2046170 and https://support.office.com/en-US/Article/Merge-items-from-multiple-calendars-0a7b4a55-ea17-4024-bc98-1766d2382780.

[160]   Dillon et al., 1993.

research group at the University of Washington. The members of the group are involved in research concerning the use of information technologies and each uses one (or several) digital calendars to coordinate with people outside the group. But the board with notes one per person placed at the entrance to the office area for the research group works just fine in this circumstance.

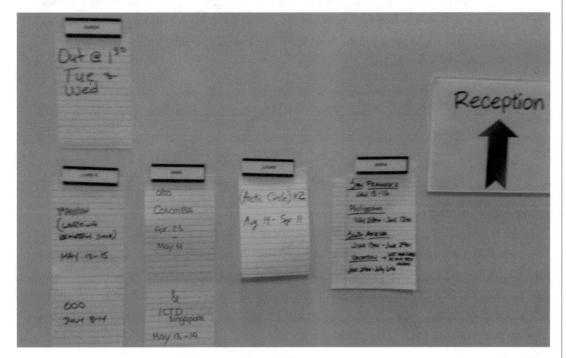

Figure 10.1: The use of attentional surfaces in a shared (physical) space.

It's about the information.

10.2.5 @LARGE

Somewhere "out there" is someone who…

> ➢ will pass by your house on the way to the airport at the same time you wish to leave for the airport and would be happy to give you a ride for the company and the option to avoid traffic by driving in the HOV (high-occupancy vehicle) lane;

> ➢ is on the way you will take to get to the airport, needs to arrive at roughly the same time you need to arrive, and would welcome a ride from you (and might even chip in for gas money or the cost to park at the airport);

➢ is a five-year survivor on the other side of an operation and treatment for a rare form of prostate cancer which it seems is the same kind of cancer you have just been diagnosed to have;

➢ has just been diagnosed with a rare form of cancer just like the one you are now happy to have survived (you just celebrated your five-year anniversary of being cancer free). You are happy to share your story to help this person. Telling your story also makes you feel better;

➢ will listen to you as you express you innermost goals—goals you won't share even with your spouse or closest friends—and will encourage you on your way to their achievement;

➢ has the courage to articulate goals quite similar to your own. You have a vested interest in seeing this person (people) achieve her/his (their) goals. If they can, then perhaps you can too?

➢ will work with you to expand the coverage of a Wikipedia article on "Chautauqua."[161]

PIM@large is about the timely communication and exchange of information with family, friends, and strangers too and, as needed, on a global scale, in order to identify whole new opportunities for coordination and communication toward "win-win" synergies of effort. PIM@large is about identifying whole new opportunities for *multi-goaling*, as I introduced the concept in Chapter 9 of Part 2 in this "Future of PIM" series,[162] i.e., accomplishing two or more goals with one effort—killing two birds with one stone, as the saying goes. I wrote:

> *In multi-tasking, we do an uneasy time-slice switching between several tasks (doing none especially well). With multi-goaling, one activity accomplishes several goals (the proverbial two birds killed with one stone). With synergy between goals we often do even better in the completion of one goal for the presence of the others* (p. 124).

The drive to the airport with a passenger (as identified through a ride share service) is an example of multi-goaling: We've decided to drive no matter what (i.e., since public transportation from where we live is not good, a taxi is too expensive, and we need our car for the return trip the very next day). But now for nearly the same effort, we give someone else a ride too. Perhaps we get rideshare credits we can use when we don't feel like driving on another occasion. Possibly we get help in paying for parking at the airport. Regardless, the drive takes less actual time for the option, with a passenger, to take the HOV lane. And the drive seems shorter still for the good conversation and interesting new connections made during the journey. Multi-goaling.

[161]   https://en.wikipedia.org/wiki/Chautauqua.
[162]   "Transforming Technologies to Manage Our Information," Jones, 2013.

It is an unfortunate irony that this section on PIM at a "large" (even global) scale is one of the shorter ("smaller") of all the sections on social situations of PIM. Its coverage is incomplete and provides only a glancing treatment of selected topics. The chapter is already long, and wider, deeper coverage would easily lead to a whole book on this topic alone, perhaps two. Here, then, is a foreshortened sampling of research and future directions relating to PIM@large.

Goal-setting, sharing, and shared-goal collaborations

Burke and Settles[163] discuss goal-setting websites relating to a diversity of activities, including writing a novel, knitting, and weight loss.[164] Sites involve a management of information that is both personal and communal:

> *These kinds of sites, in which individuals attempt to meet their own personal goals in the virtual company of others, span the boundary between purely individualistic action and social collaboration. The Internet makes it easy to track milestones, compare one's progress to others, and post encouragements* (p.1).

In their own analysis of data relating to a website offering goal setting in connection to an annual song-writing challenge[165] Burke and Settles identified overall benefits resulting from a communal sharing of personal goals with others who hold similar goals and interests:

> *Members who receive social feedback when they first join a community, and those who engage in one-on-one collaborations, are more successful long-term. Not only do they perform their goals better, they feel more "plugged in" to the group and act in ways that enable others to reach their goals, as well* (p 9).

In a later study looking more closely at the collaborations that ensue from goal-sharing at the site, Settles and Dow[166] found that "communication, nuanced complementary interest and status, and a balanced effort from both parties contribute to successful collaborations."

The power of ad hoc communities, based upon shared interests and shared goals (i.e., held in common or at least exchanged), to facilitate collaborations and an active exchange of not only information but also time and emotional support, is not new. Marchionini[167] for example writes in support of a "Sharium" as an extension to traditional libraries. In a manner analogous to the evolution of the web from predominantly read-only in its initial years (i.e., for all but a select few) to read/write,

---

[163] Burke and Settles, 2011.
[164] See for example, http://nanowrimo.org/, http://www.loseit.com/, and https://www.ravelry.com/account/login.
[165] http://fawm.org/.
[166] Settles and Dow, 2013.
[167] Marchionini, 1999; Marchionini et al., 2006.

thanks to an explosion of social media services,[168] the sharium provides not only the means for people to access information but also to contribute ideas, time, and expertise with others.

Websites that promote goal-setting, sharing, and, indirectly, collaboration based upon shared interest (as expressed through the goals that are shared) can certainly bridge conventional barriers of distance and geography. However, in place of these, new barriers can arise. Van Alstyne and Brynjolfsson[169] note that "As IT capabilities continue to improve, preferences—not geography or technology—become the key determinants of community boundaries."

Also, somewhat to the contrary, is a study described in an article by Porges et al.,[170] in which they first note that in studies of goal setting, tracking, and sharing, the benefits of goal progress logging and social feedback are often intermixed. Based upon the data from their study, which was designed to tease apart the relative effects of each, they observed that "surprisingly, social feedback has no significant advantage over progress logging. Further, participants who gave and received social feedback had a higher level of annoyance toward the study."

Gamification

In many cases, progress logging and social feedback combine nicely (not annoyingly) and are not usefully teased apart. Such may be the case, for example, with applications of *gamification* where the "social" comes in the form not only of collaboration (e.g., encouragement) but also mild forms of competition (e.g., "looks like I took more steps than you yesterday…").

Gamification is defined simply as "use of gameplay mechanics for non-game applications"[171] and with somewhat more elaboration as "the use of game thinking and game mechanics in non-game contexts to engage users in solving problems and increase users' contributions."[172] In one of the more famous examples of gamification, *Foldit*[173] an online puzzle video game representing protein folding problems, engaged a massive number of online players (57,000) in a game to fold selected proteins as well as possible following constraints imposed by the available tools for "folding." The game is credited with providing useful results that matched or outperformed algorithmically computed solutions.[174]

---

[168] See Jones, 2012, Chapter 4.

[169] Van Alstyne and Brynjolfsson, 2005.

[170] Porges et al., 2014.

[171] https://en.wiktionary.org/wiki/gamification.

[172] https://en.wikipedia.org/wiki/Gamification; see also, "Counting Every Moment," in the Economist (http://www.economist.com/node/21548493) for an entertaining though somewhat dated article on "self-tracking" and gamification. For a more scholarly treatment see an article by Luis Von Ahn (2006) or see his TED talk (http://www.ted.com/speakers/luis_von_ahn?). Von Ahn was the lead in efforts to develop reCAPTCHA (Von Ahn et al., 2008); (see also, https://en.wikipedia.org/wiki/ReCAPTCHA).

[173] https://en.wikipedia.org/wiki/Foldit.

[174] http://www.nytimes.com/2010/08/10/science/10gamers.html?_r=2&.

Principles of gamification are increasingly applied in a variety of areas ranging from education[175] to reviews of restaurants and hotels[176] and also to encourage contributions in various wikis, most notably Wikipedia.[177]

The exchange of information and services

Finally, in the category of PIM@large are various sites supporting the exchange of information and services (and sometimes goods?). Items of exchange vary widely from personal experiences and words of encouragement on health matters[178] to ridesharing.[179]

PIM is involved not only in the initial matching of items for exchange (e.g., "What do I need?"; "What can I give?") but also in subsequent bookkeeping (e.g., "How many credits?" "What must I do?" "Who must I pick up? When? Where?"). In Japan, a special "currency," *Fureai kippu*,[180] has been developed. People earn credits for helping the elderly. The number of credits earned depends upon the nature of the service (e.g., shopping for someone or taking them to their doctor's appointment) and the number of hours involved. Anyone, including elderly people, can earn credits that can be transferred or redeemed for comparable service (i.e., now or when the person providing the service is older and in need of help).

We might well imagine similar *sectoral currencies*[181] in other areas such as education or even a more general system of expertise bartering[182] as brokered by the Web. The rub is in the valuation of services. What is my expertise worth vs. yours? And there is danger in any attempt at valuation or quid pro quo. People may experience a "glow" of "Good Samaritan" feeling for time and service freely donated and may feel considerably less good (or even cheapened) should these offerings be given a value either explicitly (in units) or implicitly through exchange.[183]

---

[175]   See, for example, https://www.youtube.com/watch?v=9_XUHhi3amA, or http://www.yukaichou.com/gamification-examples/top-10-education-gamification-examples/, or https://chcgamestudies.wordpress.com/2013/03/18/video-games-in-education-final-blog-post/.

[176]   See, for example, http://www.tripadvisor.com/.

[177]   See, for example, Arazy et al., 2015; Kriplean et al., 2008; Morgan et al., 2014; Thornton and McDonald, 2012.

[178]   See Cure Together (http://curetogether.com/) and Patients Like Me (https://www.patientslikeme.com/; https://en.wikipedia.org/wiki/PatientsLikeMe).

[179]   See https://en.wikipedia.org/wiki/Real-time_ridesharing and, as an example of a website look at Lyft https://www.lyft.com/; see also, https://en.wikipedia.org/wiki/Lyft.

[180]   See https://en.wikipedia.org/wiki/Fureai_kippu.

[181]   https://en.wikipedia.org/wiki/Saber_(sectoral_currency.

[182]   https://en.wikipedia.org/wiki/Barter.

[183]   Bellotti et al., 2015.

10.3   CONCLUSIONS: INFORMATION, COMMUNICATION AND A NEVER-ENDING DIALOG TO KNOW

This chapter has broadly considered how people practice PIM in the course of their interactions with other people and especially in several distinct social situations: at home, at school, at work, at play, and "@large."

Across social situations we considered the use of information to represent, information to communicate, and information to know.

To paraphrase Aristotle (a second time): *All people by nature desire to know.* We shouldn't necessarily think that knowledge for Aristotle was solely its own reward (i.e., knowledge for the sake of knowledge). By all accounts, Aristotle was a very practical person, possibly the first empiricist,[184] the one who fled Athens rather than risk execution (so that Athens would not commit "a second sin against Philosophy").[185]

Aristotle might be comfortable with the practical story told in language by our everyday uses of the word "know." We know what time it is (and whether we should let someone know that we're running late). We know what the weather is forecast to be today (and whether or not to take an umbrella with us to the game). We know so that we can act.

We know through our information. In the ideal, incoming information informs us (at the right time, the right place, in the right form…) so that we know what we need to know (and what we need to do). Outgoing information informs others so that they know and, we hope, are better able to act in ways that are consistent with our shared interests.

Information shared can accomplish something ordinary and minor like insuring that all ingredients are available for the planned evening meal without the need for a second trip to the grocery store. Or information can accomplish the extraordinary such as communicating critical details of a rescue mission. Information as the stuff of communication and social discourse can make us more knowledgeable—smarter—and also more effective in our efforts to realize our life's goals and fulfill our life's roles.

Actually, by the preferred direct translation, Aristotle said, "All men by nature desire to know." It seems reasonable to think that he meant to say "people" both in this quote and the previous quote at the outset of this chapter. Or we might think he would have used the more inclusive "people" were he alive to speak with us today.

Scholars conclude that the words reaching us from Aristotle come originally as information in the form of lecture notes (his own or possibly taken by one of his students) that were not in-

---

[184]   http://en.wikipedia.org/wiki/Empiricism, http://yourknowledge.hubpages.com/hub/Empiricism-Aristotle-the-First-Empiricist.

[185]   http://philosophy-of-living.com/a-philosophers-life-aristotle/.

tended for publication.[186] We may never find his "lost works" that were written for publication and posterity.

Words, whether originally written for publication or only as a prompt for tomorrow's lecture, are subject to errors of transcription, translation, and interpretation. These errors may multiply as, over time and distance, the information is transformed from one language, one culture, one context to another. A limitation of the written word…

Aristotle's mentor Plato, quoting Socrates, famously wrote about the limitations of writing and the written word in his Phaedrus dialogue:[187]

> *Writing, Phaedrus, has this strange quality, and is very like painting; for the creatures of painting stand like living beings, but if one asks them a question, they preserve a solemn silence. And so it is with written words; you might think they spoke as if they had intelligence, but if you question them, wishing to know about their sayings, they always say only one and the same thing.*

These caveats ring just as true today as they did when first written by Plato some 2,400 years ago in ancient Greece. These caveats apply not only to writing and painting but also to other forms of information.

Back in 1972, I participated along with thousands of other people in an overwhelmingly peaceful demonstration against the Vietnam War. However, a video depiction of the same demonstration on the evening news focused on a little "rectangle" of the whole demonstration in which a minor scuffle broke out between the police and the demonstrators. The scuffle was over in seconds and was surely less than one percent of the total area taken up by demonstrators. But TV viewers who weren't at the demonstration easily concluded that the whole demonstration was violent. The "reality" depicted by the video for TV viewers sitting at home was very different than the one I experienced while actually at the demonstration.

But there was dialog. No, the video did not respond directly to questions (though it likely revealed more in slow motion or freeze frame). But there were letters (yes, paper letters sent by surface mail) to the local television station and to local newspapers for the town and the college. One letter writer was invited to give a short video editorial at the end of the news broadcast some days later. Doubtless many fewer people saw the video or the letters than saw the original broadcast report of the demonstration. But there was dialog.

We note the ironies that attend the information we have both from Aristotle and from Plato. Aristotle "speaks" to us via lecture notes he may never have intended to share with anyone other

---

[186]   Irwin et al., 1995.

[187]   See http://www.perseus.tufts.edu/hopper/text?doc=Perseus%3Atext%3A1999.01.0174%3Atext%3D-Phaedrus, 274e—275b. See also http://en.wikipedia.org/wiki/Phaedrus_%28dialogue%29#Discussion_of_rhetoric_and_writing_.28257c.E2.80.93279c.29. For a charming recent discussion, in dialog form, of the impacts of media on the message see Grudin, 2011.

than himself as support for the lecture of the next day. Plato quotes Socrates concerning the limitations of writing and the only reason we are privy to the thoughts of Socrates on limitations of writing is because Plato chose to make a written representation of these thoughts.

Socrates did not himself put his dialogues into writing. But in addition to Plato's written account of Socratic dialogs we also have writings by Xenophon meant to represent a significant selection of the dialogues of Socrates.[188] Where both Plato and Xenophon provide written accounts of the same event as, for example, of Socrates' defense at his trial, there is an opportunity to compare and contrast accounts. Such has been the subject of scholarly discussion for centuries.[189]

Scholars conclude that many of Xenophon's written accounts of Socratic dialogs could not have been, as Xenophon claimed, based upon his own direct experience (e.g., in one case he was far too young; in another he was off elsewhere on a military campaign) and are at best a representation of accounts received second-hand and via hearsay. For many written accounts, as provided by both Plato and Xenophon, there is reason to suspect these may be outright fabrications—a record more of what Plato or Xenophon wanted Socrates to say.

Who can ever know for sure? Scholars may someday conclude that writings we now attribute to Plato and Xenophon are outright forgeries. Perhaps these were written instead by some medieval Irish monk who, tiring of the tedium of transcribing ancient texts,[190] decided to have some fun. If so, then a dialog such as the Phaedrus dialog may be a record of what the monk *wanted* Plato to *want* Socrates to say.

Would we then curse the written word? Would we wish the forgeries had been lost or consumed in some fire of long ago set by Viking raiders?[191] I don't think so. The ideas still matter. The dialog sparked by the written expression of these ideas still matters. We are still by far the richer and wiser for the thoughts expressed and shared through a social fabric of information exchange that extends around the globe and across the millennia.

Modern technologies of information capture; manipulation and communication create many more social opportunities to inform, misinform, and wrongfully inform. Consider a sampling of incidents over the past few years (as of 2015):

> ➢ Amidst an exchange of accusations and denials, video camera surveillance footage provides damning evidence that at least some members on the New England Patriots team were responsible for wrongly deflating footballs before a critical conference

---

[188]   For more on Xenophon see http://en.wikipedia.org/wiki/Xenophon and also http://www.iep.utm.edu/xenophon/.

[189]   See, for example, Strauss, 1972.

[190]   For more on the role Irish monks played in the preservation of ancient texts see https://en.wikipedia.org/wiki/How_the_Irish_Saved_Civilization.

[191]   For entry references concerning Viking raids in medieval Ireland see https://en.wikipedia.org/wiki/History_of_Ireland_(800%E2%80%931169) or http://www.irishtimes.com/ancestor/magazine/emigration/viking.htm.

game. Discussion continues concerning a possible change in the pre-game procedure for handling footballs to be used in the regular game.[192]

The incident, which, to those who don't avidly follow the National Football League, may seem more silly than serious, has provided rich inspiration for jokes on late-night comedy shows. In a separate situation, not at all funny, but instead a matter of life and death:

> A man fleeing after a routine, daytime traffic stop for a non-functioning brake light is fatally shot by the police officer. The smartphone video taken by an eyewitness provides damning evidence in contradiction to the police officer's own report. The police officer is charged with murder.[193] The incident and several others involving the fatal use of police force spark a nationwide dialog concerning minority representation in and racial attitudes among members of the police force and concerning policies, procedures, and proper tracking of their use of deadly force.

But then there are new opportunities to spread misinformation as well. Government campaigns of misinformation are nothing new where these often have the advantage of control over the channels of mass media communication. But now in our web-widened world even ordinary people with no special power or authority have the possibility to deceive and misinform on a massive scale:

> Sitting in a London apartment, bored and with no fresh news from his homeland, an Iraqi man and his friend decide to create some of their own by putting out false reports through Twitter of a battle in the made-up town of "Shichwa" that was just recently won by the Iran-backed Hashd al-Shaabi in a struggle against ISIS.[194] The incident adds further fodder to an ongoing discussion concerning, among other things, what controls are needed for social media outlets such as Twitter, Reddit, and YouTube and whether controls should be imposed or voluntary

And then the tragic consequences of information wrongfully recorded and shared:

> "A Rutgers University freshman, distraught over a gay tryst splashed live across cyberspace by his roommate, plunged to his death from the George Washington Bridge." The incident sparks a nationwide debate concerning, among other things, our rights to privacy and a possible need for explicit protections against bullying.[195]

---

[192] http://www.latimes.com/sports/la-sp-sn-deflategate-patriots-tom-brady-20150506-story.html.

[193] https://en.wikipedia.org/wiki/Shooting_of_Walter_Scott.

[194] http://www.independent.co.uk/news/world/middle-east/isis-supporters-fight-imaginary-battle-over-iraqi-town-that-never-existed-after-twitter-hoax-10308300.html; http://www.thedailybeast.com/articles/2015/06/07/isis-loses-key-butter-churn-battle-on-twitter.html.

[195] http://www.nydailynews.com/news/crime/rutgers-freshman-kills-classmates-hidden-camera-watch-sexual-activity-sources-article-1.438225.

Note that in each of these incidents, the information—whether the video recording of a surveillance camera, a webcam, or a smartphone or the text in a series of Tweets—whether accurate, fake, or wrongfully obtained and shared—is never the whole story. The real story, the larger impact, is in the dialog that surrounds the information, connecting it in the process to many other pieces of information and to real action in the form of changed laws, policies, and attitudes. The information doesn't, ever, "speak for itself." We speak for it through the social fabric of our discussions.

Let the dialog continue. May it never stop.

But now the focus of this treatment of PIM must itself shift. How can the study of PIM "inform" the design and development of better PIM tools? This is the topic for the next chapter, "PIM by Design."

CHAPTER 11

PIM by Design

Little lamb, who made thee? …Dost thou know who made thee?

William Blake, *Songs of Innocence*[196]

11.1 TAKING STOCK. WHAT'S BEEN COVERED? WHAT REMAINS?

We are nearing the end of this series on "The Future of Personal Information Management."
 In Part 1, "**Our Information, Always and Forever**:"

- Chapter 1, **A New Age of Information**, established what PIM is both as a field of study and an everyday activity. Chapter 1 also reviews historical trends in information management leading to the creation of PIM as a field of study in its own right with its own, self-identified community of researchers and developers. The field of PIM is young[197] (just over a decade old as of the writing of this book).

- Chapter 2, **The Basics of PIM**, laid a groundwork for PIM and its discussion through a framework that includes the six senses in which information is personal and the six kinds of PIM activity as directed toward creation, maintenance, and use of a mapping between information and need.

The remaining two chapters of Part 1 explored challenges and opportunities of a world in which our information is:

- Chapter 3, **Always at Hand**, thanks to a ubiquity of devices to record and retrieve, most especially including mobile devices we carry or wear. These devices merge the digital with the physical for good and bad.

- Chapter 4, **Forever on the Web**, thanks also to ever more massive capacities for the storage and transmission of data. We're coupled to the Web 24x7 and through the web to a world of people and a world of information. Web-based services give us generous amounts of storage. But is the information we store still "ours"? Who else is using our

---

[196] The Lamb, http://www.gutenberg.org/files/1934/1934-h/1934-h.htm#page1/.
[197] For a review of the history of PIM see the section, "A Short History of PIM," in Chapter 1 of Part 1 of this series (Jones, 2012).

information? How? Will the information still be there when we need it? And in the right formats? Can we ever make it go away?

Part 2, "**Transforming Technologies to Manage Our Information**," explored the challenges and opportunities presented by enabling technologies. First we considered:

- Chapter 5, **Technologies of Input and Output** that may permit us to speak, gesture, wink, and "gaze" to communicate our information needs and that provide new ways to overlay our experience of the physical world with digital "enhancements."

Next, in Chapters 6, 7, and 8 we considered technologies, respectively, to save, search, and structure our information. (As a useful simplification, these correspond to "input," "output," and "store" in a conventional diagram of information flow.) The final chapter in Part 2:

- Chapter 9, **PIM Transformed and Transforming**, introduced the notion of a clerical tax that we each pay in the routine, often tedious, actions we perform with our information (similar to what was termed "paper pushing" in older days). How close can our Practices of PIM come to being "tax free" so that our time is mostly spent making sense and creative use of our information?

Part 3, "**Building a Better World with Our Information**," shifts back from enabling technologies to a more immediate practical look at PIM and the effective use of information in our lives:

- Chapter 10, **Group Information Management and the Social Fabric of PIM**, looks at how we represent and communicate information so that we know better what to and so that others also "know" better what to do (e.g., in accordance with shared goals). Our Practices of PIM occur in a variety of social contexts: at home, school, work, play and also "@large."

The current chapter and the next (and final) chapter pair to take contrastive slants of "innocence" and "experience" on the same general topic of designing for PIM or, we might say, "PIM on Purpose."

- Chapter 11, **PIM by Design,** looks at what the field of PIM study says, and might say, about the design (and development) of tools. What does it mean to deliberately build tools with PIM in mind? And then, also, what might the study of PIM tell us about best (or better) practices for the use of existing tools? How should PIM impact our expectations and our standards for evaluating tools? For evaluating alternate practices of PIM?

    Note: "practice" and "Practice" have different definitions in the context of PIM. A *practice* (small "p") of PIM is a technique, method, or strategy of PIM that accomplishes some purpose(s) and that is or might be a part of the person's PIM repertoire.

Taking a picture of a meeting whiteboard with one's smartphone and then sending to meeting participants and others along with a meeting notes is, for example, a practice of PIM with (among things) the purpose of representing meeting discussion and outcome (and helping those who were there to recollect meeting details).

A *Practice* (with a capital "P") of PIM is the sum total of all practices (including techniques, methods, strategies) and systems (e.g., for managing email or streaming audio or Web references) that a person uses in support of and as enabled by the information (content and structure), information channels, and tools in the person's personal space of information (PSI). (See the clarification of terms section of Chapter 12 for the meanings this series gives to "technique," "method," "strategy," "system," "practice," and "Practice," in the context of PIM.)

• Chapter 12, **To Each of Us, Our Own,** is a personal "experience" counterpart to the well-intentioned "innocence" of Chapter 11. Each of us, of necessity, practices PIM every day of our lives and mostly, so far, without guidance drawn from its formal study. Most of us have been practicing PIM longer than there has been a field of PIM study. We have considerable experience. But likely, we have each learned to do PIM in our own way, making mistakes as we go and learning through the "school of hard knocks." Can we do better? Without waiting for new and improved tools of PIM, using only the tools at hand, but possibly in new ways, can we ourselves design better Practices of PIM?

Note that the definition of "tools" as used in the current chapter and throughout this series as we consider PIM is broad: Tools needn't be digital. One of the most successful PIM tools of all time may be, for example, the paper-based *Post-It* or *sticky note*.[198]

With that noted, much of the discussion in this chapter is focused on the design of computer-based tools of PIM. But this is a very broad category including desktop applications, web-based services, and various devices (e.g., laptops, tablets, "palmtops," "wearables," etc.).

11.1.1 GETTING BETTER THAN THE GIVEN

This chapter attempts to redress an imbalance. In the media and even in our daily conversations, tools are generally the given. Take them or leave them; use them or not. The tools are "there" and the challenge is to figure out what to do with them.

Moving from tools and technologies to impacts on Practices of PIM was prominent in the previous chapters, but with some push in the other direction. Chapter 3, for example, advocated for and explored the benefits of an "i.e.log," stored securely on the Web, as a time-stamped record of all

---

[198] https://en.wikipedia.org/wiki/Post-it_note.

our "item events"—our interactions, across devices, with information (e.g., emails, sent and received, pictures, taken, web pages visited, etc.).

Chapter 4 advocated for a PIM-informed factorization of tool functionality so that, for example, a basic horizontal service to "capture and keep" information or to re-find information might be used across a range of more special-purpose "vertical" applications (e.g., apps for reference management, task management, or note-taking). Chapter 4 also explored the metaphor that our information might be like a "house on wheels":

➢ able to freely move between cloud services such Dropbox, Google Drive, Box, and Microsoft OneDrive according our assessment of their merits with respect to security, support for sharing, syncing, capacity, cost per GB, etc., and

➢ able to be worked with (viewed, maintained, expanded, "lived-in") through a variety of "surface" tools that can be applied, mix and match, to our information. Applications would make "house calls" rather than insisting that we "submit" (our information).

The pushback, to make a PIM-informed assessment of how well tools and technologies work for us and how they might work better, continued in the chapters of Part 2, "Transforming Technologies to Manage our Information,"[199] as we considered more directly the impacts of technologies of input/output, e.g., a "natural interface" (Chapter 5), storage (Chapter 6), search (Chapter 7), and structure (Chapter 8).

The title of Part 2 was, by design, ambiguous. Yes, technologies (and tools) will continue to profoundly impact our ways of managing our information and through these, the lives we lead. But Part 2 also explored the ways that the field of PIM might transform the application of these technologies. The "Why?" answer for a technology should be something better than "Because we can." The "How?" should be something better than a tool/technology-centric answer of "however things work." Can principles derived from the study of PIM give us better answers? Part 2 produces a tentative "yes" by identifying opportunities for a more directed application of technologies of storage, search, and structure.

The review of PIM studies relating to technologies of capture and storage, for example, called into question the value of a full-motion video "total capture" of all we see and hear in a waking day.[200] For all that is recorded, much is still left out (e.g., happenings behind our backs, smells, feelings, emotions, and then, more generally, for whatever is recorded there is always a larger surrounding context that isn't part of the recording). Such a recording is, of course, information "out there" rather than knowledge "in here." We should not fool ourselves that the recording just by its mere existence is some kind of external memory.

---

[199] Jones, 2013.
[200] See Chapter 6, "Technologies to Save Our Information," Jones, 2013.

As a practical matter these recordings must be indexed for selective access and, even then, we may never find the time to review them. How often do we even find time now to review digital photos and short video clips? Sellen and Whittaker[201] argue more generally for applications of technologies of capture and storage that seek not to provide "external memories" but that instead complement human memory in ways that make up for its limitations.[202]

The recording as external information cannot work as a "plug-in" substitute for internal memory but rather should work as an integral part of a larger system. There is nothing new in this. Paper and pen have long served literally as a scratchpad extension to our internal mechanisms for thought.[203] The recording, properly indexed and integrated into our Practices of PIM, may help to complement and extend of human memory and a raw ability to think "in the head." But not without limitation. For example, the ability for such an external recording to support the recollection of internal memories appears to decay with time at roughly the rates that these internal memories decay.[204]

As a practical example of this approach, I suggested that technologies of capture and storage may be better directed toward crawling and consolidating our scattered online information (think health records and financial statements across a multitude of accounts) in usable formats (e.g., as CSV transactions that could be readily imported into a spreadsheet).[205] We shouldn't be at the mercy of financial institutions and health care authorities who may decide to "mothball" our records or to convert these to a format such as PDF which is much less easy to work with.

Search too as discussed in Chapter 7, Part 2,[206] can be guided by considerations of PIM.[207] The search interaction using a search box and a list of results such as with Google may largely disappear as search is increasingly situated in our personal spaces of information (PSIs). This will happen, for example, as the people, places, topics, themes, and things that matter to us are each represented in our PSI as a personal category and also as a locus for a *situated search* that provides a list of suggestions, periodically on its own or when asked, of information items to associate to the category. Each personal category then serves as an attractor to draw in various forms of information—photographs, emails, web pages, even texts and tweets—that are otherwise scattered through the various applications and services we use.

Further, the search can be continuously fine tuned through a process of supervised learning that takes into account what we select for association and what we don't—an interplay of the extensional (items selected for association with a category) and the intensional (a representation of

---

[201] Sellen and Whittaker, 2010.
[202] For more on this argument also Jones, 1988; Jones, 1986a, 1986b.
[203] See, for example, Kirsh, 1995.
[204] Sellen and Whittaker, 2010.
[205] See, for example, Mint.com.
[206] Jones, 2013.
[207] See also Jones, 2007, Chapter 11 and Jones and Teevan, 2007, Chapter 9.

"family resemblances"[208] among the items selected for association with a given category). All of this might be accomplished using the lowly, everyday "folder"[209] as enhanced through a customizable, extensible inclusion of metadata.

Technologies to structure our information can also be guided by practical considerations of PIM. It is generally a nonstarter, for example, to require that people first make a wholesale transfer of their information to a new store or give up their existing applications (e.g., a word processor, spreadsheet app, or email client) before they can experience a better, new world of smart applications based upon semantically encoded (e.g., as RDF) personal information. A more realistic, more effective approach is to model information where it is (i.e., in the file system and existing applications and services)[210] so that a person's existing applications and methods of information management continue to work as usual.

New tools that work "in place" to provide additional ways to work with information return us to an original definition of "application" as in "The act of applying or laying on."[211] Analogous to the plumber or electrician who comes to a house, applications come to the information rather than vice versa. Alternatively, consider our information is a living, growing garden to which we apply a diversity of tools just as we might apply spade, hoe, rake, and watering hose to a physical garden. Similarly, it may be more realistic—and more useful—to structure our collective information on the World Wide Web, not by building a separate semantic Web (a "Web of data")[212] but rather within the HTML of existing web pages.[213]

11.1.2 LEARNING FROM HUMAN-COMPUTER INTERACTION

The overlap between the fields of PIM and human-computer interaction (HCI) has been noted throughout this series.[214] How can the community of PIM researchers learn from the community of HCI researchers (many of whom might count themselves in both fields)—the better to achieve real, beneficial impact on the development of tools and technologies of personal information management? What challenges distinguish PIM from HCI as a field of inquiry especially as we look to accomplish "PIM by design"?

Elements of the design process as articulated in many models in the HCI literature[215] have direct application to PIM design. Take your pick. Common to all is a break from the "Waterfall

---

[208] See https://en.wikipedia.org/wiki/Family_resemblance.

[209] "Folder" is marked off with quotation marks in recognition of the many ways in which the semantics of folders are realized across operating systems and in cloud services such as Dropbox, OneDrive, and Google Drive.

[210] For more on this approach, see the "Taking Back Our Information" series of insets in Chapter 8, Jones, 2013.

[211] https://en.wiktionary.org/wiki/application.

[212] http://en.wikipedia.org/wiki/Semantic_Web.

[213] http://en.wikipedia.org/wiki/Microdata_(HTML).

[214] Especially see Chapter 1 of Part 1 in this series (Jones, 2012) and see also Chapter 10 of this Part 3.

[215] See, for example, Dix et al., 2004; Moggridge and Atkinson, 2007; Nielsen, 1994; Seffah et al., 2005.

model"[216] that has software smoothly "flowing" in a direction from requirements specification to final product. Common to all models, instead, is the notion of iteration, i.e., a willingness to repeat previous stages until things are "right" (or at least right enough).

Gould and Lewis (1985) have one of the simpler, easy-to-understand, easy-to-remember breakdowns:

1. "**Early Focus on Users and Tasks.** First, designers must understand who the users will be. This understanding is arrived at in part by directly studying their cognitive, behavioral, anthropometric, and attitudinal characteristics, and in part by studying the nature of the work expected to be accomplished.

2. **Empirical Measurement.** Second, early in the development process, intended users should actually use simulations and prototypes to carry out real work, and their performance and reactions should be observed, recorded, and analyzed.

3. **Iterative Design.** Third, when problems are found in user testing, as they will be, they must be fixed. This means design must be iterative: There must be a cycle of design, test and measure, and redesign, repeated as often as necessary" (p. 300).

Wobbrock[217] uses the terms "investigate" and "evaluate," respectively, for stages 1 and 2. In between these stages in his model are stages to "ideate" and "prototype." The designer can select from numerous methods for each stage. The designer can investigate with surveys, focus groups, person-to-person interviews, contextual inquiry, task analysis, etc. The designer can ideate using personas, scenarios, affinity diagramming, mind-mapping, storyboarding, and sketching, etc. The fidelity of a prototype can range from rough (deliberately so) paper sketches of the user interface to interactive, functioning applications. Evaluation methods too can range widely from relatively low-cost heuristic evaluations and cognitive walkthroughs to usability testing involving a sampling of people from the targeted user groups, either in the lab or "in the wild" and then possibly over an extended time period.

In this chapter there will be no attempt at a step-by-step breakdown of the design process as it might be applied to the design of PIM tools. But discussion will consider two aspects of design:

➢ **The descriptive.** This includes all efforts to understand the what, where, and how in current situations of PIM. How do people vary in their practices of PIM? What do they do? How? What problems do they encounter? The descriptive corresponds to stage one ("Early focus on users and tasks") in the Gould and Lewis model and also to "investigate" in Wobbrock's model.

---

[216] http://en.wikipedia.org/wiki/Waterfall_model.
[217] Personal commmunication, April 4, 2015.

> **The prescriptive.** How can things be improved? What are the alternatives? Better tools? Improvements in current tools? Better use of available tools? How can we be sure that a proposed solution will work (especially before sinking too many resources into its pursuit)? The prescriptive includes stage 2 ("empirical measure") of the Gould and Lewis model or, similarly, "evaluate" of Wobbrock's model. But also, with respect to Wobbrock's model, the prescriptive includes "ideate" and "prototype," i.e., all steps directed toward addressing the problems of a current situation of PIM as "described."

11.1.3   A PLAN FOR THE REMAINDER OF THIS CHAPTER

Sections in the remainder of this chapter will cover the following:

> **Considerations (including "don'ts," "do's," and guidelines) when designing for PIM.** Many align with those of HCI but with a special informational slant. Others, if not unique to PIM, can properly be said to be distinguishing, i.e., these considerations arise when focus enlarges, as it necessarily must in the study of PIM, to consider the larger *information ecologies* in which people practice PIM. Focus must also expand to consider an informational lifecycle in which many years may separate the act to keep an information item (such as a bill of sale or a photograph) and later acts to re-find and "use" this information. Moreover, information in the form of photos, documents, or even email can have value not only in the lifetime of its owner but also as legacy. A need to take the longer view arises with other activities of PIM as well. Decisions of maintenance and organization, policies for managing privacy and information flow, easily, hurriedly made or made by default ("I accept") may have their full impact only much later.

> **Methods for PIM study and design.** The space of PIM inquiry is not only "long" (as in an informational lifecycle) but also broad. When considering, for example, how people use information to complete a project (and how they might better use information given better support), we must consider information in a broad range of forms from paper-based to email to files to a variety of new forms introduced by web services such as Facebook and Twitter. And then there is the tremendous diversity in people and their individual Practices of PIM. The space of PIM inquiry is vast. It overwhelms. In the face of this, there is a need for cost-effective methods of PIM study and design that can scale.

> **Big challenges and big opportunities.** Finally, we take a brief look at the bigger picture challenges and opportunities of PIM. We do this for fun and because challenges and opportunities take us to the very heart of what PIM is all, about. These also carry

us into a final chapter in this series where we explore the design choices each of us makes of necessity in our daily practices of PIM.

11.2   CONSIDERATIONS WHEN DESIGNING TOOLS FOR PIM

As noted above, there is considerable overlap between the considerations that apply in HCI design (i.e., design for user interface and the user experience) and those that apply in PIM design. In their own coverage of PIM evaluation, for example, Kelly and Teevan (2007) list standard usability measures (ISO document 9241) that are "relevant to any discussion of PIM evaluation because it is generally accepted that a good PIM tool should be usable."

A web search on "user experience" (or "user interface") can easily return useful "don'ts" of HCI design such as don't assume you are like your targeted user or "don't hurt anyone" (or, we might say, don't make things worse).[218] In some cases, a construct is both a "do" and a "don't." Metaphors and analogies, for example, serve to guide in HCI design and to communicate the features of software ("it's a computer desktop"; "It's just like a file cabinet"). But drawbacks in their use have also been noted.[219] Metaphor not only for teaching the user interface but also as a basis for user interface design has been critically discussed.[220]

An informational perspective can provide additional depth to a consideration of pros and cons in the use of metaphor and analogy. Consider, for example, the classic yellow highlighter that is now so standard in our digital tools as adopted from the paper highlighter. Little has been added to the digital adaptation (other, possibly, than a greater ease in switching colors). Could we do better? Note that even as the selected text is highlighted helping to make it standout from surrounding text, the highlighted text is harder to read (See Figure 11.1). In my experience, highlighted text might better be called "semi-redacted" text.

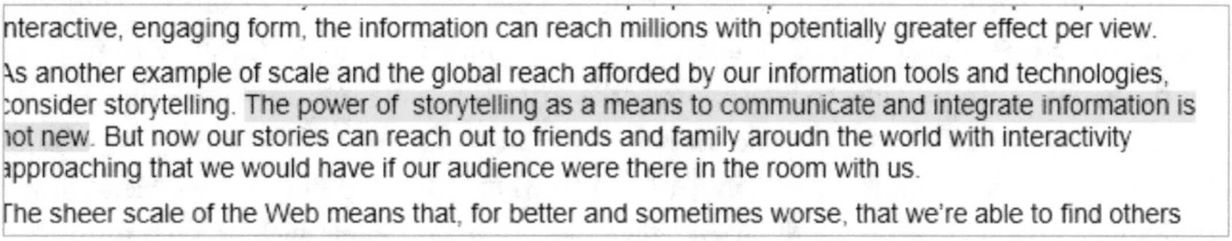

nteractive, engaging form, the information can reach millions with potentially greater effect per view.

As another example of scale and the global reach afforded by our information tools and technologies, consider storytelling. The power of storytelling as a means to communicate and integrate information is not new. But now our stories can reach out to friends and family aroudn the world with interactivity approaching that we would have if our audience were there in the room with us.

The sheer scale of the Web means that, for better and sometimes worse, that we're able to find others

Figure 11.1: The highlighted text stands out from the passage but is harder to read than surrounding text.

218   For example, see http://uxmag.com/articles/guiding-principles-for-ux-designers.
219   Halasz and Moran, 1982.
220   Gurak, 1991.

So then the challenge: How to draw our attention to one selection on the page without compromising the legibility of this selection in the process?

More generally, in designing for better PIM in our tools, we shouldn't be a slave to metaphors especially when these needlessly carry limitations from paper-based information into the digital world.

11.2.1   IT'S ABOUT THE INFORMATION…

Information and information management are the "object" in two senses of this word:

➢ **Information** items of the PSI are the things sent, received, kept, found, created, modified, and deleted. Information tools and channels of the PSI are the things selected, "installed," fostered, and discarded the better to manage our information, coming and going. At a broader scope, collections of information items (PICs) are the thing maintained (synced, saved, shared) and organized, made sense of and used (i.e., to make decisions and effect change). Our information, in all its many forms, is a complement to our senses and a projection of ourselves. Our information brings to us representations of circumstances we cannot or wish not to experience directly. In an outgoing direction, our information speaks for us, our accomplishments, our abilities, our availability, our desires, etc., to a larger world.

➢ Effective information **management** at a personal level is the object (goal, end, purpose[221]) of PIM. How can we improve our Practices of PIM? How can we keep, find/re-find, maintain (save, sync, share) and organize, manage privacy and the flow of information, measure and evaluate, and make sense of and use our information the better to fulfill our roles, realize our goals, and live the lives we wish to live?

Consider again the extent to which our interactions with our world are one step removed from direct experience and mediated, instead, through information items. As noted in Chapter 1 in this series,[222] "In deciding to take an umbrella with us to work, we may check the Web for a forecast even before we look outside. In the other direction, many of the actions we take to effect change in our world (e.g., reserving a hotel room or delivering flowers to a friend in the hospital) are accomplished through an exchange of information items such as Web forms and emails." Some of the ways that information impacts and matters to us in our daily lives as listed in Chapter 1 include:

• "Information is what we extract from the data of our senses in order to understand our world.

---

[221]   https://en.wiktionary.org/wiki/object.
[222]   Jones, 2012.

- Information is what's in the documents, email messages, web pages, MP3 files, photographs (digital and paper-based), videos, etc., that we send (or post) and that we receive (or retrieve).

- Information is for representing and referencing worlds distant from us in time or space. Information is how we learn about the ancient Egyptians. Information is how we learn of the current plight of people in a remote disaster area. Information is how we learn about the possibility of getting lung cancer in 20 years if we don't stop smoking.

- Information is how we are represented to the outside world, accurately or not, for better or worse.

- Information is a drain on our money, energy, time, and attention.

- Information is how we get things done.

- Information is an extension of us."

To "information" should be added informational tools for working with information. Add also our access communication, in various modes, that bridge large gaps in time and distance. Tools and technologies of information management extend back to the invention of writing and the persistence of information through the use of clay tablets, parchment, and papyrus.[223] Today, powerful tools of information management are available to a much larger percentage of a much larger population. It is estimated that 50% of the adults in the global population today (about 7.25 billion people) have access to a smartphone (and through this to the Internet) and this percentage is predicted to rise to 80% by 2020.[224]

Chapter 10 provides numerous examples where information, supported through tools and technology, greatly extends our ability to inform and be informed, to coordinate and collaborate. In many situations, the exchange of information is at least semi-collaborative. Senders may wish to persuade recipients to adopt a viewpoint or take an action but they usually stop short of outright deception in their efforts to do so. We, as recipients, may attend to or ignore the information of a channel. Even though the information is intended to influence or manipulate, we are often better off "subscribing" to the channel than dropping it. We may ignore or seek to block ads. But we still surf the Web.

The broader, even global, reach of our information has consequences that go well beyond mere convenience. Fishermen off the southern coast of India, for example, with a day's catch in the hull, can compare market prices via their mobile phones and so decide where to dock to get the best price for their fish.[225]

---

[223] Gleick, 2012; Ong, 2007.
[224] "Planet of the phones," 2015.
[225] "To do with the price of fish," 2007.

Somewhere out there, perhaps on the other side of the globe, is the perfect job for us (or the perfect living space or … the perfect mate). We describe the position we're looking for. We can speak of our abilities, and our accomplishments. But by traditional means we may reach only a handful of people and then under special circumstances such as at a job fair. This information in written form as a printed, photocopied resume or an email attachment can realistically be sent to a few hundred people. But placed on a website perhaps in more interactive, engaging forms with text enhanced by multi-media, the information can reach millions with potentially greater effect per view.

Or as another example of scale and the global reach afforded by our information tools and technologies, consider storytelling. The power of storytelling as a means to communicate and integrate information is not new. But now our stories can reach friends and family around the world with interactivity approaching what we would have with our audience in the room with us. Our stories told can be automatically transcribed and used as a basis for weaving in other information items such as photos, emails, and web pages.

The sheer scale of the Web means that, for better and sometimes worse, we're able to find others "out there" with similar or complementary interests and experiences to our own. We can find "tagging buddies" who share our ways of viewing (and tagging) information. We can engage others in "games"[226] to support weight loss, better fitness, or in pursuit of other goals relating to health, wealth, and well-being.

As discussed in Chapter 10 (the "PIM@large" section) our information technologies can even support a kind of "time travel" so that, for example, a cancer patient can speak to a cancer survivor who faced similar circumstances, perhaps rare, some months or years previous.[227] The chances of a patient finding their counterpart on the "other side" of treatment are small if search is local to a town or a circle of acquaintances, but chances are greatly increased if search is global.

Or consider another a kind of time travel where we might "speak" with ourselves either in the past or in the future. The photos we take, even the emails we send,[228] can aid in our recollection of reminiscences of, and reflection on ourselves at an earlier point in time. In support of travel in the other direction—into the future—are increasingly sophisticated "ghost of the future" simulations of the way we might be some 10, 20, or 30 years into the future assuming our current trajectories. These simulations can have impact. Ersner-Hershfield et al. (2008) demonstrated for example a significantly greater tendency among participants to allocate funds toward retirement vs. current enjoyment when faced with an age-morphed depiction of themselves from a computer screen vs. a comparable depiction of themselves that was not age-modified (see Figure 11.2).

---

[226] See http://en.wikipedia.org/wiki/Gamification.
[227] Costello, 2014.
[228] Zalinger, 2011.

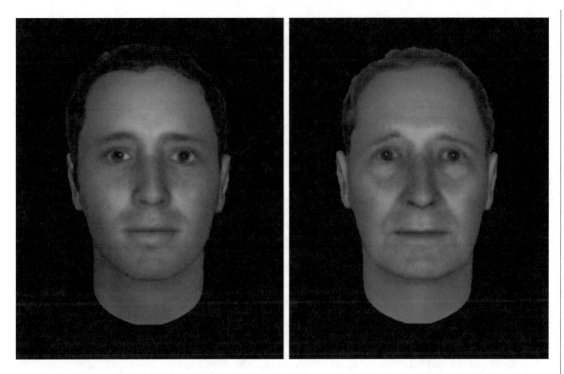

Figure 11.2: The left panel shows a representation of a person as he looks currently; the right panel shows an "age-morphed" version of the same person.[229]

In the study of PIM our focus broadens both temporally and "spatially":

➢ **Over time.** Information must be managed not just for now but for later—possibly for a lifetime and for a legacy beyond. We keep documents that we may not need again until time to complete our taxes several months from now. We take and keep photos we may not look at again until decades from now or perhaps that we will never find the time or opportunity to look at but that will prove a priceless inheritance to our children and grandchildren.

➢ **Over "space."** In the extended present (e.g., today, yesterday, tomorrow, this week), the study of PIM takes us beyond an assessment of the UI (or, more broadly, the UX) for a specific tool (application, device, web service) to a consideration of a larger context that includes other tools (paper-based as well as digital), other people, and also, for example, the attentional surfaces of our walls, shelves, and physical desktops.

[229] Ersner-Hershfield and Bailenson, 2008. Copyright (c) 2008. Association for Psychological Science. Used with permission..

It's about the information. And it's about our ability to leverage our information through our tools and technologies.

With this in mind… some don'ts and dos.

11.2.2 WE ARE NOT MACHINES: DON'T OVERLOOK THE SOCIAL AND THE EMOTIONAL IN PIM

People can get emotional about their informational tools. In a web search, type in the name of a tool—an application, a device (e.g., laptop, tablet, palmtop), or service (e.g., Facebook or LinkedIn)—preceded by "I love" and you are likely to get good matches. Now type in "I hate" for the same tool to get still more matches. People have strong feelings that they are not afraid to express.

People also have strong feelings concerning their own information within the PSI especially the information they "own" or directly control (the first or P1 sense of information). But emotions are different. Feelings now may run from pride to embarrassment and even guilt. The "P" in both PIM and PSI is, after all is, for "personal." People at a social gathering might freely talk about this or that tool, its virtues and problems. The tool is external. People are less likely to make comments such as, "My home office is a complete mess and I feel like crap whenever I go in there" or "my email is out of control and I dread clicking on the inbox."

In studies of current situations and problems of PIM, investigators will sometimes informally take on the role of coach, therapist, or member of the clergy, at least in the minds of the participants. In the Boardman and Sasse[230] study, one participant offered that "It's like a confessional getting all my computer problems off my chest" (p. 585). Mizrachi and Bates[231] noted that participants in their study "commented on how much fun the interview was, how interesting the topic was, or that they had never thought of their behaviors in such a way."

In a longitudinal study described by Bruce et al.,[232] the investigator visited with participants in several 60–90 minute sessions over a period of several weeks to track their progress on a project (selected by mutual agreement) and to track the management of project-related information. As the study came to its conclusion, participants would often express a desire to continue possibly with another project. Participants made comments such as, "having you visit me every week or so really helps me to keep on track." Another common experience is that though participants may be initially reluctant to give of their time, as an interview session proceeds, participants often don't wish for the session to stop and are happy to continue talking even after the session has officially concluded.

Common to these studies is an interview process that calls upon participants to give "guided tours" of portions of their PSIs—digital and paper-based. A Boardman and Sasse participant commented that *"this is a high-trust exercise!"* (p. 585). One participant in the Boardman and Sasse

---

230   Boardman and Sasse, 2004.
231   Mizrachi and Bates, 2013.
232   Bruce et al., 2010.

study offered of one PIC, "some of the things I'm quite proud of" (p. 585). On the other hand, participants as they tour may be faced with and even overwhelmed by the detritus, the clutter, and representations in their information for the many unfinished projects that they have otherwise learned to ignore. In a Jones et al.[233] 2005 study ("Don't take my folders away!") participants on occasion felt compelled to delete information during the guided tour of the interview—not because it was private and personal but because "it really shouldn't be here."

These examples illustrate both the emotional nature of personal information (especially P1 information that we "own") and also the desire for social support. Why indeed should we struggle alone? Descriptive studies, especially longitudinal studies, are likely to get richer data and suffer less from participant dropout to the extent that these are able to engage participants in an active, emotional involvement in the study.

On the prescriptive side, we can imagine a service designed to guide users toward better Practices of PIM. Perhaps the "coach" in this interaction doesn't need to "have all the answers" nor even to be very directive. Perhaps it is enough for the coach simply to observe, support, and, in the spirit of patient-centered therapy,[234] to evince unconditional positive regard. The client in the structured circumstances of the interviews can figure things out. Interviews, especially after the first one, might even take place remotely through a service such as Skype.

11.2.3 "TOO MANY INFORMATION!" DON'T MAKE INFORMATION FRAGMENTATION WORSE THAN IT IS ALREADY

Don't I mean "too much information"? Bear with me. The choice of wording should make more sense as we proceed through this section.

In even the earliest discussions toward building a community of research for PIM, the fragmented nature of our information was targeted as "PIM enemy #1." In a "Personal Information Management Group Report"[235] for a National Science Foundation (NSF) Information and Data Management (IDM) 2003 Workshop in 2003, we listed as the first challenge that "information is scattered" and that "so too, is the study of PIM":

Gathering the information needed to complete a task can then be a major chore in its own right.

With multiple locations, devices and information organizations the chances for confusion and inconsistency increase as well (so that, for example, a person ends up looking in all the wrong places for a desired piece of information) (p. 4 of 6).

Our information often cleaves by the divisions set by the applications, devices, and web services we use. In arguing for PIM as a field of study in its own right, the report noted a state of

---

[233] Jones et al., 2005b.

[234] http://en.wikipedia.org/wiki/Person-centered_therapy.

[235] Jones and Maier, 2003.

research in which studies were similarly divided one from the other by boundaries established by current tools, i.e., researchers were often implicitly letting the tool developers and designers set the conditions for the discussion:

> *Many excellent studies focus on uses of and possible improvements to email; other studies similarly focus on the use of the Web. Of course no single study can address PIM in its entirety. But in defining a study along the lines set by existing applications and information forms, we may miss important opportunities for information integration.* (p. 4 of 6).

In 2004, partly as a metaphorical reference to disk fragmentation,[236] I referred to the situation as one of *information fragmentation*:

> *A wide range of tools and technologies are now available for the management of personal infor-mation. But this diversity has become part of the problem leading to* information fragmentation. *A person may maintain several separate, roughly comparable but inevitably inconsistent, organi-zational schemes for electronic documents, paper documents, email messages, and Web references. The number of organizational schemes may increase if a person has several email accounts, uses separate computers for home and work, uses a PDA or a smart phone or uses any of a bewildering number of special–purpose PIM tools. New tools often introduce still more schemes of organiza-tion…*[237]

Just as disk fragmentation means that "your computer slows down as it has to look in differ-ent places to open a single file,"[238] information fragmentation means that "the assembly or 're-col-lection' of information "can be time-consuming and error-prone."[239] We may have to look in many different places in our PSI in order to assemble the information needed to complete a single task.

As we noted in the summary report for PIM 2005,[240] "A seemingly simple decision, such as whether to say 'yes' to an invitation, often depends upon information in several forms—from a digital calendar, from a paper flyer, from websites, from a previous email conversation, etc."

Problems of information fragmentation are frequently experienced when completing basic tasks or making simple decisions. These problems are a near certainty in our efforts to complete larger projects involving the coordinated completion of several tasks. A number of descriptive stud-ies show that, in the completion of a project, people struggle to manage the separate stores and the organizations of several distinct forms of information including paper documents, e-documents,

---

[236] http://en.wikipedia.org/wiki/Defragmentation.
[237] Jones, 2004.
[238] http://windows.microsoft.com/en-us/windows/what-is-disk-defragmentation#1TC=windows-7.
[239] Jones et al., 2005a.
[240] PIM 2005 was sponsored by the NSF and was the first in a sequence of PIM workshops occurring roughly every 1.5 to 2 years that continue to this day (Jones and Bruce, 2005).

emails, web references, and other more "irregular" items of information such as thoughts, to-dos, mind maps, etc.[241]

For example, the Jones et al. (2006a) study looked at how people organize project-related information. Participants listed projects that they were actively working on in the current week—i.e., projects for which they completed project-related tasks in the week or "touched" information relating to the project. Projects divided between the work-related (e.g., "online training course"), financial non-work-related (e.g., "set up 529 for kids," "taxes"), and fun (e.g., "camping trip"). For each participant, one project was selected for closer inspection and an inventory was taken of information relating to this project.

The inventory revealed that information was scattered across the "usual suspects"—files, emails, web references. In addition, though the 12 participants were conversant with computing technology (half had related jobs), three quarters of the participants still preferred to jot down project-related notes and to-dos on paper. All participants described problems of information fragmentation and each expressed, in various words, a desire for better integration of their information (e.g., "some way to unify information across separate tools").

Problems of information fragmentation may be most apparent in finding/re-finding activities of PIM as when people struggle to gather together task- or project-related information. As described in Chapter 4 (of the *Keeping Found Things Found* book)[242] fragmentation is especially problematic when all relevant information must be assembled, e.g., all events and previous commitments that might conflict with a proposed meeting time. In addition to the time and hassle, when all items in a set must be retrieved, each additional item represents one more chance to fail. Assuming a very high likelihood (say 95%) to retrieve one item (e.g., email, calendar appointment, web page with event information) and assuming independence of retrievals, the likelihood of failure goes from 5% to 23% as the set of items to retrieve goes from 1 to 5.

But in some cases the likelihood of failure is still greater. In situations of output interference, the items a person remembers to retrieve first may interfere with the retrieval of later items in a set—perhaps because the act of retrieval itself strengthens, in a person's memory, the items first recalled at the expense of unrecalled items.[243] Some of us may experience this effect when we try to think of everyone in a group of eight or nine friends. No matter whom we list first—and this can vary from time to time—the last one or two people are often the hardest to remember.

If problems of information fragmentation are most apparent in finding/re-finding activities, problems of information fragmentation are experienced for the other major kinds of PIM activity as well:

---

[241] Bergman et al., 2006; Boardman and Sasse, 2004; Jones et al., 2006a.
[242] Chapter 4, Finding and Re-finding: From Need to Information," Jones, 2007.
[243] Rundus, 1971.

> **Keeping**. Where to put newly encountered information? People may encounter information in the form of a web page, an email message, or even a thought that comes into their heads while driving or in a meeting. Where to put the reference to an interesting website when there is not time currently for close examination? Where to "put" the email message people mean to respond to later when they have time or after they've done some background work first? People might like to place newly encountered information together with related information already under their management in the PSI but this may be difficult to do, especially when existing information is widely scattered. A keeping activity often translates into a finding activity—"where is that folder?" or "what did I do with that other information I already saved?"

> **Meta-level activitie**s too are made more difficult by information fragmentation. Multiple organizations, multiple devices, multiple stores mean that activities to maintain and organize are also multiplied. Maintaining consistency is harder still. As the number of channels, incoming and outgoing, increases (think Facebook, Twitter, LinkedIn, websites, personal blogs, and one or several email accounts), so too do the actions required to **manage privacy and the flow of information**. Similar, actions to protect personal data are multiplied by the number of separate services that keep personal information on the web. **Measuring and evaluating** activities to assess basic questions such as "where did my time go today?" become more difficult when the time is scattered so widely across the organizations and tools of a PSI. **Making sense of and using information** becomes more difficult with information fragmentation even when (if) finding activities have successfully gathered together the relevant information. When information comes in so many different forms from so many different sources, an integrative understanding of the information and its implications can be much harder to achieve.

In Chapter 1 of this series[244] it was noted that "Task/project management and information management are two sides to the same coin." As information tools and channels multiply and as personal information fragments, we would expect a corresponding fragmentation in a person's efforts to complete a task or larger project. A person's "META" (money, energy, time, attention) resources fragment, it would seem, into ever smaller units as people become more "connected."

Indeed, in a workplace study, Gonzalez and Mark found that people spend an average of 3 minutes on one task before switching to another.[245] Well before the dawn of personal computing, Mintzberg[246] noted that "Managerial Activity is characterized by Variety, Fragmentation, and

---

[244]   Chapter 1, "A New World of Informmation," Jones, 2012.
[245]   Czerwinski et al., 2004.
[246]   Mintzberg, 1971.

Brevity" (p. B-99). Perhaps all people in our times are of necessity becoming "managers" not only in the workplace but elsewhere too. At the dinner table or while driving, people may switch from the "task" of being a pleasant dinner guest or attending to traffic to the task of viewing a text message or answering the phone. Switching can bring negative consequences that range from mild (e.g., annoying other dinner guests) to extreme (e.g., a fatal automobile accident).

But as Mark[247] notes, "task switching may be beneficial at times. It could serve to refresh one if tired, and can provide new ideas" (p. 22). We can add other reasons. Work on one task might have reached a natural stopping point pending additional information. The completion of a task to reserve airline tickets, for example, might have reached the point of identifying viable alternatives with final purchase pending review by a person's travel partner. And there are, of course, cases where switching is imperative no matter what the state of the current task, such as when a fire alarm goes off or the boss drops by with a special request.

Some division of information and information channels may also do more good than harm. A separation of information between two different laptops or tablets—one for work and the other for non-work activities, for example—may have a generally beneficial effect (e.g., compliance with company policy) even at the expense of some extra hassle when non-work and work activities over-lap (as, for example, when scheduling the family for a corporate holiday party). Similarly, people may maintain separate email accounts, one for work, and the other for non-work. Or people may keep separate Facebook accounts—one for business contacts and casual acquaintances and the other for close personal friends. Divisions such as these, though crude and imperfect, can be useful. People may need to monitor their work email account continuously throughout the day, for exam-ple, but may check the non-work account less often, or more often only for fun and not necessity.

Often, though, the partitioning of a person's information is not a good thing. A partition may be a by-product of using different tools each with its own "silo" of information. Or perhaps the partition arises because the person decides to switch from one way of organizing information to an-other (and then to another…). Regardless, the costs of the partition greatly outweigh any benefits. This is information fragmentation. There is no precise boundary between partitions of information that are, on balance, beneficial and information fragmentation. But information fragmentation, as used in this book and in the KFTF book, is always a bad thing, i.e., costs greatly outweigh benefits.

Similarly, even as the benefits of and necessity for task switching are noted, Mark goes on to write that task fragmentation or, what she terms, *work fragmentation*, "can inhibit innovation, as people need time and attentional resources to develop deep thought and creative solutions" (p. 80).

What to do? How can "PIM by design" with its informational approach lead to less of both information fragmentation and task/project fragmentation? Or how at least, as we design and build new tools, can we avoid making matters worse?

[247] Mark, 2015.

Here are some general principles to follow in the development of tools to avoid making information fragmentation worse (and to begin making it better):

> **Don't add yet another way of organizing information.** Evernote has its "notebooks" and "tags." Microsoft OneNote has its "sections" (tabs) and "pages." Bookmarking facilities of browsers provide essentially a secondary file structure. People must already maintain "Too many hierarchies!" as Boardman et al. wrote (2003).

> **Do leverage existing organizing structures instead.** In particular, leverage the file system folder structures we all maintain.

> **The "folder" lives.** The demise of folders was seen as imminent a decade ago.[248] But rather than disappearing, the folder model has made the journey from the desktop to the Web in all the major cloud storage services. Gmail which once was strongly tag-based ("labels") now provides support for folder organization. Though their implementations may differ, all the cloud storage services support folder semantics (e.g., move a folder and its content moves, too).

> A folder structure shared has many new possible uses. For example, a folder structure as shared through a cloud service such as Dropbox can serve as a useful kind of scaffolding or structure for single-page (web) applications. One way to do this is through the itemMirror platform as this was described in the "Taking Back Our Information Series" of Chapter 8, Part 2 of this "The Future of Personal Information Management" series ("Transforming Technologies to Manage Our Information).[249] The itemMirror platform can leverage a cloud service's support for sharing. itemMirror also provides the means to associate metadata with a folder and its "links," i.e., to files, subfolders, and "notes" (called "phantom associations" in the itemMirror object model).

> **Don't add still more "places" to monitor.** LinkedIn, Facebook, Reddit, Twitter, multiple email accounts, multiple calendars, multiple websites for viewing bank and financial information, tax information, utility bills, etc. Enough! People already have far too many places they must monitor.

> **Do leverage existing places and existing habits instead.** Consider task and to-do list management. As discussed the section, "Moving On Out: From Vertical Highrises to Bands of Horizontal Integration," Chapter 4 ("Our Information, Forever on

---

[248]   See for example, Christopher and Faden, 2005; Economist, 2005.
[249]   See also https://keepingfoundthingsfound.com/itemmirror/#/; https://github.com/KeepingFoundThings-Found/itemMirror and http://keepingfoundthingsfound.github.io/itemMirror/classes/ItemMirror.html.

the Web") in Part 1 of this series, the Web is "littered" with applications for task and to-do list management.[250] But many people speak of these apps either in the past or future tense, not the present tense (as in "I tried a task management app but couldn't keep up with the discipline" or "I really should try one of these apps to get on top of my tasks and to-dos)".[251] Better chance for long-term success may come through the leverage of existing attentional surfaces that people already routinely visit throughout a typical day. In particular, leverage and extend email and calendaring applications. This is the approach that Bellotti and her team[252] take for example with their introduction of "thrasks" (a task realized as an email conversation thread) to an email application.

> Another approach as exemplified in a service like Slack[253] is to attempt to "wrap" other streams of notification (e.g., from Dropbox, GitHub, Google Drive, Gmail, etc.) into a single "super stream" of notifications. But are other services willing to be "wrapped"? And how good is the wrapping? Users of Slack seem to love it (just search for "I love Slack"). But whether Slack will prove popular over the long run remains to be seen. Does it consolidate other streams of information or just add another one to monitor?

➤ **Do support reliable cross-linking** to files, folders, and other semi-private information. Web addresses, i.e., URLs, are a powerful mechanism for the integration of public information as reviewed by Karger[254] and as I review in Chapter 11 of the *Keeping Found Things Found* book.[255] Desktop links (e.g., shortcuts in Windows platforms, aliases in the Mac OS) worked after a fashion (subject to breakage) and could be used to better integrate information in a personal file system. With the advent of services such as Dropbox, Google Drive, and Microsoft OneDrive and the ability to save, sync, and share information in the "cloud" comes a need for new ways to create and share links that can integrate the information within and between cloud stores. Links need to work with the addressing schemes of the cloud services to provide, when appropriate, read/write access to the information of a store.

---

[250] For example, http://www.capterra.com/task-management-software/ lists over a hundred. See also, http://www.pcmag.com/article2/0,2817,2419258,00.asp and http://lifehacker.com/5924093/five-best-to-do-list-managers, http://productivityist.com/the-problem-with-not-using-email-to-manage-tasks/; http://web.appstorm.net/roundups/task-management/task-management-on-the-web-in-2010/; http://www.cyberciti.biz/tips/open-source-project-management-software.html.

[251] See Bruce et al., 2010; Jones et al., 2015.

[252] Bellotti et al., 2003.

[253] slack.com.

[254] Karger, 2007.

[255] Jones, 2007.

➢ **Do support one PIM activity well rather than several activities poorly.** The "Moving On Out: From Vertical High-rises to Bands of Horizontal Integration" section, referred to above, described a situation where many vertically integrated applications—desktop and web-based—try to do a number of things but don't do any of them especially well. Task management and note-taking applications, for example, typically each provide for the capture (keeping) of new items (notes, tasks, or to-dos). These apps also provide for support to organize, order, and make sense of existing items (notes, to-dos, tasks). And for notifications (to manage the flow of information). And many other functions as well. But when a vertically integrated app is responsible for providing so many functions, it is unlikely to do them all well. Moreover, its ways for supporting these function is likely different than that for other apps—different conventions, different methods, different store, etc.—thus increasing the user's overall experience of information fragmentation. Why not instead have tools that each do one thing extremely well as defined by basic activities of PIM (capture and keeping, finding/re-finding, maintaining and organizing, managing privacy and information flow, measuring and evaluating, making sense and using information)? These tools might then be used across various special-purpose applications that vertically integrate horizontal services to support special-purpose activities such as note-taking, task management, and reference management.

➢ **Do make it easier to stay on or get back on track.** People switch tasks. Frequently. As already noted, this is a kind of fragmentation that can be very costly. Information tools can help in several ways: 1. Decrease the number of interruptions. 2. Shorten the time spent on the interruption. 3. Make it easier to resume the primary task. With respect to #1, generalizations of the "out of office" message have considerable potential to reduce the number of interruptions. Ideally, a person's PIM alter ego is at the ready to provide answers and status update that would otherwise translate into interruptions of the person. With respect to #2, some tools support very quick capture of the interrupting thought or to-do possibly as spoken.[256] A step further are tools that suggest and make connections from the information captured to relevant tasks and projects in the person's PSI.[257] #3 in turn can be supported by preservation of state on the primary task ("now where was I?").

---

[256] See, for example, *Scraps,* Bernstein et al., 2008; Van Kleek et al., 2011.

[257] See, for example, Knitter (https://chrome.google.com/webstore/search/knitter?hl=en-US; https://www.youtube.com/watch?v=zpE95b_J8oE;) and Tagether (https://chrome.google.com/webstore/search/tagether?hl=en-US; https://www.youtube.com/watch?v=THtEvolyGh8).

➤ **Do help people to stay in the flow.** Even with attention focused on a single task or larger project, there are distractions galore. Take the writing of a document using a word processor such as Microsoft Word. The writing of a document, whether a how-to manual, a marketing report, a research article, or a book like this one, goes through different phases from initial "get the ideas down" (possibly in an outline) to a first pass at prose with fully formed sentences to later stages of copy-editing, proof-reading, and formatting. But note that word processor features supporting later stages of editing are mixed up with basic features used at the outset of writing. When formatting is so readily available, there is a temptation to use it for example to get the formatting "just right" in a sentence or paragraph even though this may very well later get cut. Likewise, with "check spelling as you type" (the Microsoft Word feature) it takes strong will power not to correct a word underlined with the "red squiggly." But doing so takes us out of our flow. Applications designed with a greater sense of flow might make it much easier for people, for example, by simply disabling "check spelling as you type" for the initial stage of a document's creation. (This was a feature I wrote about first in Chapters 7 and 15 of the *Keeping Found Things Found*" book.[258])

What About Information Overload?

Like information fragmentation which draws meaning from other uses of the word fragmentation as in "disk fragmentation," "information overload" draws meaning by metaphor from reference to the overload (and damage) done to a circuit through which too much current (think "information") is passed.[259]

Whether or not we suffer permanent damage we've all likely experienced the psychological trauma of information overload. Too much information! Too many things to look at! It never stops! "Information overload" has gained widespread media acceptance and is now the topic of a conference.[260] It's even a dictionary entry.[261]

The concept is useful as a description of our feelings. But it does little to map a course of remediation. Yes, we are overloaded. Now what? What can we do to make things better? Less information? Which information don't we want? That's the rub, of course. Which information to leave out?

---

[258] See also Bederson, 2004; M. Csikszentmihalyi, 1991.
[259] https://en.wiktionary.org/wiki/overload.
[260] http://iorgforum.org/overloaded2014/.
[261] In Wiktionary, https://en.wiktionary.org/wiki/information_overload, and in the Oxford English Dictionary (OED), http://public.oed.com/the-oed-today/recent-updates-to-the-oed/previous-updates/march-2004-update/#oos.

PIM meta-level activity can help. As mentioned above, an "Out of office" notice can give people "cover" so that they feel less compelled to answer emails immediately. People may even elect to exit email for a time. Or even to disconnect from the Internet. But so many activities depend upon a connection so that disconnecting could actually hinder the progress toward completing a task.

But then consider a well-organized library or a beautifully designed book. A person's first reaction is not likely to be "Wow! Information overload!" Since ancient times we've had more information than any of us could possibly consume even in a lifetime devoted to this and little else.

The problem is not too much information but rather "too many" information. If information is scattered in disorganized piles, people see not one well-organized whole but rather clutter of many different parts. In other situations too, we don't directly perceive amount. Rather our perceptions are based upon number. Consider time. Though the perception of time is a very complicated matter involving many areas of the brain,[262] we have all likely had the contrastive experiences of a day at the beach vs. a day with event-filled activity such as a tour of a city we have not visited before. In retrospect, we're likely to judge the second day as longer than the first. The explanation is that we mark the time experienced in retrospect by the number of events we can recall.[263]

If we think in terms of information overload or "too much" information there is no obvious remedy (Which piece of information to leave out?). If we think, instead, in terms of information fragmentation and "too many" information, then an obvious remedy is to organize and integrate our information better. With integration come fewer "chunks" of information to manage and by which to be overwhelmed.

A comparable benefit of integration has been observed in studies of human memory, including the work that I did for completion of my doctoral work at Carnegie-Mellon University.[264] The set-size and fan effects tell a grim story of interference: The more separate facts we know (e.g., about a person or a place) or the more things (to-dos, shopping list items) we need to keep in our heads (in working memory) the more error prone we are in the retrieval of these items/facts and the slower we are to verify the truth of any one of them (vs. foils such as things that aren't true of the person or things that we're not supposed to buy at the grocery store). However, if items can be related even in a subtle thematic way, then the effects of interference (set size or fan effect) are substantially reduced and may even plateau as the number of items to remember increases.

---

[262] See, for example, Allan, 1979; Grondin, 2010.
[263] Our experience during the day may even be in reverse as the day in present tense at the beach, for example, goes on and on.
[264] Jones and Anderson, 1987.

11.2.4 DO COVER THE "CHECKLISTS" OF PIM

A kind of "checklist" methodology—call it *"six by six (6x6)"*—can be devised from the framework described in Chapter 2 ("Some basics of PIM") of Part 1 of this series ("Our Information, Always and Forever")[265] with its provision for six senses in which information can be personal (1. controlled by/owned by, 2. about, 3. directed toward, 4. sent/posted/shared by, 5. for things done or experienced by, 6. potentially relevant/useful to "me") and its six-part factorization of PIM activity (1. keeping, 2. finding, 3. maintaining and organizing, 4. managing privacy and the flow of information, 5. measuring and evaluating, 6. making sense of and using information).

Table 11.1: A depiction of the 6x6 checklist methodology. A tool can be assessed with respect to its impact (good or bad) on each of the six senses in which information is personal, each of the six activities of PIM, and also for potential interactions between specific senses and specific activities.

P1, Owned by		Keeping
P2, About		Finding
P3, Directed toward	X	Maintaining and Organizing
P4, Shared by		Managing privacy and information flow
P5, For things experienced by		Measuring and evaluating
P6, Relevant to		Making sense of and using

With reference to Table 11.1, any tool, technique, or larger strategy of PIM, real or proposed, can be assessed for its likely impact, for better or worse, on personal information in each of its senses. For example, a "cool new tool" (desktop or web-based) that promises to deliver information potentially "relevant to me" (P6, the "sixth sense" in which information is personal) may do so only at the cost of a distracting increase in the information "directed to me" (P3) and by keeping too much personal information "about me" (P2) in a place not under the person's control. Similarly, a tool, technique, or strategy of PIM can be considered for its impact on PIM activity. Tools of personal informatics and digital tracking, for example, may do a great deal to improve "measuring" but if such improvements are accompanied by extra hassles in maintaining and organizing or in managing privacy and the flow information, then the tradeoffs may not be worth it.

The two checklists are not independent of one another. There is substantial overlap between senses of personal information and activities of PIM. For example, managing privacy and flow of information relates directly to senses P2, P3, and P4 (information about, directed toward, and shared by "me"). And some of the cells in the "cross" between senses and activities either don't make sense or aren't particularly interesting. But others do offer an interesting perspective. For example, a personal informatics application that tracks footsteps and pulse (a subset of P5 information) can

---

[265] Jones, 2012, first described in Jones, 2007.

be assessed for each of the activities of PIM. How, for example, can people make sense of the data collected and what can/will they do with this information?

The 6x6 methodology is complemented by other methodologies identifying other noteworthy considerations. Bergman et al.[266] for example, reports good success in the application of a *user-subjective approach* in PIM system design. The user-subjective approach advances three design principles. In brief, these are that design should allow that: 1. All project-related items no matter their form (or format) are to be organized together (the *subjective project classification principle*); 2. The importance of information (to the user) should determine its visual salience and accessibility (the *subjective importance principle*); and 3. Information should be retrieved and used by the user in the same context as it was previously used in (the *subjective context principle*).

In a similar vein is research by Elizabeth Jones et al.[267] (no relation) identifying five factors that determine whether a promising new system of PIM will be successfully adopted:

1. **Visibility**—more generally do users notice the system and remember to use it?;

2. **Integration**—does the system connect and work well with what the user already has in place?;

3. **Co-adoption**—is it necessary for others to use the system as well? (Lack of co-adoption is a major source for failure in CSCW applications);[268]

4. **Scalability**—does the system still work over time and especially as the amount of information continues to increase?; and

5. **Return on investment (ROI)**—after the hopeful enthusiasm with which a system is initially embraced has waned, the system has to prove its value such that the costs of its use are more than compensated for by benefits.

The trouble with the adoption of PIM systems is twofold:

1. Some may be discarded prematurely before the daily habit of their use has been established (e.g., for lack of visibility or integration); and

2. The problems with other systems (e.g., lack of scalability or return on investment) are apparent only much later after a system has been deeply embedded in a person's overall practice of PIM making its removal a costly hassle.

Consider, for example, a "perfect" folder organization that turns out to be too much trouble to maintain but can't be undone without many hours of re-organization.

---

[266] Bergman et al., 2008b.
[267] Jones et al., 2008.
[268] Grudin, 1988.

Finally, there is the notion of "roads" and "walls" as introduced in Section 1.4 ("Roads and Walls") of the very first chapter in this series: Chapter 1 ("A New Age of Information") of Part 1 ("Our Information, Always and Forever").[269] As people use tools to "go Neolithic" with permanent settlements on the Web for their information, we need to consider these tools both with respect to their "road" qualities (do they support communication to and from the "settlement" and a larger world of information?) and their "wall" qualities (do they protect against attacks or theft?).

11.3   TOWARD PRACTICAL METHODS WITH PRACTICAL IMPACT

PIM requires the study of people, with a diversity of backgrounds and needs, over time as they work in many different situations, with different forms of information and different tools of information management. This scope of PIM inquiry brings a need for practical, cost-effective methods that can scale. Further, there is a need not only for *descriptive* studies aimed at providing a better understanding for how people currently practice PIM but also for *prescriptive* studies aimed both at evaluation[270] and also toward the recommendation of improved tools and practices of PIM.

The nature of PIM makes its study challenging in the extreme. We seek to understand how people manage information using tools of information management. Not just any information but rather their information. Traditional laboratory tasks risk abstracting away the "personal" from PIM. People don't just keep information; they keep information within the established organizations of their personal spaces of information (PSIs)—the folder structure of their laptop, or the drawers and layout of their physical desktop or a Facebook "Timeline." Likewise, people can be said to re-find information, whether this information is in a private store or is public information on the Web, only to the extent that this information is "personal" through previous encounter.

The study of PIM, therefore, is necessarily "in the wild," i.e., the people can't be said to be doing their Practices of PIM unless they can do so with their information, their tools, their channels of communication, their overall PSI. The context matters.

The study of PIM should also be longitudinal. So many activities of PIM unfold over time. In *Keeping Found Things Found: The Study and Practice of PIM*, I likened an act of keeping, for example, to passing an American football to oneself at some future place and time. The business card is placed in a pocket in anticipation that the pocket will be checked later (before the pants go to the laundry). The email is self-sent with a reminder in anticipation that it will appear and be noticed in the inbox. Sometimes the pass, the interaction with self, succeeds. Sometime it doesn't. The bookmark saved, for example, may never be seen again or not, anyway, in time to be used as anticipated.[271]

---

[269]   Part 1, *The Future of Personal Information Managemenet: Our Information, Always and Forever,"* Jones (2012).
[270]   Kelly and Teevan, 2007.
[271]   Jones et al., 2003.

For how long should the longitudinal study be? It's hard to say. Obviously some actions, some interactions with self, aren't completed until years or even decades later.

An observational study should be unobtrusive lest the observation impact the behavior being studied. We might hope for an electronic variant of the proverbial "fly on the wall" that records the participant (full motion video) even as device logs are kept for the participants interactions with information and information tools. But then the fly had really better be able to fly—a micro-drone perhaps—since so much of PIM is now practiced on the go or in "stand-up" mode. And then likely the fly will need to have good interview skills as well since there may be a need on occasion to break through the observational "one-way mirror" in order to ask questions of clarification while the action is still fresh in the participant's mind. Or perhaps the participant is asked to "think aloud." This might work in short bursts but will surely be tiresome as time goes on.

And then how can the study of one sampling of people generalize? Over which populations? There is a natural tendency for researchers to study people who are like themselves or at least "nearby." Professors study other professors or, if not, then students in the same academic setting. Researchers in company research labs tend to study other researchers at the same company. How can results generalize to people outside the university or the research lab? How can results generalize to people who don't have Ph.D.s, haven't graduated from college or perhaps not even from high school? What about people in other age groups? From other ethnic backgrounds? Other countries?

And then, how do results obtained from people using one platform generalize to other platforms? What about the social fabric so important to PIM (as explored in Chapter 10)? The choice of smartphone can surely impact a Practice of PIM. So too the choice of laptop or tablet and its OS. So too the choice of browser or browsers (are different browsers used in different ways?). And the choice of email provider and client. And the choice of word processor, and spreadsheet package, and cloud storage service, and other web services (such as Evernote). And then what about the physical environment? And so on…

Each participant of a study is a unique point when "placed" in the very large space defined by all the dimensions that are potentially impactful to a practice of PIM.

Similar considerations apply to studies focused primarily on evaluation of a new or improved tool. For whom will it work? Under what circumstances? For how long? How does it scale as the amount of information increases? How is the use of a new or improved tool impacted by a PSI that already includes other tools and practices? And then how is the use of this tool impacted as the PSI changes (constantly) with the movement of information? With the addition of other new tools?

A person's point in the space of PIM possibilities is not only unique, it is also constantly moving as the person acquires new tools and practices of PIM.

And then how will we even know even for a single participant, even for a single point in time, whether things are better for the use of a new tool or practice? How are improvements measured?

How do we avoid a situation where improvements by one measure are countered by deterioration in other measures?

Especially difficult are prescriptive conclusions with impact not only in tool design and development but also in the selection of "best" (or at least "better") practices of PIM that might be recommended and taught in training programs. Each individual study is necessarily limited in scope and can only assess a small subset of the many situations of PIM activity and tool use that occur in the wild.

"What should I be doing to do better PIM?" "How should we build this tool to make it more useful in PIM?" If PIM researchers are asked these or similar questions, there is an understandable tendency to demur with responses like "Well that depends" or "It's hard to say" or "We really need to do more research…"

If only a small number of specific guidelines either for tool design and development or for the selection of everyday practices of PIM have emerged so far from the formal study of PIM, we PIM researchers have a ready excuse. We can "sing a song" of exculpatory innocence: The field of PIM is young and "inexperienced."[272] The ability to prescribe, to make specific recommendations (or at least assessments) in matters of tool design and with respect to better practices of PIM will surely improve as the field of PIM gathers more experience from formal study.

But the discussion here gives us reason for concern. Given an enormous space of PIM circumstances, given the difficulty of assessment, given a landscape that is constantly changing with advances in technology, the introduction of new tools and shifts in personal habits and preferences and given also the limits (often severe) on the resources available for any given study, will we researchers forever be saying "that depends" and "more research is needed"?

For this not perpetually to be the case, we need to consider a wide range of approaches to the study of PIM and to PIM "by design." In-depth studies involving on-site interviews and observation can be very useful but are also generally very expensive to conduct, especially if these involve repeated visits over an extended period of time. Given cost and availability, the number of participants is likely to be very small, thus making it unlikely that any results are statistically significant and also limiting the generalizability of these results.

Some kinds of study are not only prohibitively expensive but may also, given the nature of PIM, be inappropriate. Consider, for example, the classic "gold standard" of the double-blind laboratory experiment. The model may not fit. Our intention is to understand how people do PIM, the problems they encounter, and ways things might be improved. But this does not generally mean that people should be the *subject* of this or that experimental manipulation. Rather, people must be engaged as active participants.

---

[272]   See "A short history of PIM" in Chapter 1 ("A New World of Information") in Part 1 (*Our Information, Always and Forever*) of this series (Jones, 2012).

This applies certainly when it comes to programs for training and teaching PIM. For any program to succeed, whether a short half-day, day-long program of training (aka "tutorial" or "seminar"), or a semester/quarter-long program of teaching, the recipient of the training or teaching, the student, must be involved to an extreme degree—more so than if the topic were, say, "quantum mechanics" or "colonial America." It is, after all, the student's Practice of PIM that is meant to change, and, through this practice, the student's life that should improve (@home, @school, @work, @play…@large), through better use of information in pursuit life's goals and roles.

But involvement is needed even in efforts to design better tools of PIM. The tool, any tool, isn't administered the way, say, a drug or a change of lighting, is administered in the experimental condition of the classic double-blind experiment. The tools must be actively incorporated into a person's Practice of PIM.

In this regard, analogies can be made to efforts at "knowledge transfer." Some years ago, concerned by what I saw as some very broad claims being made for a so-called field of "personal knowledge management." I wrote a piece for *First Monday* titled "No Knowledge but through Information" (Jones, 2010). The article had three key points:

> *1. Information is a thing to be handled and controlled; knowledge is not. 2. Knowledge can be managed only indirectly, through the management of information. 3. Personal knowledge management (PKM) is, therefore, best regarded as a subset of personal information management (PIM)—but a very useful subset addressing important issues that otherwise might be overlooked.*

Chapter 10 reviewed literature characterizing knowledge as "no thing." Knowledge is distributed (in the head, in an organization too); knowledge is everywhere and nowhere in particular. We infer the presence of knowledge from actions taken, i.e., knowledge is information in action. All our efforts at an external representation of knowledge—whether simple text or if-then rules—yields one form or another of information instead.

The transfer of knowledge, from one person (or the people of one organization) to another, is mediated by information and happens only through the active involvement of the intended recipient(s). When transfer succeeds, we say that the recipient is "learning." But as a counterpart to the knowledge management term *knowledge elicitation* and also to make a point concerning the essential active nature of learning, I used the term *knowledge instillation*:

> ***Knowledge instillation.*** *"Instillation" comes from "instill" as in "to cause to become part of someone's nature." Instillation neatly contrasts with "installation." Much as we might like to, we can't simply "install" a new body of knowledge in our brains or in an organization as we might install a new software program on our computers. Knowledge elicitation is only step one. Knowledge instillation is often the more difficult step in the transfer of knowledge.*

Likewise, I'll argue that in the study toward better PIM by design in tools and practices of PIM, the methods with most impact are those that promote an active involvement—an *observant participation*—in a study's sampling of the people who are the intended beneficiaries of the better tools and practices of PIM.

In the remainder of this section and also its "experience" counterpart in the next and final chapter (Chapter 12, "To Each of Us Our Own") discussion centers on what methods might work best:

> ➢ For PIM researchers in their studies of PIM with a goal of better PIM by design in better tools and also in teachable practices of PIM (this chapter).

> ➢ For individuals in a program of self-study (or perhaps involved with others in a program of collaborative study) and with the goal of better PIM through the active integration of tools and practices into their overall Practices of PIM. (The next chapter—Chapter 12).

For the remainder of this section (here in Chapter 11), we first consider some studies of PIM for the methods of empirical inquiry they illustrate and for the pattern of results they have generated. We then consider, all too briefly, two additional approaches that complement these methods of empirical inquiry: (1) Cognitive modeling through which alternatives in PIM practices and tool design might be simulated and their performance numbers compared and (2) A massive open, online approach that leverages the Web and the ubiquity of our means to connect to it to engage much larger samplings of people in an ongoing dialog toward better practices and tools of PIM.

11.3.1 A FEW STUDIES OF PIM AND THE METHODS THEY HAVE USED

We can consider only a small subset of the many methods that have been used in PIM research or might potentially have use in PIM research. Each method is illustrated through its use in a PIM study.

Note: *method* is another word whose meaning varies in subtle but significant ways depending upon context. In the context of a PIM Practice, a method is a sequence of actions, possibly involving several techniques as supported by several tools, toward some desired end. For example, sending an email message to yourself with a to-do or task reminder is a method for task management. In the context of the study of PIM (or study in other fields, for that matter), a distinction can be made between the "Method" (uppercase "M") of a study and the various "methods" (lowercase "m") that are used in the study. (The distinction is analogous to the distinction between a person's overall Practice of PIM and the various practices that are included in this Practice.) Throughout the discussion of this chapter, focus is on study methods (lowercase "m") that might combined in various ways in a study's overall Method.

"How Do People Organize Their Desks?"[273]

Noteworthy methods:

- ➢ Guided tour;

- ➢ Setup/test of a cued re-finding task.

As of June 7, 2015, Google Scholar lists nearly 850 citations of this article. Though the article itself was published before the phrase "personal information management" was coined[274] it is cited by a good percentage of articles since that do self-identify (e.g., with keywords) as dealing with PIM. The article's characterization of unnamed "piles" and named "files" as distinct methods of organizing information and of "neat" and "messy" styles of organizing have become a standard part of PIM terminology. The article also notes the important "reminding" function that a good organization can provide and the inherent difficulty in categorizing information.

The article still makes good reading and many implications it draws are relevant even today. The potential of auto-classification to keep encountered information for example or the use of visible attributes such as color, location, and size to remind have yet to be fully exploited in support tools of PIM. All this from a study that involved only 10 participants! Good methods of data gathering coupled with creative, thoughtful analysis, can go a long way. As Malone notes,

> *This study illustrates a form of exploratory observation, like that often used by anthropologists, that can be an extremely useful prelude to designing computer systems for human users … This study is not, and is not intended to be, a controlled experiment or a large sample survey. The goal of data gathering here is to obtain qualitative insights and compelling examples, not statistical proof of a priori conjectures. Where traditional experiments and surveys rely on the skill of the study designer to reduce the effect of biases of the observers, this methodology relies more on the skill and insight of the observer to discover unexpected phenomena and illuminating examples in the human systems being observed. Sometimes (as in this case), carefully controlled studies or more extensive naturalistic observations are suggested by the insights obtained from exploratory observation, and these are certainly worth performing. In other cases, the needs for designing systems (or time and budget constraints) do not justify other studies.*

The study included a *guided tour* of regions of a person's PSI, notably the visible regions of paper "piles" and files on and near a person's workplace desk. Participants provided a running commentary on regions of their offices and the interviewer occasionally asked questions of clarification. The guided informational tour has become a mainstay method of PIM inquiry.[275] As personal

---

[273] Malone, 1983.
[274] The first use I know of was in Lansdale, 1988.
[275] Boardman and Sasse, 2004; Jones et al., 2002; Whittaker and Hirschberg, 2001.

information moves to digital form, the tours must follow. Guided tours face a challenge to provide proper prompts for information that, while important, is not always immediately visible (e.g., the information in a Dropbox account or sent and received via Twitter).

Also of interest was the set-up/test *cued re-finding task*. A subset of participants were observed as they sought to retrieve a specific item of information where probes were chosen for a participant by a co-worker.

> *Six of the interviewees were asked to find several documents in their office. These "probe" documents were chosen for each person by one of his or her co-workers... The co-workers were asked to choose some documents they thought would be easy to find and some they thought would be hard to find.*

"How a Personal Document's Intended Use or Purpose Affects its Classification in an Office"[276]

Noteworthy methods:

> ➤ Prompted in-situ completion of a real information task (sorting mail);

> ➤ Think aloud.

Kwasnik's article established the very important point that people often keep according to later anticipated use. One noteworthy method was what here will be termed the *prompted in-situ completion of a real information task*. Participants were asked to "sort through a day's (surface, paper-based) mail simulating as closely as possible the usual way in which this task is done." Participants were requested to *think aloud* as they did so. The validity and effectiveness of the think-aloud method as a relatively low impact means to acquire valuable data (i.e., reflecting the participant's sub-vocal thoughts) was carefully established in the course of early work into human cognition and problem-solving.[277]

"The Character, Value, and Management of Personal Paper Archives"[278]

Noteworthy methods:

> ➤ Life-change timing.

A noteworthy method in this study is what we might call *life-change timing*... Participants were interviewed in connection with a large planned move of offices within a research organization:

---

[276]   Kwasnik, 1989.
[277]   Ericsson and Simon, 1980, 1998.
[278]   Whittaker and Hirschberg, 2001.

We timed our investigation to coincide with an office move, which had important implications for data collection. Workers had all recently sorted through their paper data in preparation for the move. The new offices had slightly less storage space within each office, although extra storage was provided in public locations. This reduction in local storage seemed to motivate careful discarding and sorting of existing data. In interviewing and surveying workers when we did, we capitalized on the fact that they had very recently handled most of their paper data. Furthermore, they had recently been forced to identify criteria for determining what to keep and what to discard. The move also meant that we could collect quantitative data about volumes of data that people moved, and estimates of how much paper people discarded. All workers packed their archives into identical-sized professional movers' boxes, making it easy to quantify and compare different archives. Workers were also given control of the layout, but not the size, of their new offices. We were therefore able to collect data about aspects of people's physical set-up that are relevant to managing paper data.

The study provided very useful results concerning the percentage of archived information (still largely paper-based in 2001) that had ever been used or was worth keeping "in case." (Participants often downsized in office area necessitating some corresponding reduction in size of their paper archives.)

Would a similar study today, some 15 years later, be as revealing in a world where so much more of a person's information @work is in digital form?

But the method could certainly be applied in circumstances where people are facing a move from one house or apartment to another. What is tossed? What is kept? How is it organized in the new location? How are decisions impacted by the assessed informational value of the object in question—the old photograph, for example, or the frying pan which, though no longer used, is evocative of college days and the first time living away from home?

In particular, are the downsizing pressures often experienced by people of a "pivotal age group," which now roughly coincides with people of the baby-boomer generation. The age group is pivotal for several reasons: people are nearing retirement or recently retired; and people are or will soon become "empty-nesters" as children go off to college. But in other cases, children who have graduated from college may elect to stay home for a time while they seek gainful employment. People of a pivotal age may also elect to care for their parents at home. People of this age group must often make pivotal choices concerning health care and wealth management. These and other life choices may be associated with a downsizing move to a smaller house or possibly the re-purposing of rooms in the current house to accommodate an elderly parent (or even a renter who can provide extra income). These life changes equal opportunity: people of necessity much make decisions.

Many of these decisions relate to the management of their information or an informational-influenced management of physical objects.

"Once Found, What Then?"[279]

Noteworthy methods:

> ➢ Guided tour;

> ➢ Think aloud;

> ➢ Contrastive analysis of different people by professional category;

> ➢ Follow-on survey;

> ➢ Functional analysis.

Similar to Kwasnik et al., the study involved *the prompted in-situ completion of a real informational task.*

> *In this questionnaire, participants were also asked to list at least three work-related, web-intensive "free-time" tasks they might like to work on over the next week should they have a half-hour or more of unscheduled time. During the subsequent observational session, one of these tasks was selected, by agreement between the observer and the participant. The participant then spent the next 30 minutes working on this task. Participants were instructed to think aloud while performing the task. An "over-the-shoulder" video recording was made to capture screen contents (at very coarse resolution), the participant's hand movements and the participant's think-aloud commentary.*

> *Participants were asked to handle office interruptions (phone calls, visitors, etc.) as they normally would. Participants were also encouraged to do what they would normally do in the face of serendipitous discoveries (e.g., web pages of relevance to other aspects of their lives such as upcoming vacations, purchases, health insurance, child care, etc.). The observer did not speak except to answer questions of procedure or, as needed, to remind the participant to continue to think aloud.*

Also methodologically noteworthy in this study was the deliberate sampling from four distinct populations defined by profession, where professions differed from one another in their typical relationship to information and the gathering of information:

> ➢ Researchers have traditionally been direct consumers of information (in large quantities).

---

[279] Jones et al., 2002.

➢ Librarians and corporate information specialists make information available to others (including managers and researchers).

➢ Managers, traditionally, have a preference for oral communication and depend heavily on colleagues and subordinates for their information.

As an illustration of a *mixed-methods approach* to descriptive study, keeping behaviors as identified in the study were listed in a follow-on, online survey[280] with the aim to engage a much larger number of participants, more cheaply (surveys after their initial formation are nearly "free" to administer online) in a more quantitative assessment of relative frequencies of usage for different keeping behaviors overall and for each of the professions initially studied (librarians, researchers, and managers). Efforts were also made in the survey's advertisement to engage another population of information users: Students (also with their own distinct relationship to information and information gathering).

Finally, the study employed a *functional analysis* in which each observed keeping behavior was compared with respect to desirable features such as "portability" (can information kept in this way be carried with people wherever they go?) and "communication and information sharing" (can information kept in this way be easily shared with others?).

A note about the functional analysis and its tabular representation

The utility of the table as a representation of information was illustrated in Chapter 10 in, for example, the work of Day et al.,[281] showing the benefits of a tabular representation of instructions for taking a set of medications (each medicine was in its own row with columns representing times of the day and cells checked or not according to whether a given medicine should be taken at a given time of day).

The tabular representation for the functional analysis is what we've seen on many occasions in, for example, product comparison articles, where rows are product alternatives and columns represent features such as price, capacity, reliability, etc. Tables are a commonplace format for information representation, i.e., nothing special.

However, on occasion a table and its feature/functional analysis can do more. Table 10.3 of Chapter 10 in the *Keeping Found Things Found* book[282] for example provided a comparison of different modes of communication each in its own row with features of comparison such as "interactivity" and "permanent record" as columns. The table made apparent what had already, back in 1999, come to pass: the demise of the venerable telegram as a mode of communica-

---

280   Jones et al., 2003.
281   Day et al., 1988.
282   Jones, 2007.

tion.[283] For no column in the table did the telegram hold any advantages to other modes of communication.

We might hope that tabular representations of feature/functional analyses might do more than merely represent or explain. These might have predictive value as when, for example, some combination of useful features as represented by columns is not met by any current tools as represented in tabular rows.[284]

The ultimate illustration of predictive value in a good tabular representation is Mendeleev's periodic table of chemical elements.[285] Not all chemical elements were known back in 1869 when the periodical table was first published. This meant that some cells in the table were empty. Referring to one such gap, Mendeleev was able to predict with confidence that the missing element must exist. Moreover, likely features of the element based upon its position in the table (atomic weight and ability to combine with other elements) greatly facilitated its subsequent discovery. The element is now called scandium (SC).[286]

"The Perfect Search Engine Is Not Enough"[287]

Noteworthy methods:

> ➢ Experience sampling.[288]

The study was groundbreaking for establishing the limits of a direct or teleporting search and for a cognitive analysis of why people might often prefer a slower, stepwise orienteering approach in the retrieval of information. The study made use of the *experience sampling method*:

> *We interviewed each participant twice daily on five consecutive days, interrupting them in their offices at unspecified times. We asked them to describe what they had most recently "looked at" and what they had most recent "looked for" in their email, their files, and on the Web. Each semi-structured interview lasted about five minutes.*

This method proved very useful as a way to uncover everyday instances of searching for information that might not otherwise, days later, have been recalled by the participant or, if recalled, considered noteworthy. More generally, the method provides a way to achieve a kind of bottom-up

---

[283] https://en.wikipedia.org/wiki/Telegraphy.

[284] One effort in this regard a student project to build a better "Add Favorite" dialog (Jones et al., 2003).

[285] https://en.wikipedia.org/wiki/Periodic_table.

[286] https://en.wikipedia.org/wiki/Scandium.

[287] Teevan et al., 2004.

[288] Csikszentmihalyi and Larson, 1987; Larson and Csikszentmihalyi, 2014. **See also** https://en.wikipedia.org/wiki/Experience_sampling_method.

understanding for a PIM behavior that might not arise in a more top-down direction of inquiry (e.g., one focused on web search or the search for a local file).

> *Although earlier studies of directed search focused on keyword search, most of the search behavior we observed did not involve keyword search. Instead of jumping directly to their information target using keywords, our participants navigated to their target with small, local steps using their contextual knowledge as a guide, even when they knew exactly what they were looking for in advance.*

"A Diary Study of Task Switching and Interruptions"[289]

Noteworthy method:

> ➤ Diary keeping.[290]

The study made use of a *diary study* method wherein participants were charged over a period of a week to record their activities row by row as they switched from one task to another (and then back again). For a given activity, participants recorded attributes such as start time, completion time, tools used, and information needed. Results indicated a large number of shifts in task over the week. As prompted by their own reflections on their diaries and the "stories" told through these (about interruptions and task-switching), participants identified the need for a preservation and rapid restoration of state for a task interrupted and then returned to.

Participant engagement must be very high in a diary study, otherwise the data collected is likely to be spotty and incomplete. Czerwinski et al. note:

> *On the negative side, diary studies suffer from the problem that they are tedious for the recorder and they can invoke a "Heisenberg-style" challenge: the process of observing may influence the observations in that journaling tends to add to the interruption of the flow of daily events.*

"Stuff Goes into the Computer and Doesn't Come Out"[291]

Noteworthy methods:

> ➤ Guided tour;

> ➤ Multiple-form breadth (PIM was considered for files, emails, and web pages); and

> ➤ Longitudinal tracking.

---

[289] Czerwinski et al., 2004.
[290] **See also,** Bolger et al., 2003; Brown et al., 2000; Terry, 1988.
[291] Boardman and Sasse, 2004.

The study used a *guided tour* method of data collection as in the Malone study. The focus was however, on a participant's digital collections of information and in this regard two additional methods are noteworthy:

1. **Multi-form breadth:** The study applied what the article termed a cross-tool focus, for a given participant, on "file, email, and bookmark collections on (participants') main work computer." Studies prior to Boardman et al. had tended to focus only on the management of information in one form, e.g., the management of paper documents, or emails, or web bookmarks. This *cross-form investigation* of PIM practices has subsequently been used in many other studies[292] and, indeed, can be considered to be characteristic of PIM studies, i.e., in seeking to understand a person's Practice of PIM we look at a larger context involving multiple forms of information.

2. A **longitudinal tracking** of PIM practice. For a subset of the participants, Boardman and Sasse

   tracked the evolution of the three collections and the strategies used to manage them. We developed a tool to capture snapshots of the folder structures, including counts of items within folders. Details of specific items—such as filenames—were not recorded. Participants were asked to manually initiate snapshots to lessen the infringement of their privacy.

Longitudinal tracking is expensive (though less so to the extent that the participant can stay actively engaged such as through diary entries or by taking snapshots). However, longitudinal tracking is essential if we're to understand how personal information collections (PICs) evolve over time—especially as these are used in support of specific projects.[293]

The study provided a rich and multi-faceted view into the ways people practice PIM for an increasingly digitized PSI. Participants were, for example, more inclined to invest in the organization of files than in emails or bookmarks. It is perhaps this inclination to organize files (into folders) that accounts for the persistence of navigation as the preferred means of return to files[294] even as people are shifting to search as a primary means of return to emails.[295] Boardman and Sasse note:

   The folder hierarchy is often criticized for not being easily adaptable to fast-changing user needs, …Our findings suggest a contrasting perspective: the slow-changing nature of the hierarchy may benefit users by promoting familiarity with the personal information environment (p. 590).

---

[292]   Bergman et al., 2006; Bruce et al., 2010; Jones et al., 2009.
[293]   See also Bruce et al., 2010.
[294]   Bergman et al., 2008a; Bergman et al., 2012.
[295]   Jones et al., 2014; see also Whittaker et al., 2011.

The study also revealed a strong emotional character PIM and its practice. Participants some-time expressed considerable pride, for example, in their PICs and the organizations of these: "*some of the things I'm quite proud of ...*" p. 585. The interview itself could take on an additional emotional charge: "*It's like a confessional getting all my computer problems off my chest*" p. 585.

"Don't Take My Folders Away! Organizing Personal Information to Get Things Done"[296]

Notworthy methods:

➢ Guided tour;

➢ Project focus; and

➢ Socratic method.[297]

The study used the *guided tour* method but with focus, by discussion and mutual agreement, on a project that the participant was actively working on. The project then provided a basis for a "slice" across the PSI with focus on information, across tools, and across forms that related to the selected project.

One novel method was the use of what can be characterized as a variation of the Socratic method. At the conclusion of the interview, participants were asked a series of questions:

➢ "First, participants were asked why they created folders and what purpose created folders served." A high percentage of participants initially answered that folders helped them to find the content within later on, i.e., folders were for finding.

➢ Then the interviewer described an ideal search utility and gave the participant what we termed the "Google option." "Suppose that you could find your personal information using a simple search rather than your current folders." "Note that the study was conducted in 2005 when index-based desktop search built as supported by the operating system was not yet the norm. Participants all responded very positively to the thought that they might retrieve their local file as easily as they could retrieve information from the web.

➢ But then the "punch line." Participants were asked, "Can we take away your folders? Why or why not?" Participants were able to stipulate additional features of the search service that would replace their folders. No matter. An overwhelming majority (13 of

---

[296] Jones et al., 2005b.

[297] For more on the Socratic method see https://en.wikipedia.org/wiki/Socratic_method and https://sites.google.com/site/entelequiafilosofiapratica/aconselhamento-filosofico-1/the-structure-and-function-of-a-socratic-dialogue-by-lou-marinoff.

14 participants) answered that they would not part with their folders and sometimes with emotion ("absolutely not!").

The exchange served its purpose. Since find/re-finding, the "obvious" reason for using folders was taken away, participants were prompted to dig deeper concerning their reasons for using folders. Responses were very interesting. Participants had considerable trust in the folders. Folders gave them a greater since of control. Folders have often been criticized for hiding the information within but participants provided an alternate viewpoint that folders, with descriptive names at least, could actually improve visibility/understandability for the information organized within. "Folders help me see the relationship between things." "Folders remind me what needs to be done."

Other studies have indicated that folders often correspond to projects a person means to complete. The Jones et al. study went a bit further in demonstrating that for some participants, the structure of subfolders (and sub-subfolders) within a project could serve as a rough kind of problem decomposition for a project with sub-folders corresponding to tasks and sub-projects of the project. In other words, folders were not just a means of organizing information; folders and the folder structure were information in their own right.

"Mobile Refinding of Web Information Using a Voice Interface: An Exploratory Study"[298]
> Noteworthy methods:

> ➤ Wizard of Oz.

Noteworthy in the study described is a clever variation of the *Wizard of Oz* method[299] done to investigate the use of voice as a means to search for information:

> *The study consisted of two sessions that each lasted approximately one hour. In the first session, one of the participants (who we will refer to as the User) completed a set of tasks that involved finding information on the Internet using a web browser. The second session was scheduled about a week later and involved both the User from the first session, and a second participant (who we will refer to as the Retriever). In the second session, the User was located away from the computer and used a telephone to call the Retriever—who was seated at the computer used in the first session—to enlist their help to refind information that was found during the first session. This arrangement was designed to explore how an automated telephone-based intelligent agent with a voice interface could support users' remote refinding needs by observing the interaction between two human participants in a similar configuration.*

The study revealed a two-stage approach to information retrieval over a mobile device:

[298]   Capra and Pérez-Quiñones, 2005.
[299]   Kelley, 1984, see also https://en.wikipedia.org/wiki/Wizard_of_Oz_experiment.

1. Get to desired source of information and then,

2. with source confirmed, continue to search within the source for the specific information desired.

"Better to Organize Personal Information by Folders Or by Tags?: The Devil Is in the Details"[300]

Noteworthy methods:

➢ Real tools, abstract contrasts;

➢ "Within-subjects" design;

➢ Observant participation; and

➢ Longitudinal.

In this study, participants were engaged in a comparison of tagging (labeling) vs. the use of folders as a means of organizing emails. Participants experienced each condition via actual web-based versions of Hotmail and Gmail (as these were offered in 2007/2008) in an ordering counter-balanced across participants.

Participants experienced each condition for five days. During the period for a given condition (represented by Hotmail or Gmail) participants would receive through the email service a series of 25 articles on a topic of interest to them (selected ahead of time from a menu of topics). Participants received the articles in batches of five, one batch per day, and were encouraged to organize these according to the organizing constructs (labels/tags vs. folders) provided in the service. At the conclusion of a condition, participants were tested first for their memory of some aspect for the articles received and were then cued to re-find five articles selected randomly. At the conclusion of each condition, participants were also interviewed using an open-ended set of questions to assess their experiences of and reflections on the condition just experienced.

Participants were encouraged to keep a diary of their experiences in each condition. Few did. But more important, participants understood the point of the comparison and were able to abstract beyond the specifics of features of a given email service to identify underlying benefits and drawbacks of both tags and folders. The study provided a very useful set of considerations and some unexpected drawbacks in the use of tags (e.g., with the freedom to tag items in several ways comes the potential tedium of then consistently using multiple tags for every new item).

The methods provided a kind of heuristic for identifying issues that would not have been apparent without the reflective ability to compare each condition hands-on for a period of time.

---

[300] Civan et al., 2008.

Note also that the study leveraged actual services in place (Hotmail vs. Gmail) even though the desired comparison ("label this" or tagging vs. "put that there" or "foldering") was not tool-specific. It was originally suggested that we mock up a tagging and a foldering prototype but even a cursory consideration of this approach revealed its unsuitability for our purposes. Prototypes of even reasonably stability and utility would have taken months to complete and would still have lacked essential features of a real service. The approach taken was much more cost-effective.

"Easy on that Trigger, Dad"[301]

Noteworthy methods:

> ➤ Setup/test of a cued re-finding task.

The method used involved a two-stage re-finding task. An initial interview gathered information that was then used to define a subsequent retrieval task:

> *we first asked participants why they take pictures of family events, and elicited their views about the value of their photo archives. We used a mixture of open-ended and Likert style structured interview questions. Without explaining the subsequent retrieval task, we then asked them to name significant family events from more than a year ago that they had photographed digitally. To avoid having the participants choosing events that they could easily retrieve, this part of the interview took place away from their computer.*

And then…

> *After identifying these key events, the interviewer asked the participants to sit at their computer and show him pictures relating to these events. Sample requests were "Find me a picture of your son's birthday," or "Find me a picture of your holiday in Y." Participants themselves judged whether or not they found these pictures, and it was very obvious from participants' reactions whether they thought they had been successful or not. The interviewer was careful not to bias the results by suggesting participants moved on to the next task when they found difficulties retrieving pictures. The participant was solely responsible for determining whether the search had failed.*

Study results indicate that people find the organization of their photos to be "onerous" and that participants made "only rudimentary attempts to organize their collections." The author concluded that "user practices associated with digital pictures have yet to catch up with what the technology offers."

Note that the method is especially effective when there is a high likelihood that pictures were indeed taken of an event and that these are still on the participant's computer (or possibly on the

---

[301] Whittaker et al., 2010.

Web), i.e., the question is then not whether the photos exist for the queried event but whether the participant can reliably find these photos again. The method would seem less useful for other forms of information (e.g., emails, web pages, files) where it is less certain for any given event that there are corresponding information items of these forms to query.

"Folder Versus Tag Preference in Personal Information Management"[302]

Noteworthy methods:

> ➤ Real tools, abstract contrasts;

> ➤ Observant participation; and

> ➤ Longitudinal.

The study described a contrastive use of real features (support for tagging vs. folders) in real tools that is similar to the use of Gmail vs. Hotmail as described earlier in the Civan et al. study. In addition, the study endeavored to create a "naturalistic setting" in which "participants managed their own information items on their own computers as part of their daily routine":

> *In the Gmail study, we informed 75 participants about both folder-labeling and tag-labeling, observed their storage behavior after 1 month, and asked them to estimate the proportions of different retrieval options in their behavior. In the Windows 7 study, we informed 23 participants about tags and asked them to tag all their files for 2 weeks, followed by a period of 5 weeks of free choice between the 2 methods.*

The study revealed:

> *a strong preference for folders over tags for both storage and retrieval. In the minority of cases where tags were used for storage, participants typically used a single tag per information item. Moreover, when multiple classification was used for storage, it was only marginally used for retrieval. The controlled retrieval task showed lower success rates and slower retrieval speeds for tag use.*

"How Do People Re-find Files, Emails, and Web Pages?"[303]

Noteworthy methods:

> ➤ Setup/test of a cued re-finding task;

> ➤ Think aloud;

---

[302] Bergman et al., 2013.
[303] Jones et al., 2014.

➢ Multiple-form breadth (PIM was considered for files, emails, and web pages); and

➢ Longitudinal tracking.

A *needs-simulated* variation of the *setup/test of a cued re-finding task* method was used to study return to files, emails, and web pages. The procedure is involved:

1. "Participants completed a set-up session followed by a test session, two to four weeks later. Each session lasted about an hour. The procedure involved personal information—files, emails (received), and web pages actually viewed by the participant….

2. Participants, under observer direction, generated three different lists—one for files, one for email, and one for web pages—in an ordering that was counter-balanced across participants. Each list was sorted by date (i.e., received date or last accessed date) so that more recent items were topmost….

3. The attempt was also made, for each list, to create a sampling of test items that was distributed, roughly, over the previous 7-day period. This meant sampling from a list beginning with items viewed "Today" until two acceptable test items were selected. Items were then sampled from "Yesterday" until two test items were selected and so on until 14 items test items had been selected for each form of information….

4. To select items in a list within a given time period, participants worked through items one by one. The observer did not see the items during this stage of the set-up session. Participants were instructed to bypass items that, for whatever reason, they preferred not to include in the study…

5. For items not skipped, participants rated the likelihood that they would want to re-find this item again over the next twelve months…

6. For items where the likelihood was rated as 75% or higher, participants were then asked to briefly describe a reason for re-finding the item. Participants were encouraged to be as specific as possible but without referencing the item by "name" (e.g., file name, domain name, sender name, or subject tagline).[304] Participants were not told that they would later be tested on these items…

7. The test session involved selected testing of five items randomly chosen from each list (file, email, web page). … For a given item, participants were given the "reason for return" which they had provided during the set-up session. With reference to a

---

[304] Examples of reasons included "to use as reference for what wife wants for birthday next year," "want to change prescription to mail order; need to use form attached to email," "use receipt when filing income taxes next year."

reason, participants were instructed to imagine a situation "now" where the item was needed.[305] Participants were then asked to re-find this item as quickly as possible by whatever method or combination of methods they chose. Participants were instructed to think-aloud…Participants were timed and their method(s) of re-finding were noted…"

The procedure enabled us to generate cues (as reasons for return) in a set-up session which could later be used in a test session to cue items for a re-finding effort. The study revealed systematic differences between files, email, and web pages in the preferred method of re-finding: Search was the most common "first choice" for return to email message while navigation (from folder to folder) was the preferred method of return to files. Web pages were somewhere inbetween. Results also suggest that support for re-finding begins with support for the initial "keeping" of information.

"'For Telling' the Present: Using the Delphi Method to Understand Personal Information Management Practices"

Noteworthy methods:

> Delphi method;

> Second-order "research the researchers;" and

> Focus on "notable" PIM behavior.

The study involved focus on a different kind of participant: researchers who themselves study people in their daily practices of PIM. Researchers have been studying personal information management (PIM) for many years, but little exists by way of practical advice for how individuals should manage their own information. We employed the Delphi Method to engage PIM researchers with expertise in a variety of relevant areas in a five-round extended dialog about PIM practices. All interactions occurred on the Web using Google Docs, Google Forms, and Google Sheet.[306]

The study was done cheaply on a part-time cost-free basis by the facilitators (also co-authors) of the Delphi method. All panelists participated voluntarily as motivated by an interest in the topic and the opportunity to have an extended dialog with fellow researchers (often anonymous but sometimes not depending upon the round of the study).

The first round involved an identification of "notable PIM behavior" whether as seen among participants in some study or as observed more informally in self, friends, or colleagues. Behaviors identified were then grouped for subsequent rounds of discussion leading ultimately to a set of 36

---

[305]   On those occasions where a participant had no recollection of an item given the reason for return, they were instructed to "give it a shot," i.e., by imagining some item they had previously encountered that would fit the "reason for return" and then to return to this item.

[306]   https://support.google.com/docs/answer/49008?hl=en; https://www.google.com/forms/about/.

PIM practices, along with pros, cons, and recommendations for or against each practice. The study also produced a list of straight-forward, near-future improvements in tool support (i.e., "low-hanging fruit").

A common theme among suggested improvements was an ability to annotate and, more generally, to associate metadata with files, folders, applications, and tasks. Metadata might then be leveraged to support new kinds of keeping (e.g., the semi-automated matching of new information to existing folders as described in Chapter 7), finding (e.g., searches targeting metadata), measuring and evaluating (e.g., reflection concerning tasks and the pattern of task completion), and making sense of and using information (e.g., through simple support for the ordering and placement of items in view for a folder or other object).

Perhaps most important, the study provided:

> detailed description of how we applied the Delphi Method to study PIM and how it might be used more widely in HCI research as a complement to more established methods of inquiry.

Plans are underway to apply variations of the Delphi method in an extended discussion among "extreme PIMsters" i.e., non-researchers who have a strong interest in PIM and have developed their own systems, sometimes elaborate, for the management of their information.

11.3.2 SOME RESULTS, THEIR IMPLICATIONS, AND THEIR IMPACT

In this admittedly selective, limited sampling of PIM studies, some 21 methods have been identified. In order of mention, these are:

1. **Guided tour.** "Please show me your information."

2. **Setup/test of a cued re-finding task.** "Find a photo from last year's Thanksgiving dinner."

3. **Prompted, *in-situ* completion of a real information task.** "You've been waiting for a good time to do that web research. Pretend that that time is now."

4. **Think aloud.** "Speak the words topmost in your mind."

5. **Life-change timing.** Moving offices. Downsizing living facilities.

6. **Contrastive analysis of different people by professional category.** How do people vary in the ways they approach their information?

7. **Follow-on survey.** With practices of PIM identified in a qualitative study, now let's get some larger numbers.

8. **Functional analysis.** What features, functions, purpose(s) are served by different observed PIM behaviors? In different tools?

9. **Experience sampling.** "What PIM-related things have you done recently or are you doing right now?"

10. **Diary keeping.** "Track your switches from task to task; note the problems you've had in finding, keeping or other activities of PIM."

11. **Multiple-form breadth.** Look across information forms (paper, digital files, emails, and web pages) especially as these relate to a project.

12. **Longitudinal tracking.** How are things changing over time? Note this especially with respect to personal information collections (PICs) such as for projects or for a lasting area of interest.

13. **Project focus.** Everyone has projects, @home, @school, @work, and @play. How do tools and practices of PIM impact the ability for people to complete their projects in a timely manner?

14. **Socratic Method.** Coming closer to what matters through dialog.

15. **Wizard of Oz.** Tools of the future simulated now with people "behind the curtain."

16. **Real tools, abstract contrasts.** Real tools, exemplifying different approaches (e.g., use of folders vs. tags). Can people look beyond the many incidental differences in features to underlying differences in approach?

17. **"Within-subjects" design.** Let the same participant experience different conditions (but possibly at different points in time).

18. **Observant participation.** "Yes" (the answer to the question above for method #16). With the right motivation, the right instructions, people, as participants in a study, can be "observant" and can make thoughtful comparisons and contrasts between conditions. Participants can identify considerations that are not apparent to the researchers (or to anyone without actually experiencing the conditions).

19. **Delphi method.** Consensus forged (or at least a deeper understanding and better articulation of essential differences) through structured rounds of deliberation.

20. **Second-order "research the researchers."** Leverage the knowledge (insights, generalizations, case examples) that researchers have acquired from years of study.

21. **Focus on "notable" PIM behavior.** What function does the book by the door or the leading "_" character in a file name serve?

These methods (lowercase "m") combine to form the Method (uppercase "M") of a given study. Few, if any, could comprise the Method of a study on their own.

The methods listed above are but a subset of the methods relevant to the study of PIM. Many other methods come to us from the field of HCI as already noted at the outset of this chapter. In turn, many of the methods listed above are by no means specific to the study of PIM. Methods such as "think aloud," or "Wizard of Oz," or the use of follow-on surveys, obviously have had much broader application.

Other methods such as the "guided tour," or the "setup/test of a cued re-finding task," or the "prompted, in-situ completion of a real information task" are more central to PIM study. These methods combine with others such as "longitudinal tracking" and "multi-form breadth" to meet two essential challenges of PIM study—that it should consider changes in a Practice of PIM over time (e.g., as a function of changes in tool support, progress of a project, overall amount of information to manage, etc.) and that it should focus not only one tool or one form of information (e.g., email, or the bookmarking facility of a web browser) but rather broadly consider various forms of information, including paper, and especially as these relate to the completion of a given project.

What have these methods helped us to discover concerning not just how people practice PIM now and the problems they encounter but also how things might be improved through adoption of better practices of PIM and the development of better supporting tools of PIM?

More than a little. These and other PIM studies tell us, for example, that:

➢ Across emails, files, and other forms of digital information, we need to accommodate digital analogs to the paper notion of "piles" and "files."[307] The same information might have both representations in different views or elements of both in a single view (e.g., "large icons"). Features of the pile that are important to realize for digital forms include ease of initial keeping, a reminding function (as long as the pile is visible) and an ability to delay the naming or tagging of information until more is known about the information and its likely use(s).

But realization of all affordances of a paper pile has not proven easy. Ease of initial keeping, for example, often works against the reminding function. "Do nothing" methods for keeping web information[308] such as "count on search" (or navigation or return via auto-complete of the web address) have a pile-like feature of ease of keeping ("do nothing" is, after all, pretty easy) but lack a reminding function. Automatic forms of clutter control also work against the reminding function. Most email appli-

---

[307] Malone, 1983.
[308] Jones et al., 2002.

cations, for example, have a kind of piling mechanism where incoming emails simply "pile" on top of previously received emails, displacing less recent emails in the portion that is visible in the display. Out of sight is also, unfortunately, often "out of mind."

➢ People keep much more information than they are ever likely to use.[309] This is the case for paper information (e.g., as made manifest in an office move) and is even more the case for digital information. Storage is cheap and plentiful. Capture is quick and easy. The result, which is especially true for photos, is that support for keeping information has far outpaced follow-on support to maintain, organize, make sense of and use this information.[310]

➢ People keep information in many different ways partly because no one tool or method now realizes all features that might be useful. A "super keeper" tool for managing information newly encountered (e.g., web pages, emails), thought of (e.g., to-dos, reminders) or created (e.g., pictures) would provide, among other features, for an immediate ability to *communicate* this information with others (e.g., via emails, "tweets," and Facebook posts), an ability to place this information in a calendar or to-do list (*reminding*), fast, easy *integration* of this information into structures already commonly used (e.g., project and task folders), and an ability elaborate and annotate this information for better *context*.[311]

➢ If people are going to spend time organizing for any form of information it is mostly likely to be for their files and folders. There are benefits in having folder structure stay relatively static as a structure people can learn and build upon.[312] Folders, and presumably other forms of structuring information too, are information in their own right.[313] Folders represent and summarize their contents. Folders can correspond to projects and so group together project-relevant information (document files but also emails and links to web pages). Subfolders can represent tasks and then serve as reminders for what needs to be done. The structure of subfolders under a project folder can represent an informal, but often effective, problem decomposition for a given project.

➢ People keep information in accordance with anticipated need and subsequent use.[314] However, determining—we might say "divining"—circumstances of subsequent use

[309] Whittaker and Hirschberg, 2001.
[310] Whittaker et al., 2010.
[311] Jones et al., 2002.
[312] Boardman and Sasse, 2004.
[313] Jones et al., 2005b.
[314] Kwasnik, 1989.

is fundamentally difficult.[315] Moreover, the mechanics of "hook-up" (e.g., connecting new information into an existing structure of folders, sending email to self, creating a bookmark, etc.) can represent a serious source of distraction in "self-inflicted" interruptions from the task at hand.[316] Greater visibility and understanding of eventual need might help not only keeping decisions but also, by reducing the costs of keeping,[317] promote a quicker return to and resumption of the task at hand.

➤ Tagging with labels vs. placing in folders? Both models for structuring information have their pros and cons. Though people often say they would prefer tagging, study results indicate that people rarely use more than one or two labels for a given item of information and may actually perform better under a placement model (e.g., place in only one folder) requiring more initial cognitive effort but less subsequent mechanical effort, i.e., to tag consistently.[318] Beyond either model or even a "best of both worlds" hybrid may be wholly new forms of structuring that allow people, for example, to sketch their understanding of relationships between key concepts shared by items in the collection they are forming.

➤ People often prefer stepwise, *orienteering* approaches to find new information and also to return (re-find) information already experienced. Smaller steps reduce the cognitive burden to specify the query and these also help to preserve a context in which to understand the results that are returned.[319] People may, for example, first use search to find a "waypoint" such as a website and then navigate from or within this source for the specific information desired.[320]

➤ However, first-choice preferences in method to find or re-find may shift as a function of the available tools. There is, for example, an observable shift toward search as a first choice for the return to emails that is coincident with a OS-level support for fast, index-based search.[321] This shift is also coincident with other factors of impact such as an overall increase in the amount of email received and an increasing tendency not to organize this email into folders.[322]

---

[315] See Bruce, 2005.
[316] Czerwinski et al., 2004.
[317] See Jones, 2010.
[318] Civan et al, 2008; Bergman et al., 2013.
[319] Teevan et al., 2004.
[320] Capra and Pérez-Quiñones, 2005.
[321] Jones et al., 2014.
[322] See Whittaker et al., 2011.

➢ The apparent enduring preference for navigation as a preferred method for return to personal files may be due to factors that will apply regardless of tool support such as, for example, a need for a sense of location.[323] However, some results are consistent with a primacy or "first impressions matter" effect that closely ties preferred methods for re-finding information to initial methods for keeping information. People prefer navigation as a method of return to files because these were initially "placed" (i.e., in folders). Tools providing better and, more important, universal, OS, and cloud store independent support for tagging as a means to initially keep files might yet effect a shift that better search support alone has not yet been able to effect—from navigation as the preferred or primary method of return to files to search as the preferred method of return.

➢ With its focus on researchers rather than end users and on achievement of consensus concerning "better practices" of PIM, the Delphi Method study[324] last described in the studies reviewed above, might be regarded as, methodologically speaking, the most unusual of the studies reviewed. The study not only provides a list of recommended practices (and also practices that researchers "advised against") but also reveals "low hanging fruit" in directions for near-future tool support. A common theme among suggested improvements was, for example, an ability to annotate and, more generally, to associate metadata with files, folders, applications, and tasks. Metadata might then be leveraged to support new kinds of keeping (e.g., the semi-automated matching of new information to existing folders as described in Chapter 7), finding (e.g., searches targeting metadata), measuring and evaluating (e.g., reflection concerning tasks and the pattern of task completion), and making sense of and using information (e.g., through simple support for the ordering and placement of items in view for a folder or other object).

As evidenced by the studies reviewed in this section then, progress in understanding how people do PIM, the problems they encounter, and even specific implications for tool design, has been substantial—especially so over the past decade or so coincident with the start of a self-identified community of researchers who do PIM research. Moreover, the pace of research appears to be accelerating.

But… could the pace be faster? Could implications be more practical? When asked, at a dinner party for example, "So what should I do (to better my Practice of PIM)?" I'm still hard-pressed to provide more than a few basic suggestions. "Use a cloud store for saving, syncing, and sharing." "Create folders for each of your active projects and place not only project-related files but also

---

[323] See Bergman et al., 2008b.
[324] Jones et al., 2015.

emails and web references inside." "Create 'self-appointments' in your calendar as a visible means of basic task management".... Some of these practices are likely already a part of the person's Practice. Others may simply not apply.

Another concern is that methods of PIM study are expensive, most especially those methods identified above as key methods for PIM study. The "guided tour," the "setup/test of a cued re-finding task," and the "prompted, in-situ completion of a real information task" can each be very expensive, requiring, for example, same time and typically same location coordination between participant and researcher. If we factor in the additional methods for "longitudinal tracking" and "multi-form breadth" then costs are further multiplied.

These methods, even with their expense, are likely always to have a place in the study of PIM toward better "PIM by design" in tools and also in practices of PIM. Methods are useful both to explore and to confirm. But can these be supplemented with other methods providing greatly broader reach and potential impact for the same cost or comparable reach and impact for considerably less cost? In the next two sub-sections we consider two possible approaches toward practical methods with practical impact:

1. Cognitive modeling through which alternatives in PIM practices and tool design might be simulated and their performance numbers compared and

2. A massive open, online approach that leverages the Web and the ubiquity of our means to connect to it to engage much larger samplings of people in an ongoing dialog toward better practices and tools of PIM.

11.3.3   WHAT ABOUT COGNITIVE MODELING?

At the outset of this section on methods of PIM inquiry and design, we considered a fundamental—daunting—challenge: "PIM requires the study of people, with a diversity of backgrounds and needs, over time as they work in many different situations, with different forms of information and different tools of information management." Study must be "in the wild"—in the places where people practice PIM. Not just @work and @home but also @school and @play. Not just when people are doing PIM "sit-down" in a conventional office (work or home) but also when people are engaged with their smartphones or other mobile devices or when people are doing PIM in a coffee shop or the library.

The study of PIM should be "broad"—considering not only digital but also physical forms of information. The study of PIM should be "long"—i.e., studies should be longitudinal to allow for changes in a Practice of PIM as a function of growing expertise, new tools, and ever more information. A study should be unobtrusive (mostly). People, moreover, vary greatly with respect to background, personality, current job and living situations, and constellation of PIM tools.

In the space of possibilities defined by all factors of reasonable relevance to PIM study, it would seem that each of us might very well occupy a unique point—albeit a point that is moving constantly as we acquire more information, more information tools, and more experience. How can results, dearly bought from the study of one sampling of people (usually quite small), possibly generalize to other people with other backgrounds from other countries and other cultures? The results of a study might not even apply to the study participants some months or even weeks after the study is concluded!

But then, let us dream a little. Suppose we had a magical machine. Call it a "computer." For any given person, we researchers might put in the relevant data—educational background, current job, job history, social networks, personality type, current configuration of tools, current state of information, age, gender, ethnicity, etc. … anything of potential relevance to a person's Practice of PIM and its improvement.

Or, better, the computer might acquire this information directly, with permission, from various existing data sources (certainly companies like Google and Facebook could help) and, as needed, through an interview with the person.

And then, with a few rounds of cogitation, the computer might put forth a sequence of recommended changes that are tailor-made for the person in question—new practices, new tools to acquire, old practices, old tools to abandon. Possibly a new system for the organization of information (in all its many forms). Recommendations might cover each sense in which information is personal to the person (i.e., owned by, about, sent to, sent by, recording experiences or potentially relevant) and each activity of PIM (most notably the meta-level activities that are so often overlooked).

Or, instead, the computer might be used by a tool designer interested in identifying the tool or tool improvement likely to have the largest, demonstrable impact on the largest number of people. The computer might then, with its ability to sample from and simulate PIM Practices for a diversity of people, produce a profile showing which groups to target with which tools. The computer might even adjust recommendations depending upon the designer's objectives (e.g., pure profit or more altruistic pursuit of tool support "for the masses").

Even the most optimistic, enthusiastic among researchers in the fields of artificial intelligence and cognitive science would probably allow that such a computer is not likely any time soon. But were it to exist, it would likely be based upon *cognitive engineering models*[325] of people, their internal cognition and their interactions with their environment, most especially with the information and the information tools in their PSIs. The approach involves *cognitive engineering* as defined by Norman[326] to be a "type of applied Cognitive Science, trying to apply what is known from science to the design and construction of machines."

---

[325]   Pirolli, 2006.
[326]   Norman, 1986.

More specifically, the approach would involve computer-based simulations of the ways people do PIM or, more generally, the way people process information to do smart things (and not-so-smart things too). The diversity of ways to model people is large.[327] This diversity won't concern us here... Call the general approach *cognitive modeling*. Most notably in the field of HCI, the approach is manifest in GOMS (Goals, Operators, Methods, Selections rules).[328]

Pirolli notes the benefits of cognitive modeling: "Cognitive engineering models ... [are]... founded on the twin notions that (a) prediction is a sign of understanding and control over the phenomena of interest, and (b) a designer with an engineering model in hand can explore and explain the quantitative and qualitative effects of different design decisions before the heavy investment of resources for implementation and testing."

John and Suzuki[329] note that "Predictive human performance modeling has been an HCI 'holy grail' for decades. If the field had a computational model of a human that could perform like a human (including perception, cognition and motor action), make errors like a human, learn like a human, and experience emotions like a human, then we could test our design ideas as they emerge in the design process, quickly and inexpensively" (p. 267).

If cognitive modeling, regardless of approach, cannot yet realize the scenarios described above nor the "holy grail" as described by John and Suzuki, are we getting closer? Pirolli paints an optimistic picture of steady progress toward the predictive modeling of ever more complicated situations of human-information interaction—from modeling to answer basic questions ("What is the time it would take to perform elementary tasks, like inserting, deleting, or moving text?") to the much more sophisticated modeling required to answer questions such as "How long will it take an experienced user to find an answer to a question using their PDA?" or "How difficult will it be for a user to find information on a World Wide Web site?"

Pirolli offers that "Recent progress allows us to begin to address [these] last ... questions" and that "The continual accumulation of knowledge and progress in predictive power is a measure of the fruitfulness of the marriage of psychology and human-information interaction."

Maybe. But now, nearly a decade later as I write this, there is little evidence that I'm aware of that such advanced instances of cognitive modeling are commonplace or have had any significant impact in the routine design of, for example, websites or smart phones (as successors to the PDA).

The weaknesses of the GOMS approach are nicely summarized in the Wikipedia article on GOMS (https://en.wikipedia.org/wiki/GOMS#Weaknesses_of_GOMS_Overall):

> *All of the GOMS techniques provide valuable information, but they all also have certain drawbacks. None of the techniques address user unpredictability—such as user behavior being affected by fatigue, social surroundings, or organizational factors. The techniques are*

---

[327]   See, for example, Gray, 2008, and also Pirolli, 2006.
[328]   Card et al., 1983; John and Kieras, 1996.
[329]   John and Suzuki, 2009.

very explicit about basic movement operations, but are generally less rigid with basic cogni-tive actions. It is a fact that slips cannot be prevented, but none of the GOMS models allow for any type of error. Further, all of the techniques work under the assumption that a user will know what to do at any given point – so they apply only to expert users, not novices.

And...

Functionality of the system is not considered, only the usability. If functionality were considered, the evaluation could make recommendations as to which functions should be performed by the system (i.e. mouse snap). User personalities, habits or physical restrictions (for example disabilities) are not accounted for in any of the GOMS models. All users are assumed to be exactly the same...

More generally, Landauer[330] asserts that a useful theory needed for predictive modeling of "human-computer systems" (e.g., vs. simply an ever-lengthening list of special-case if-then rules) is "mostly" impossible because such systems are "chaotic or, worse, highly complex, or dependent upon many unpredictable variables" (p. 60).

As an example of these "many unpredictable variables," Grudin observes:

My very first HCI experiment was a very simple cognitive task that enabled me to use a clever method developed by Tony Deutsch in studying rat behavior. It showed that sometimes people reliably selected input methods that were not optimally efficient because they were a little more fun or more challenging. It also showed reliable individual differ-ences—some people preferred an approach that was less cognitively demanding even if it took longer, whereas others were the opposite, they relished the more demanding approach when it led to faster performance. This was a situation in which the context was very sim-ple and the task purely cognitive (Jonathan Grudin, personal email communication, June 9th, 2015).

Learning to use a cognitive modeling system like GOMS, effectively, consistently, can itself present a major learning challenge. Once this skill of modeling is acquired, the would-be modeler may be faced with a modeling task that itself requires major investments in time and in other resources too if, for example, studies are done to validate and to calibrate. If the model then falls short of the predictive capacity needed in order to prescribe effectively (e.g., better practices of PIM or better tools), then far from realizing the "holy grail" as described above, the cognitive modeling approach may represent a sink hole of researcher time and money. We may be left with a model that in its own complexity falls short even in descriptive utility to give insight or understanding of the "thing" (people doing PIM) being modeled notwithstanding the simplifications—some unrealistic (e.g., no errors, little or no decision making or creative mental effort)—that are made along the way.

---

[330]   Landauer, 1991.

But this assessment is too harsh. Discussion continues concerning the nature of the roles cognitive modeling can usefully play in efforts toward prediction with application to HCI and PIM.[331] But modeling efforts of more modest scope—focused more narrowly on a specific PIM behavior, for example, and forsaking an aggregative attempt toward an ever more precise description and prediction of overall human information behavior—have steadily borne fruit over the years. Bergman et al.,[332] for example, use a basic predictive model to identify an "optimization point" in the tradeoffs between folder depth and folder size. Gray and Fu,[333] using a rational analysis framework,[334] were able to show that, in the logic of "least effort tradeoffs," even the saving of a few milliseconds can motivate people to settle for the "imperfect knowledge in the head" in preference to the look-up of external information (and also to settle for associated higher rates of error).

Many other tipping points of PIM might be amendable to this kind of analysis. Where, for example, is the tipping point in a preference for search vs. navigation as the method of choice for the retrieval of a personal file? How is this point affected by search speed and search success rate? By size of the corpus of files under consideration? More ambitiously, and as an extension of the research of Gray and Fu, what factors in general might influence a person to rely more heavily on "near knowledge" (i.e., information close at hand as described in Chapter 10) vs. knowledge in the head? And how might near knowledge help to compensate for observed age-related increases in memory retrieval times? (Note that increases are gradual and themselves may be a consequence not of age per se but rather of age-related increases in the amount of knowledge to "sift through" in order to retrieve a specific fact. See, for example, the articles in an edition introduced by Gray and Hills.[335])

11.3.4 MIXED METHODS MADE "MASSIVE OPEN ONLINE"

So where does that leave us? Cognitive modeling certainly has a role to play in our efforts toward better "PIM by design." But the role is much more limited than the "holy grail" vision of a system able to predict and prescribe across the vast space of PIM possibilities. If there is no "silver bullet" method (e.g., cognitive modeling) able to cover this space, then perhaps the answer instead is to bring existing methods "to the masses," i.e., to adopt existing methods in various combinations for "do it yourself" study by interested people.

Over the years, I have "met" (usually through email) a large number of people who express strong interest in PIM. Some have spent considerable time thinking about and developing their own systems for management of information in various forms (especially electronic documents, paper documents, and emails). I believe many of these people and more might be willing, with a

---

[331]   See, for example, Peebles and Cooper, 2015.
[332]   Bergman et al., 2010.
[333]   Gray and Fu, 2001.
[334]   Anderson, 1990; see also Jones, 1988.
[335]   Gray and Hills, 2014.

little training (web-based) and encouragement (e.g., a community of others also interested in PIM), to invest significant effort in studies of themselves, their friends, and families. People, through various forums and discussion boards, are already sharing their stories, thoughts about, tips, traps, etc., of PIM (see, for example, http://hci-user-advocate.blogspot.com/2010/01/my-pim-part-ii. html). And PIM-related discussions concerning "how to organize files and folders" or how best to use PIM tools like Evernote can be very lively (see, for example, http://www.asianefficiency.com/ organization/organizing-files-folders-documents/ or http://lifehackerbook.com/ch2/).

With a little more structure, there might be a better basis for collecting and sharing data on Practices of PIM across a very large and diverse group of people and for a wide range of circumstances. But then we note some caveats:

> In the web-widened world of "do it yourselfers" in PIM study, how to promote ethical behavior (especially with respect to the dissemination of results)? Packages for a "do it yourself" study of PIM, if provided through a university or corporate research facility, would need to be reviewed first (i.e., by the appropriate Institutional Review Board or IRB).

> The quality of studies could vary widely. Results of any consequence would need to be reproduced in more formal studies done by trained researchers.

With these caveats in mind, let's have a little fun as we consider in turn each method, in the order of its introduction earlier in this section, both for its expense now in a formal study and for how the method, in new variations, might "go massive" as it mixes with others in massively open, online studies of PIM.

1. A **guided tour** is expensive when observer and participant need to be in the same place at the same time. But the method is less expensive if it can be done remotely (e.g., via a service like Skype). The method goes massive (i.e., "massive open online") as people begin to create their own videos and post these on YouTube.com (or even Twitch.tv). And why not? Better than yet another "my cute cat" video.

2. A **setup/test of a cued re-finding task** can be moderately expensive if done informally in the manner of the Malone study[336] or very expensive if done in a longitudinal study such as that described in Jones et al.[337] The method might go massive in at least two different ways:

    2.1. As part of a self-administered "PIM checkup" (e.g., "now please time yourself as you look for a digital photo of last year's Thanksgiving dinner…");

---

[336] Malone, 1983.
[337] Jones et al., 2015.

2.2. As part of game played by two or more people. For example, two people might each share substantial portions of their folder structures with each other via a service like Dropbox. Each person then, after a review of the other person's information, might pose questions of varying degrees of difficulty.

3. A **prompted, *in-situ* completion of a real information task** is expensive, as with other methods, when observer and participant must be in the same place at the same time. Again the method is less costly if observation can be done remotely. The method might go massive in the context of a "PIM task of the week" that interested people agree to do, video record (with voice over), and post.

4. **Think aloud.** Of course! This is the voiceover for #1, 2, and 3.

5. **Life-change timing.** There are many reasons to think this method might go massive. For each of the social situations discussed in Chapter 10, for example, there are life changes that might prompt changes in or at least a reassessment of a person's Practice of PIM: @home (moving), @school (graduation, or perhaps completion of an academic year that was less successful than hoped for), @work (loss of job or job change or "no change," i.e., the feeling of being stuck in one's current position), @ play (a breakup or a divorce or marriage), or @large (reaching out for advice in the face of a serious illness). Baby boomers, in particular, as they are now in a pivotal age, face several different kinds of life changes. They are recently retired or nearing retirement; empty nesters but perhaps now needing to provide for home care of an aging parent; possibly downsizing with a move to a smaller house, and so on.

6. **Contrastive analysis of different people by professional category.** As people share not only information concerning their Practices of PIM but also demographic information, there can be a possibility for comparisons not only by professional category but by age, gender, ethnic background, culture, country, and so on.

7. **Follow-on survey.** Certainly. Call them polls.

8. **Functional analysis.** Yes. People are already well accustomed to the review of products by feature and function. Surveys formatted as tables with room for commentary might provide just the right degree of open-ended structure.

9. **Experience sampling.** As with #3 above, people might very well sign up for these (if not too frequent) especially for the promise of seeing comparable date from others upon completion.

10. **Diary keeping.** Perhaps not the traditional "dear diary" but people need to tell their stories and do so now in pieces via Facebook posts, LinkedIn updates, and tweets. #PIM anyone?

11. **Multiple-form breadth.** Certainly. As prompted by example "tours" and "self-assessments."

12. **Longitudinal tracking.** Yes, serious "PIMsters" are in it for the long-run.

13. **Project focus.** Of course. Everyone has projects. And as noted earlier ("Don't overlook the emotional and social in PIM") people may gain real value from sharing their projects with others.

14. The **Socratic Method** happens now, to some degree, on discussion boards. This can happen more systematically through facilitated discussions and especially in the context of the Delphi method (below).

15. **Wizard of Oz.** It's not clear (to me) how this would go massive.

16. **Real tools, abstract contrasts.** Yes. Serious users do this all the time.

17. **"Within-subjects" design.** Yes, this is called life only with a time confound (i.e., different conditions are generally experienced at different points in time).

18. **Observant participation.** People can learn to be "observant" not in the sense of being "diligently attentive in observing a law, custom, duty, or principle" but rather in the sense of being "alert and paying close attention; watchful" (see https://en.wiktionary.org/wiki/observant) and…reflective concerning what works and doesn't in tools and practices of PIM. Use of participant observation is well-established in the fields such as sociology and anthropology.[338] But here the phrase is inverted and the interest is in observant participation, i.e., having participants who are sufficiently engaged to reflect upon a PIM tool or practice, the good and the bad, either in a single session or over an extended period of time. Given engaged (by self-interest) observant participants, several other methods could possibly work well on a much larger scale than attempted so far. Observant participation relates to but is distinct from approaches in participatory design[339] wherein there is an attempt to "actively involve all stakeholders (e.g., employees, partners, customers, citizens, end users) in the design process to help ensure the result meets their needs and is usable" (http://en.wikipedia.org/wiki/Participatory_design).

[338] See, for example, Jorgensen, 1989.
[339] See, for example, Muller, 2003; Schuler and Namioka, 1993.

19. The **Delphi method** as an extended facilitated discussion (incorporating elements of the Socratic Method as well), works very well for online use. But massive? Not really. The number of "panelists" for any given instance of use would probably not exceed 30 or so (possibly less).

20. **Second-order "research the researchers."** Yes, or by extension, why not engage others who are doing work relating to PIM—web designers, for example, or professional organizers?

21. **Focus on "notable" PIM behavior.** This can be the basis for many instances of online sharing via diary entry, for example as in "I do this funny PIM thing and wonder if others do as well."

This exploration into what might be called "the crowd-sourcing of PIM study" has been fun and somewhat fanciful. But the possibilities and the potential are real enough. We are thinking "outside the box." We will need to—especially if we are to meet the big challenges and the big opportunities in PIM design, some of which are outlined in the next section.

11.4 BIG CHALLENGES, BIG OPPORTUNITIES IN PIM DESIGN

So far, we've explored general considerations (dos and don'ts) of PIM design.

We've explored a few (of the many potential) methods for descriptive and prescriptive inquiry that might scale for PIM research. How best (effectively, efficiently) to understand what people do now in their Practices of PIM? What problems do they encounter? What might they be doing if only they had better tool support? What do they go out of their way to accomplish now even without tools designed, explicitly, to help? And then, what implications can be drawn concerning the design of better tools?

But dos and don'ts and methods can be piecemeal. Observed and practiced on their own, absent an awareness of big picture challenges and opportunities, these considerations and methods may produce only small incremental improvement: The penny under the lamppost when gold is nearby in the shadows.

Big challenges, big opportunities of PIM include these:

➢ **Putting more "meta" into a Practice of PIM**. The more meta the better to manage personal "META" as in money, energy, time, and attention. These life resources, most especially time and attention, are fragmented in ways that align with and are caused by the fragmentation of information. Informational tools (devices, applications, services) that are meant to help may in fact make matters worse. Tools are the master rather than the servant. Mastering informational tools and properly managing personal information means going beyond an interrupt-driven, reactive level of keeping and finding to a more proactive, strategic meta-level of PIM that includes activities of maintenance and organization, managing privacy and the flow of information, measuring and evaluation and, above all, making sense of and using larger personal information collections (PICs). But how? Meta-level PIM activities are not only "above" or involving a larger perspective. These are also "after" as in later as in, all too frequently, not at all. The informational tools, such a source of problematic fragmentations, most notably our smart phones and other mobile, wearable devices also provide opportunities not yet realized to "go meta" with our information.

➢ **Storytelling to weave personal information together.** Storytelling is our most ancient, most human way to represent, communicate, and know that which we can't perceive directly with our senses. Our stories provide lessons. We learn. Our stories are entertaining. Stories well told are a pleasure to hear and to tell. Stories represent the world as we remember it and as we would like it to be. Future stories express intention and, properly told, can greatly increase our chances of fulfilling these intentions. Moreover, in an age of digital information stories can do much more. These can provide a basis for weaving information fragments into more coherent wholes. Stories can usefully ground, embody, and "reify" information that may otherwise "float" out of reach in the cloud. But can people tell their stories in chunks of 140 characters, or emails where expectations are to keep it short and get to the point. When it is safe to share more than superficial "look at me; life is great" Facebook posts? Again, the tools and technologies that have taken diminished people's willingness and ability to tell good, integrative stories can also form the basis for a renaissance realizing the best of oral traditions combined with the ability to persist and project through words and pictures.

➢ **Multi-goaling, not multi-tasking.** Multi-tasking is a myth as already noted. But multi-goaling—the notion that a single activity might realize several different objectives—is definitely possible. Multi-goaling means better planning, better realization of synergy, and serendipity, most especially, better communication (see the @large sub-section in Chapter 10).

➢ **At home on the Web.** With respect to information, the Web is increasingly where people are. When we begin to think in these terms, it is no longer acceptable that a switch from one tool to the next should require an export and then an import. The process is too time-consuming and too likely to result in error. People can't convert all their information and the portion converted loses, at minimum, its original context. We look, instead, for tools that can make "house calls"—tools that can work with our information in its place. Using the metaphors introduced in Chapter 1, we look for tools that can help people to build "roads" i.e., connections to and from their homes on the Web and also "walls" to protect their privacy and to secure against attacks and break-ins (e.g., "viruses").

➤ **Support for an aging population.** To live is to age. Age is a lifetime giver of experiences, knowledge, and wisdom. But age takes, too. After bringing us to a peak of raw ability, mental and physical, sometime in our late 20s, age begins to take from the accumulated credits for each. In the normal course of aging, people experience a gradual decline in raw cognitive ability as measured, for example, by tests of short-term working memory capacity and processing speed.

The ultimate, inevitable end to a person's life story is never in doubt. But a growing body of research provides intriguing, suggestive indicators that people might compensate for and counter declines in raw cognitive ability through methods that better leverage both information "out there" and a person's accumulated knowledge "in the head." Ideally, methods combine so that the net effect of age is minimal and people remain active, engaged, and self-reliant up until the very end of their biological lives.

We consider a few of these challenges in greater depth before reaching some conclusions for this chapter.

11.4.1 PUTTING MORE "META" INTO A PRACTICE OF PIM

From Chapter 2 (Section 2.2) in Part 1 of this series we have that "PIM activities are an effort to establish, use, and maintain a mapping between information and need."

The everyday, every minute, reactive activities of keeping and finding need to complement one another. Keep information encountered or created for a later, anticipated need; find (re-find) information later to meet a need. It makes little sense to take the trouble to keep information if this information can't be found again later when it's needed.

The effectiveness of keeping and finding activities depends, indirectly, on the effectiveness of an underlying organizational system and the strategies we apply to implement and maintain an organization over time. Lots of time can be wasted with bad systems and bad strategies. Worse, information may be effectively lost even though it is right there—somewhere—neatly filed away. A bad organization can be worse than no organization at all.

Considerations of organizational schemes and strategies for keeping and organizing move us to the metalevel where the focus is more directly on the mapping between information and need. Which organizational schemes and strategies work best? How can we know? By what measurements and evaluations? Do our practices of maintenance ensure that the information, once found, is correct and current? Do we get the right version of a document? Or do we face a confusing "none of the above" choice between several documents versions? Can we manage the flow of information, incoming and outgoing, in ways that reduce the occasions to find and keep information? For example, subscriptions, RSS feeds, even our friends and colleagues can provide us with useful information we might otherwise need to find on our own (if we think to look in the first place).

Meta-level activity operates broadly upon collections of information (PICs) within the PSI, the configuration and effective use of supporting information tools, and on the mapping that connects need to information. The daily actions of keeping and finding are largely reactive (i.e., faced with a need, find the information to meet this need; faced with information, identify if and what need it might meet). In contrast, meta-level activity is more proactive. Meta-level activity focuses not on the need or information immediately at hand but on a larger consideration of information collections, supporting tools, and the overall mapping. Alternatively, meta-level activity can be seen to move to a more strategic level in people's efforts to manage their information.

One factorization of meta-level activity makes the simplification that the PSI is one big store to be maintained and organized, and for which input and output should be managed. People might also benefit from an ability to take measurements in support of various evaluations of the store (e.g., does it have the right information in the right forms, sufficiently current and complete?). This approach leads to the following overlapping kinds of meta-level activity: *Maintain and organize; manage privacy, security, and the flow of information* (incoming and outgoing); and *measure and evaluate*. Implicit in each of these activity types is an effort to *make sense of* and *use* the available information.

But then we can note that:

> ➤ Any actual PIM behavior we would wish to observe and analyze is likely a combination of meta-level activity types (and keeping and finding too). The sharing and synchronization of information in a cloud service such as Dropbox, for example, has elements of *maintenance* and *organization* (i.e., information is automatically backed up) and managing for *privacy*, *security*, and *information flow* (can people trust that their information is secure and safe from snooping? With whom should people share what?). Meta-level activity types might, then, be thought of as vectors—independent but not necessarily orthogonal from one another—forming a basis for the description of a "point" of actual PIM behavior (in a large space of possibilities).

> ➤ A consideration of meta-level activity makes clear the point that information is not an end in itself but rather a means to an end. PIM is about managing information to realize life's goals and roles. Further, information provides people with a way of managing their limited resources. So then, having a little fun with letters and words, consider "META" as an acronym for money, energy, time, and attention. Each of these resources must be managed if people are to be effective in the realization of

their goals and the fulfillment of their roles and responsibilities. But people don't "touch" (manage) these resources directly. People manage via their information. Financial statements tell people whether their expenses are under control and whether they are on track for retirement. Their calendars help them to manage their time. The use of open windows and the tabs of a web browser can be considered as a way of managing attention.

➢ Similarly, aside from what people can keep "in mind," people don't work with tasks or to-dos directly but instead through their information in various forms—a planning document or a spreadsheet list, for example, or a "self-appointment" placed in a calendar (perhaps only approximately by time and day according to a rough notion of when the task should be completed).

➢ Information is evermore so likely to be in a digital form. People then don't "touch" (manage) their information directly but instead via their information tools. (Even for information in paper form, people use tools, of course, including staplers, filing cabinets, and their own hands). An investment to select, configure, and learn to use information tools is a critical aspect of each meta-level activity.

But then, as another sense of "meta," meta-level activity is the "after" activity. Actions at this level such as "spring cleaning" or "clean-up," notwithstanding their overall importance, are seldom urgent and so easily postponed and avoided. In considering how to put more "meta" in a Practice of PIM, this sub-section takes a closer look at each of these meta-level activity types.

Maintaining and Organizing

Several studies have now looked at how the same person manages across different forms of information.[340] The following composite emerges:

➢ People do not generally take time out of a busy day to assess their organizations or their PIM practice in general.

➢ People complain about the need to maintain so many separate organizations of information and people complain about the fragmentation of information that results. People struggle to organize their information so that they can keep their focus of attention and avoid "getting lost."[341]

[340] Boardman and Sasse, 2004; Jones et al., 2005b; Ravasio et al., 2004.
[341] Hanrahan, 2015; Hanrahan et al., 2014; Hanrahan and Pérez-Quiñones, 2015.

➢ Even within the same personal information collection (PIC), competing organizational schemes may suffer an uneasy coexistence with each other. People may apply
one scheme on one day and another scheme the day after.

➢ Several participants in one study reported making a special effort to consolidate
information in their PICs,[342] for example, by saving web page references and email
messages into a file folder organization or by sending e-documents and web page
references in email messages.

➢ People don't, in general, have reliable, sustainable (i.e., automatic) plans for backing
up their information.[343]

Even if digital forms of information can be integrated, people must still contend with paper
forms of information. The integration of paper and digital forms of information can be troublesome.
As noted in Chapter 10, for example, Diekema and Olsen[344] found that the teachers' dualistic system of digital and physical information was especially challenging. While some teachers tried to
standardize their organization schemes across material type, some teachers resorted to digitizing
all materials. Others printed out their digital materials so they could be filed with the rest of the
paper files.

Managing Privacy and the Flow of Information

We continue with the useful simplification that a person's PSI is one large store. If maintenance and
organization activities are concerned with the store itself and its contents, the activities to manage
privacy, security, and, more generally, the flow of information are concerned with the input and
output to the store. What do people let in? What do people let out?

Letting the wrong things (information, data) into a PSI or letting the wrong tools access
or modify a PSI can, at minimum, be a major hassle (e.g., a need for "disinfection"). At worst, the
computer may be hijacked to nefarious ends and all its data corrupted. Indeed, problems of malware
("viruses," "worms") are endemic. By some estimates, 30% or more of the computers in the U. S.
are infected.[345] Letting the wrong information out to the wrong people can also be a costly source
of trouble—e.g., if credit cards are compromised or worse a person's identity is stolen wholesale.

And yet, the exchange of information, incoming and outgoing, and increasingly in digital
forms, is an essential part of living in the modern world. To order goods and services online people
must be prepared to "let out" their credit card information. To try out a potentially useful, new
information tool, people may need to "let in" a download that could potentially make unwelcome

---

[342]   Jones et al., 2002.
[343]   Marshall et al., 2006; Marshall et al., 2007.
[344]   Diekema and Olsen, 2014.
[345]   Samson, 2012.

changes to the web browser or the desktop. Providing for adequate control over the information, coming into and out of a PSI, is a major challenge. Even more challenging is the user interface to make clear the implications for various choices in privacy control and in clicking the "Accept" button for use of services such as Facebook.[346]

Also of relevance are the daily challenges associated with sharing information with others in various social situations ranging from the home, to school, to work, to play and "at large" (e.g., via open-ended discussion boards on the Web). (See Chapter 10). ·

Measuring and evaluating

People need to ask, at least occasionally, "Is my Practice of PIM working? Is it helping me to make the best use of my limited resources (money, energy, time, attention) toward meeting my goals and fulfilling my roles and responsibilities? Can it work even better? If so, what should change?"

These questions depend both upon the measurements that can be made and also on the evaluations people must make in cases where measurements (and the underlying objectives these measurements reflect) are in competition with one another.

Actions of measuring and evaluating are often high-level and qualitative. For example, as people are driving home from work, much later than they'd planned for and with no time, or energy, to exercise at the gym, they may reflect on a day of non-stop meetings and interruptions as they ask themselves "What did I really accomplish?"

But increasingly evaluations can be based upon numerical data. Questions such a "where does the money go?" or "where did the time go today?" needn't be only rhetorical. Increasingly detailed, consolidated data is becoming available to answer these and other questions concerning not only how people manage their resources but also how effectively they're living the lives they wish to live. Detailed financial data can tell people "where" the money is going. Calendars consolidated with activity logs can tell people "where" the time went and much more besides. On which devices? Which applications? Relating to which people or which projects? Involving physical activity as well? Or, conversely, the intake of calories (e.g., a business lunch)? How did physical measures of heart rate, blood pressure, blood sugar levels, etc., vary during these activities?

People's every action can be tracked and a digital trace formed. The nearly constant use of computational devices (even as people sleep) creates opportunities to capture additional data about themselves and their environment for purposes of correlation and, potentially, deeper understanding. Associated issues of privacy are enormous and beyond the scope of this article to address.[347]

On a more positive side, how can measurements be used to a person's advantage?

---

[346]   Ackerman and Cranor, 1999; Al-Shakhouri and Mahmood, 2009; Bauer et al., 2009, Bos et al., 2009; Boyd and Hargittai, 2010; Egelman et al., 2009; Hoofnagle, 2009; Iachello and Hong, 2007; Karat et al., 2007.
[347]   But see Moore, 2010, 2011; Tunick, 2013.

The increasing capture (by intention or incidentally) and availability of data in digital form to measure everything from heart beats to gaze duration to affective response give rise to notions of · the quantified self and personal informatics.[348] Definitions of personal informatics or PI vary. Some would tightly connect PI to enabling devices and applications for tracking.[349]

But self-efforts to track personal activity—the better to understand and make adaptive changes in behavior—are not new. In Chapter 12 we'll consider the example of Benjamin Franklin's attempts at a weekly tracking of the "seven virtues"—this back in the 1700s. Rapp and Cena provide a more flexible definition: "Personal Informatics (PI), also known as Quantified Self (QS), is a school of thought which aims to use technology for acquiring and collecting data on different aspects of the daily lives of people."[350]

PI applications are often affiliated with health information and many times have a dedicated hardware device. But some examples also include systems that collect personal information over time from a variety of sources to provide more integrative summaries of the many scattered events happening that relate to a person in one way or another. A popular example of this second variety is Mint.com, which collects information from all of one's financial accounts (checking, saving, credit cards, etc.) and summarizes this data into an integrated dashboard.

Personal informatics is properly regarded as a subset of PIM where special focus is given to activities of measuring and evaluation and also to making sense of and using the data collected. For example, Li et al.[351] decompose a personal informatics system into five stages: preparation, collection, integration, reflection, and action. The first three stages fit well under the more general activity of measuring and evaluating while the last two stages fit well under the more general activity of making sense of and using information. Not surprisingly, users of PI systems also face challenges to manage for privacy and information flow and to maintain and organize the large amounts of data collected. According to Li et al.,[352] users face information fragmentation problems comparable to those already discussed earlier in this chapter (and through the series). More recent work in personal informatics seems to acknowledge a need to think more broadly and to place efforts at "self-tracking" in the larger context of an overall PIM practice.[353]

Making Sense of and Using Information

Making sense of information represents another kind of meta-level activity. People must often assemble and analyze a larger collection of information in order to decide what to do next. For

---

[348] Choe et al., 2014; Elsden and Kirk, 2014; Froehlich et al., 2014; Gurrin et al., 2014; Rooksby et al, 2014; The Economist, 2012.

[349] Li et al, 2012.

[350] Rapp and Cena, 2014, p. 613.

[351] Li et al., 2010.

[352] Li et al., 2011.

[353] Burns et al., 2012; Froehlich et al., 2014; Khovanskaya et al., 2013.

example, among the choices available in houses for sale (new smartphones, a pool of job applicants, etc.), which will best meet a person's needs? Which treatments to select in the aftermath to surgery for prostate cancer? Does radiation therapy "make sense"? Which kind?

Making sense of information is "meta" not only for its broader perspective but also because it permeates most PIM activity even when the primary purpose may be ostensibly something else. For example, people organize information in folders ostensibly to insure its subsequent retrieval but then also as a way of categorizing and so making sense of the information. In the Jones et al. study,[354] as noted earlier in this chapter, folder hierarchies developed for a project often resembled a project plan or partial problem decomposition in which subfolders stood for project-related goals and also for the tasks and subprojects associated with the achievement of these goals. Similarly some teachers organize their files by utilizing the structure as established in their curriculum standards.[355]

Barsalou[356] has long argued that many of a person's internal categories arise to accomplish goals. His research demonstrates an ability of people to group together seemingly dissimilar items according to their applicability to a common goal. For example, Weight Watchers might form a category "foods to eat on a diet." Rice cakes, carrot sticks, and sugar-free soda are all members of the category, even though they differ considerably in other ways.

Folders and tags (and piles, properties/value combinations, views, etc.) can form an important part of external representations which, in turn, can complement and combine with internal representations ("in our heads") to form an integrated cognitive system.[357] Finding the right external representation can help in *sense-making*,[358] i.e., in efforts to understand the information. For example, the right diagram can allow one to make inferences more quickly.[359] The way information is externally represented can produce huge differences in a person's ability to use this information in short-duration, problem-solving exercises.[360] Different kinds of representations, like matrices and hierarchies, are useful in different types of problems.[361]

We're back to the original challenge. Meta-level activity, though very important to any Practice of PIM, frequently happens "after" the interrupt-driven activities of keeping and finding and that means, all too often, that these activities never get sufficient time and attention in a busy day. How to get more "meta" into a Practice of PIM?

Tools designed for PIM can help by considering three "I"s:

---

[354]   Jones et al., 2005a.
[355]   Diekema and Olsen, 2014.
[356]   Barsalou, 1983, 1991.
[357]   Hutchins, 1994; Kirsh, 2000.
[358]   Dervin, 1992; Russell et al., 1993.
[359]   Larkin and Simon, 1987.
[360]   Kotovsky et al., 1985.
[361]   Cheng, 2002; Novick, 1990; Novick et al., 1999.

> **Incidental.** For example, given proper tool support many, if not most, measurements needed to evaluate a person's PIM Practice can be collected automatically, as an incidental by-product of the daily use of information and information tools.

> **Incremental.** A meta-level activity is easier to do if it can be done in small chunks spread over time. How can people accomplish something within a few seconds here and there when people are unwilling to take a longer period of time out of an already busy day? People do one kind of meta-level activity—managing the flow of information—every time they designate that an email message is "junk." An email application should use this designation to update and fine-tune its definition of what "junk" is to the person managing the email. The designation of email messages as junk is an incremental activity. People can designate as many or as few as they want, depending on their time or inclination.

> Similarly, with respect to management of privacy and information flow, people may ultimately want a more comprehensive privacy policy customized to their needs, with fine-grained distinctions drawn according to who wants what, when, and why (under what circumstances). But if they had to create such a policy in a single sitting, they might never do so. And the policy created might not be that good either. Questions relating to privacy are more likely to get answered (with better answers) if these are distributed over time as the occasion arises.

> **Integrative.** Meta-level activities are more likely to be done if these are integrated into other activities people do anyway and perhaps even like doing. Consider maintaining and organizing. People talk about it ("These folders don't make sense any more. I need to re-organize." "I should weed out these older versions of the document." "I need to be sure my financial data is getting backed up.") but may seldom find the time to take action. Part of the problem is that activities to maintain and organize are separate from other daily activities. Can we do better? Can activities to maintain and organize be an integral part of other activities? Consider, for example, planning. People plan all the time. Planning—whether planning a party, a vacation, or even a weekly meeting—can be fun and, anyway, it needs to be done. The Planz prototype[362] was built around the notion that an effective organization of information can emerge as a natural by-product of the planning people must do in any case.

Planning might be regarded as a meta-level activity in its own right and one that involves all PIM meta-level activities described above. Planning a summer vacation, for example, involves maintaining and organizing information relating to the plane flights, hotel reservations, and rental

---

[362] Jones et al., 2010.

cars. Issues of privacy and information flow arise as credit card information is sent and reservation confirmations received via the Web and email, respectively. People need to measure and evaluate—is the schedule realistic? Are costs reasonable and within the budget? And, as always, there are efforts to make sense of the plan and its information. Does it make sense? Will it be fun… to plan a road trip with so many stops?

Meta-level activities of PIM relate closely to the notion of task management *metawork* as described by Gonzales and Mark:[363] "People periodically conduct metawork throughout the day, which involves coordination, checking activities, organizing email, organizing their desk at the start or end of a working day, and catching up with teammates on what they have missed."

11.4.2 STORYTELLING TO WEAVE PERSONAL INFORMATION TOGETHER

Planning can be regarded as a kind of storytelling told in the future tense, i.e., people's plans are a story of what will or is meant to happen.

Why storytelling? For one thing, stories told in the future tense as expressions of intention—especially if these contain specifics concerning the "how" of execution—are more likely to come true than if we merely expressed a vaguely worded desire to "finish the re-model."[364] As our story develops into a plan, we're more likely to experience moments of serendipity where relevant information or the right person just "happens" to appear. There is often little that is accidental about these encounters. We may be constantly encountering information that could be useful to us in our efforts to reach this or that goal. But unless thoughts of a goal and the steps we need to take toward its fulfillment are active in our minds, we may easily overlook the information.[365]

For another thing, we love to "tell a good yarn."[366] We tell stories all the time and enjoy doing it. When asked to tag something—an article, a picture, and a video—people may take time and struggle. They are not sure what tags they should use. But people readily tell stories for the same objects. And from the words of these stories come tags that are often of better quantity and quality than those generated during an explicit exercise to "tag."[367]

Stories, as indexed for fast search, can be an excellent way to organize related materials—photographs, drawings, email exchanges, etc. And these days, the recipients of our digital stories can talk back—encouraging us to clarify or elaborate on this or that point.

As we work across devices (phone, pad, laptop, desktop, etc.) and applications (device-installed and web-based), we struggle with the various manifestations of a general challenge of information fragmentation. Where is "our" information (e.g., information about us; information we've

[363] Gonzales and Mark, 2004.
[364] **See research on intention,** Gollwitzer and Sheeran, 2006; Sheeran et al., 2005.
[365] Seifert and Patalano, 2001.
[366] Hsu, 2008.
[367] Marshall, 2009.

created, provided, or posted)? Is it still correct and current? Who can see it? Who do we want to see it? ... Our information may be scattered in many, many different places. How to check them all? How can we bring our information together in ways that make sense for us?

A log of our information interactions is a critical first step toward a better management and integration of our information ... and ourselves. A log that includes GPS encoding, near-field interactions with devices, pointers to pictures we've taken, or videos we've recorded begins to approach the fidelity of a lifelog with a potential to serve as a lifelong complement to our internal memory.

So far so good. But a log may overwhelm with its detail. And a temporal sequencing of events can't be expected to tell the "whole story". We often want to relate an event or event sequence to a project, a purpose—a story—in ways that jump across time. For example, we encounter a website that directly relates to "Project A" even though we're not working on this project now. Or we take a picture that would fit perfectly into a photo album we wish eventually to share with our family. In these and many other examples, we seek to impose structures on our information that take us from the given "sequential" of a log to the "consequential" of a story. For any given sequence of events, there may be many different story overlays and a given event may be involved in no story, one story or many stories.

11.5 CONCLUSIONS: PIM ON PURPOSE

If you were queen or king for a day what PIM tools would you "command"? If you had three wishes (or seven), what PIM tools would you "wish" for?[368]

We might first go "meta" in our responses. We'd command that our tenure as queen or king were extended, for a day, a year, or indefinitely. One of our wishes would be to have three more wishes, or an infinite number.

We do this for good reason. Like the start of most projects, a project to build a better tool is often begun in hopeful innocence with an eye on the goal and less thought for the difficulty of the journey along the way. It might be too hard to start otherwise. Our commands, our wishes, our designs, on first attempt are likely to be wrong or at best only partly right. Even features that work as designed may also have unintended, undesirable consequences.[369]

Investigate, ideate, prototype, evaluate... the most important word in the sequence is "iterate"—the equivalent of having another day, another wish, another try to get things right.

---

[368] The motif that one is granted, through magic or a deal with the devil, the power to command or wish for "anything" is common in literature, film, and popular culture. See for example, https://en.wikipedia.org/wiki/Deals_with_the_Devil_in_popular_culture. The results frequently turn out badly. See, for example: https://en.wikipedia.org/wiki/The_Monkey's_Paw, https://en.wikipedia.org/wiki/The_Lathe_of_Heaven, https://en.wikipedia.org/wiki/Faust:_The_First_Part_of_the_Tragedy, http://www.gutenberg.org/files/14591/14591-h/14591-h.htm.

[369] https://en.wikipedia.org/wiki/Unintended_consequences.

But in real life, we don't have absolute command, not even for a day. Nor can we wish for "anything." Our capacity to effect change as individuals or even in large corporations—a Google, a Microsoft, an Amazon, or an Apple—is limited. We don't have unlimited time to iterate either. R&D budgets are tight. Products must ship.

On the other hand, "we" (as individuals and in larger organizations) are not alone. The iterative progression toward better tools of information management can be seen to happen globally in billions of places, in billions of different ways, large and small, motivated by a desire for money, fame, or simply to make a positive difference. The modern effort toward better tools started in the 1940s with the advent of the full programmable, automatic computing machines[370] and inspired by the writings of people like Vannevar Bush,[371] J.C.R. Licklider, Douglas Engelbart, and Ted Nelson.[372] The effort will surely continue to the end of time or, at least, until the end of the world as we know it.

Each new tool—each new desktop application, web service, or mobile device—carries costs as well as benefits. Some costs are clear. Some much less so. A friend of mine, for example, sometimes goes solo skiing in the winter at a local ski resort when he finds himself with a free weekday afternoon and his ski buddies are all at work. He commented on how much more lonely the experience is now. In earlier times, pre-smartphone and MP3 player, other skiers were generally "unplugged" and casual, impromptu conversations on the ski lift going up were likely to happen. Not so now. My friend is a knowledgeable, interesting guy with lots to offer in even a casual conversation that takes place in the few minutes on the ski lift ride. The other skiers, plugged into the same music they heard yesterday and the day before, don't know what they are missing.

But on balance we would likely agree that things, with respect to information, are steadily improving. In Chapter 9 I noted that the *clerical tax* I'm paying to complete this series of books is (by rough estimate to be sure) much smaller as a percentage of total time than what I "paid" back in 1983 as I worked to complete my dissertation at Carnegie-Mellon University. We are not, aside in any case from the rare ascetic among us, going back.

But then the question arises: As tools show steady improvement bringing overall benefits to our Practices of PIM (and the quality of our lives?), how much of the credit will be seen to come from the field of PIM? A case can be made that progress proceeds largely by a process of economic selection analogous to an evolutionary process of natural selection and is largely unaffected by academic efforts toward more "intelligent design."[373] People vote, with their pocketbooks, their downloads, their "visits," and the market responds.

---

[370]   See https://en.wikipedia.org/wiki/History_of_computing, http://www.computerhistory.org/timeline/?category=cmptr, http://homepage.cs.uri.edu/faculty/wolfe/book/Readings/Reading03.htm.
[371]   Bush, 1945, though his Memex machine was not a digital computer, https://en.wikipedia.org/wiki/Memex.
[372]   Licklider, 1960, 1965; Engelbart, 1961, 1963; Engelbart and English, 1968; Nelson, 1982; Nelson, 1999.
[373]   See, for example, Winter, 1964.

As noted in the introductory remarks to this chapter, PIM, as a field of inquiry with a community of researchers engaged in its study, is young. Human-computer interaction (HCI) as a field of inquiry is several decades older and yet people continue to raise similar questions about HCI and its real beneficial impact on the development of computer-based tools (i.e., applications, devices, and services).[374]

If better tools of HCI and PIM are certain to happen regardless "in the long run"—the product, perhaps, of a semi-random "walk" through marketplace possibilities—a counterpoint in favor of some guidance from the academic sidelines toward a more timely, more direct pathway to better tools can be borrowed from the field of economics as expressed in the famous quote by John Maynard Keynes: "this long run is a misleading guide to current affairs. In the long run we are all dead."[375] Keynes goes on to say, "Economists set themselves too easy, too useless a task, and if in tempestuous seasons they can only tell us, that when the storm is long past, the ocean is flat again."

The argument here, however, is not for a Keynesian-style intervention (e.g., through some analog to government spending and monetary policy). Rather, the argument is that considerations of PIM might be factored into assessment of tool alternatives toward fewer false starts and a more direct path to better tools for PIM. New efforts should at least not be "innocent" concerning previous efforts, especially those that failed.

In this regard, a problem exists in PIM and HCI research that is reflective of a larger problem with research and development and the general pursuit of science in an academic world of "publish or perish"[376]: "Success" is published; failed efforts, even if well-motivated and methodologically sound, are too often not published. This is particularly true for efforts to build better tools. I organized a panel at CHI 2007 titled, "'Get Real!' What's Wrong with HCI Prototyping And How Can We Fix It?"[377] to discuss the problem of tool R&D as this relates to PIM as well as HCI. In his position statement, Jonathan Grudin called into question what "success" is with respect to tool R&D:

> Demand characteristics and confirmation bias prevail in evaluation. Our visions, enthusiasm, and hopes are communicated to participants who respond accordingly. Our quickly published assessments note that things generally went well, participants liked the experience on the whole, and that we discovered how to improve our promising systems. When a system disappears, all that remains are those optimistic papers, luring future researchers like the sparkling water above a tar pit. Woe to the

---

[374] See for example, Juristo et al., 2007; Kuutti, 2009.

[375] See https://en.wikiquote.org/wiki/John_Maynard_Keynes; from *A Tract on Monetary Reform* (1923), Ch. 3. For references to readings on Keynesian economics see: https://en.wikipedia.org/wiki/Keynesian_economics.

[376] See, for example, http://www.economist.com/news/leaders/21588069-scientific-research-has-changed-world-now-it-needs-change-itself-how-science-goes-wrong and http://www.economist.com/news/briefing/21588057-scientists-think-science-self-correcting-alarming-degree-it-not-trouble.

[377] Jones et al., 2007.

researcher who tries to publish a reflective, objective paper describing why things did not work out: Reviewers tend to say "you should have known better than to try that in the first place!"

Indeed, we might do much more to learn from failure. One proposal I put forth during the panel discussion was to have papers submitted initially with no result, discussion, or conclusion sections and have these papers reviewed, at least in an initial round of review, solely on the merits of the "proposed" research as described in the paper's introduction, literature review, and method (or approach or planned development) sections.

We should also consider that the "waters" in a PSI may continue to be "choppy" for a long period of time. Once tools and systems of organizing are adopted, these are often very difficult to change even after serious problems emerge, most notably problems of scalability. People may suffer the daily hassles of working with a system of filing documents, for example, or a word processor that gets in the way as much as it helps because the costs to change are so large.

This chapter reviews considerations (don'ts, dos, guidelines) that apply to any effort to build or improve upon tools of PIM. In particular are the checklists that apply to any PIM tool and that might be reviewed the way the checklist of "things to do or take" is reviewed before a family vacation. Methods, too, especially methods that engage a large and diverse sampling of people as "observant participants," may help to reduce considerably the number of false starts before a tool succeeds with its targeted user group. Advanced or "super" users may increasingly program their own tools in the form of, for example, web applications making use of HTML, CSS, and JavaScript.

Most important in the discussion of this chapter, is the coverage of "big" challenges and opportunities of PIM. We seek to design tools that help people to:

> Put more "meta" into their Practices of PIM so that they are less reactive, more pro-active, more strategic in matters of maintenance and organization, measuring and evaluating, managing privacy and information flow and, especially, in making sense of and effectively using their information.

> Tell their stories, big and small, of the past, the extended present, and the future, first incidentally and through the capture of small incremental fragments (emails, tweets, posts, texts, notes spoken to self, etc.) but ultimately in flowing coherent, complete stories that integrate their information into an integrated whole.

> Plan and coordinate the better to realize synergies that help them to realize the most of their "META" recourses (of money, energy, time and attention) by multi-goaling, i.e., rather than a largely futile effort to do two actions at the same time (poorly) accomplish several objectives through the same action (done well).

➢ Build their houses of information on the Web as only one (but a key) part of larger information ecology that includes their social networks and their physical spaces too.

➢ Manage their information for a lifetime including the golden years of advanced age; manage also for legacy.

Better tools sooner is a fine objective for people involved in the design and development of PIM tools.

But sooner is still not now. Meanwhile each of us on a daily basis must do PIM. How can we do better? What can we do now, using existing tools, to improve our Practices of PIM?

This is the topic for Chapter 12, the last chapter of the third and final book in this "The Future of Personal Information Management" series.

CHAPTER 12

To Each of Us, Our Own

Tyger, tyger, burning bright, In the forests of the night:
What immortal hand or eye, Could frame thy fearful symmetry?

—William Blake, *Songs of Experience*[378]

This is the concluding chapter of the last book, Part 3, of a series titled "The Future of Personal Information Management." In the conclusion to an academic chapter or article, discussion often reverts to the future, and one of the most frequent phrases we're likely to encounter, no matter the discipline, is some variation of "future research is needed to…"

But in a book series that has the future as an overriding theme enough space has already been given to explorations of the future. It's time to bring discussion back to the present and the *near* future.

We practice PIM every single day of necessity and mostly without the guidance of research. The field of formal PIM study is young. Most of us have been practicing PIM much longer. We have considerable experience.

At the same time, many …most? … of us have the feeling our Practices of PIM could be better. What about your PIM Practice? Do you waste time keeping information (as files, bookmarks, self-sent emails, paper notes, notes in Evernote, etc.) that you never seem to ever use again later? Do you spend time trying to find (re-find) information you "know is here somewhere"? Do you feel guilty for not spending enough time on maintaining and organizing your information? Or, worse, do you experience worry, even panic, at the thought that you have no good provisions for backup? (Where are those photos, anyway?). Conversely, do you feel a little embarrassed for spending too much time organizing your information?[379] Do you spend too much time monitoring email? Too little (to the point that others are mad at you)? Are you easily distracted? Do you distract yourself in the middle of your work with visits to Facebook, Reddit, or Twitter? Do you frequently reach the end of the day and wonder, perhaps as you are driving home from work, "where (on earth) did the time go? Why didn't I get more done?"

If you are like me, you answer "yes" to many of these questions.

This chapter is long on questions and short on answers. It is for you to provide the answers filling in the blanks, so to speak, according to the circumstances of your own life. The chapter can

---

[378] The Tiger, http://www.gutenberg.org/files/1934/1934-h/1934-h.htm#page1.
[379] Bruce et al., 2010.

do little more than what I do when I occasionally give a training session/tutorial (day-long or half-day) on PIM. Though some in the audience might want a list of specific tools and methods for practicing PIM, no such list exists. Or rather, it might be made but would work for no one. Even the customized list I might make for myself would be dated almost as soon as it was generated. I'm constantly trying new tools, new techniques, new methods, and new strategies of PIM. You too?

The best this chapter can aspire to accomplish is to explore at least some of the considerations, methods, and the big challenges and opportunities that apply as we each design (and constantly re-design) our own Practice of PIM. With this in mind, the structure of this chapter mirrors that of Chapter 11 ("PIM by design") only here with a different slant. In this chapter we shift away from the "innocence" of possibility in new tool design (where at the outset, a little like the start of summer, all things seem possible). In this chapter, we shift to the practical present and the leverage of our hard-won experience with PIM.

Sections are as follows:

> **Considerations (including "don'ts," "dos" and guidelines) when designing your Practice of PIM.** Considerations reviewed in Chapter 11 apply to you and me as we design our own Practices of PIM.

> **Methods you might use.** Depending upon your level of interest, many of the methods discussed in Chapter 11 can apply to you in your efforts to design your own Practice of PIM. You might keep a diary or do experience sampling. You might pair with someone else so that they observe as you give a guided tour of regions in your PSI and then, in turn, you observe as they give a guided tour within their PSI. Guided tours can be very "therapeutic." But many of us simply don't have the time. Most important is to remain an *observant participant* in your own Practice of PIM. Your observations and reflections concerning what does and doesn't work for you, when, where, and how can be very useful to you as you design your Practice. These may be worth sharing with other people too.

> **Some ways to challenge yourself in your Practice of PIM.** Finally, we consider some ways that each of us can challenge ourselves in our Practices of PIM, for lifetime and legacy.

Consider this final chapter then to be a kind of self-paced "open-book exam" we each might follow as we each strive to build a better world with our information.

12.1   A CLARIFICATION OF TERMS

It is useful to clarify the terms of our discussion including terms first introduced in Chapter 2 of this series.[380]

Our information sent and received takes many *information forms* in accordance with a growing list of communication modes, supporting tools, and our customs, habits, and expectations. People still send paper-based letters, birthday cards, and thank you notes. But ever more so, people communicate using digital forms of information including emails, documents shared (as attachments or via a service such as Dropbox), and "tweets," text messages, blog posts, Facebook updates, and personal web pages.

Across forms, it is useful to speak of an *information item* as a packaging of information. An item encapsulates information in a persistent form that can be managed. An information item can be created, stored, moved, given a name and other properties, copied, distributed, and deleted.

The concepts of information item and information form have been useful abstractions in our discussions of PIM. For example, an email message, as an item, packages together information such as a sender, receiver, subject, body text, and date sent. All emails, as befits their form, share in common characteristics such as the expectation of a timely delivery (i.e., in seconds not days) and a timely response (i.e., within a day or two, not a month later). An email message can be transformed, i.e., it can be copied to create a new information item of a different form. For example, a user may print the email and view it in a paper form. Each form is associated with distinct set of tools, techniques, habits, and expectations for interacting with and managing the information.

There are several senses in which information can be personal. Each represents a different relationship between the information and the person and are labeled for convenience of reference P1 thru P6: Information can be owned by/controlled by (P1), about (P2), directed toward (P3), sent (posted, shared) by (P4), representing things experienced by (P5), or (potentially) relevant (P6 to) "me." (See Table 2.1 and Figure 2.1 of Chapter 2.)

Each person has a single unique *personal space of information* (PSI) defined to be the union of personal information in each of its six senses, all informational tools used to manage this information and also the various channels by which information is sent and received. A PSI affects the way its owner views and interacts with the rest of the world (P3, P5). A PSI also affects the way its owner is seen, categorized, and treated by others (P2, P4).

At its center, a person's PSI includes all the information items that are, at least nominally, under that person's control (P1). Documents, emails, bookmarks, auto-completes for URLs and email addresses, etc., are information "close at hand" (near knowledge) that a person can work with and modify (directly or indirectly via actions) to serve as a kind of support "scaffolding" to complement and extend a person's internal memory and cognitive processing. At its periphery, the PSI

---

[380] Jones, 2012.

includes information that the person might like to know about and control but that is under the control of others. Included is information about the person that others keep (P2). Also included is information in public spaces, such as a local library or the Web, which might be relevant to the person (P6).

Personal information collections, referred to as PICs or simply collections, are personally managed subsets of a PSI. PICs are "islands" in a PSI where people have made some conscious effort to control ("pick") both the information that goes in and how this information is organized. PICs can vary greatly with respect to the number, form, and content coherence of their items. Examples of a PIC include:

- The papers in an office and their organization, including the layout of piles on a desktop and the folders inside filing cabinets.

- A collection of projects each represented by a folder stored in a cloud storage service and accessed from different devices.

- A collection of information items related to a specific project that are initially "dumped" into a folder on a person's notebook computer and then organized over time as the project takes shape.

- A reference collection of articles in digital format, organized for repeated use across projects.

- Digital songs managed through a laptop computer or smartphone.

- A collection of media (TV shows, movies, music) stored in a streaming service under a personal account, organized by genre or play list and including information such as ratings, watched/unwatched, and other notes.

A PIC includes not only a set of information items but also their organizing representations including spatial layout, containing folders, properties, and tags.

Just as the information item is self-contained as a unit for storage and transmission of information, the PIC is self-contained with respect to the maintenance and organization of personal information. People typically refer to a PIC when they complete a sentence such as "I've got to get these [papers | emails | photographs | documents] organized!" The organization of "everything" in a PSI is a daunting, perhaps impossible, task. But people can imagine organizing a collection of web bookmarks, their email inbox, their laptop filing system (but probably only selected areas), and so on. Likewise, in the study of PIM, PICs are a tractable unit of analysis, whereas consideration of a person's entire PSI is not.

Other common words as used in the context of the PIM discussions of this series have the following informal definitions:

- A **tool**—refers to software applications (especially designed for the end-user), web services, mobile devices, and any other thing we use for management of digital information. But the term also refers to tools for working with paper-based information including a stapler or a highlight marker. Other objects can become information tools in certain contexts such as when an office door and its current state of openness (closed, nearly closed, half-open, wide-open) communicates degrees of readiness of the office's occupant to engage in a "drop-in" discussion.

- A **technique** is the use of a particular feature or characteristic of a tool. For example, the use of the "high importance" tag and the "follow-up" flag in Microsoft Outlook are techniques. Similarly, the placement of a smartphone to "vibrate" (e.g., while at a concert) is a technique. The placement of a door to a certain degree of openness is also a technique (which, in drafty circumstances, may be reinforced by the technique of kicking a rubber doorstop to wedge the door to a fixed position of openness).

- A **method** is a sequence of actions, possibly involving several techniques as supported by several tools, toward some desired end. My inclusion of my email address in the bcc: field followed by my flagging of this message as it appears in my inbox is a method which has the desirable effect of reminding me to followup as needed on the conversation.

- A **strategy** is the conscious use of one or more methods of information management toward some desired state of affairs. A choice of strategies of information management involves a consideration of costs, benefits, and tradeoffs. For example, an effort to "go paperless" with all documents (bills, bank statements, credit card statements, etc.) is a strategy of information management that realizes benefits (e.g., less physical clutter) but with some cost (e.g., less visibility, possibly less control). A strategy must be articulated in some way by the person who uses this strategy. Observable states (e.g., of information organization) alone are not enough. That all paper-based financial and tax-related documents are, for example, in one big pile may be happenstance or it may be a part of a strategy as expressed by the documents' owner (i.e., "it's not worth it for me to sort these since I'm not likely to need to look at them again until I file my tax return").

- A **system** involves the use of tools, techniques, methods, and strategies toward the management of one or more forms of information. We may have (or not) a system for managing our emails or for managing the documents and other digital files on our laptop computer.

- A **practice** (with a small "p") refers to a technique, method, or strategy of PIM that was initially selected by the person to accomplish some purpose and is now a part of the person's PIM repertoire. For example, the use of "self-appointments" in a calendar to manage and remind of tasks and to-dos is a practice of task management. The use of leading characters in file and folder names to move their file or folder up or down in a name-based ordering is a practice of PIM.

- A **Practice** (with a capital "P") refers to the sum total of all techniques, methods, strategies, systems—all practices of information management—that a person uses in support of and as enabled by the information (content and structure), information channels, and tools in their personal spaces of information (PSIs). This is the sense intended in phrases such as "An overall Practice of PIM" or "A person's Practice of PIM." All of a person's PIM practices combine to form a single "Practice" of PIM for that person. Just as a person has only one PSI she/he has only one Practice of PIM.

What is the relationship between people's Practices and their PSIs? If the PSI is the "object" then we might say that the Practice is the sum total of all "methods" (and techniques, strategies, even whole "systems") to be applied to this object. Alternatively, with reference to the letters in the acronym "PIM," we might say that the PSI is for the "I" in PIM, i.e., all information in aggregate that relates to the person (the "P") in one way or another and also all information tools and information channels. A Practice is for the "M" in PIM.

In the sections that follow in this final chapter we'll look at:

➢ Considerations when designing your Practice of PIM;

➢ Methods you might use as you design your Practice of PIM; and

➢ Some ways to challenge yourself in your Practice of PIM.

12.2   CONSIDERATIONS WHEN DESIGNING YOUR PRACTICE OF PIM

As you read this now, congratulations. You are a survivor. If you are reading this in sequence after reading all 11 chapters that precede this one in the Future of PIM series then extra congratulations! You are a survivor indeed! But even if you alight on this in a skimming pattern (as so many of us do these days when reading anything other than a novel) you still deserve congratulations. You are a survivor in your Practice of PIM.

Everything you've learned still applies. Nothing written here is meant to diminish from the value of your lessons learned, hard won over the years, from your daily struggles with your information and with the tools you use to manage this information.

The best you can expect from this book, from any book, is to acquire a few new perspectives, a few different ideas, some of which may prove useful to you in your Practice of PIM.

Information is power. Information and its effective management can transform the ways we live our lives and, through these, our world. Information is our means to build a better world. This is one of the most important messages of this series.

A related message of the series is that we should all become (better) students of our own Practices of PIM. What's working? What isn't? What can we change for the better?

We are all still learning. I, for example, just learned (as of June 15th, 2015) that when looking at a long listing of files and subfolders for a folder in Windows Explorer (I use the "Details" view), typing the leading letters of the name for a specific file or subfolder, in rapid succession, can take me directly to its entry in the listing. I then have only to press the return key to open the file or subfolder. This often proves faster for me even with the desired file/subfolder in view than moving the pointer, and double-clicking to open. The method works even better when the desired item is not in view and especially for views that contain lots of items (files and subfolders) which, for reasons I will elaborate on later, is increasingly the case for me. I'm surprised I didn't know that before. But I didn't.

12.2.1 IT'S ABOUT YOUR INFORMATION…

Information is at the center, literally, of the phrase "personal information management." Place information at the center of your Practice of PIM.

Your information. Take an inventory. Be sure to consider all six senses in which information can be personal. I've started my own inventory in Table 12.1.

	Relation to "me"	Description, location, tools (app, service, device), questions/issues
		Table 12.1: My (rough, in progress) inventory of my information
1	Controlled by, owned by me	Laptop (MacBook); Laptop (Lenovo IdeaPad) Smartphone (Android), with lots of photos and video clips waiting to be "curated" Email for work (Outlook/Exchange); email for non-work (Gmail); email I never use (Hotmail) Facebook account, Twitter, LinkedIn, ResearchGate… Dropbox (for nearly all my digital information), Google Drive, OneDrive Piles and piles of paper bank statements and financial reports in my home office waiting to be sorted through some day… Photos… what am I going to do with my photos
2	About me	Credit history (?? Did the credit card payment we missed a few months back have impact?) Medical records with primary care physician (still all paper-based) Online account with my cardiologist (what's in there?) Blood draw results (available if I ask for it from the lab as a paper print-out…are my PSA levels higher than last time?) PayTrust account Account for electrical utilities Financial statements, bank statements, tax returns all online at various places … are they secure?…
3	Directed toward me	Nice to have the out-of-office message on… gives me "cover" to finish this chapter.… Are we on the "do not call list"? It doesn't seem so. Does it make any difference? Should we put a "no solicitors" sign in our driveway? Do the ad-block utilities work for my browser? Are they worth it? Are there ads I'd really like to see?

4	Sent (posted, shared) by me	I should update my blog (http://keepingfoundthingsfound.com/blog); does anyone actually read it? http://keepingfoundthingsfound.com/; http://talesofpim.org/; http://kftf.ischool.washington.edu/; http://pim.ischool.washington.edu/, http://faculty.washington.edu/williamj/ … Too many "properties"! Too many appearances! Most are out of date. Few are properly connected to one another Facebook, Gmail, Outlook….and Twitter too (but who has time to tweet?)
5	(Already) experienced by me	My Outlook calendar, Outlook emails, mails—great resource. Half of my memory is in these accounts! And then my photos. I wish I had time to organize these in some good way…
6	Relevant (useful) to me	What did I miss at the last faculty meeting? (Not in the minutes just "in the air") Time to schedule another lunch with David? (I always find out about things I would'nt know otherwise)

I just did so (again) and found the experience useful and somewhat distressing—each item in the table carries with it one or more "to-dos" for me. The table is rough and very incomplete. As I worked through its cells adding items, more and more kinds of information occurred to me so that a cell that I thought might have only a few items ended up having many. And I'm not done…

12.2.2 DON'T THINK YOU'RE SO SPECIAL (EVEN IF YOU ARE A LITTLE DIFFERENT)

I live in the Seattle area. One of my most favorite ad campaigns is the "Northwest types" series from PEMCO insurance with its tag line: "We're a lot like you. A little different."[381] The ads are funny and sweetly accurate in their caricatures of the traditional Northwesterner.

So too in our Practices of PIM. We're each a little different but often in similar ways. This is apparent to me whenever, as I often do when I teach or give a tutorial on PIM, I poll the audience concerning their practices of PIM. People are hesitant at first. But as they, with encouragement and sometimes with evident embarrassment, relay this or that practice of PIM, there are almost always nods of recognition and agreement from other people in the audience.

This sense of being "different" but in similar ways, was also apparent among the researchers who gathered at a recent PIM workshop.[382] In an afternoon breakout session, workshop attendees

---

[381]   See for example, https://www.youtube.com/user/NorthWestTypes.

[382]   *PIM 2013* (http://pimworkshop.org/2013/), the sixth in a series of workshops concerning PIM.

took turns sharing details of their own practices of PIM and discussing their observations from formal studies of PIM behavior. As one person presented, other workshop participants would frequently offer, "I do that too!" or, "That's a lot like something I've seen participants do in my studies."

A point here is that practices of PIM that we may think are unusual or even a little "weird" are often much more widely shared than we might suspect. In Chapter 2 of the *Keeping Found Things Found* book[383] and as inspired by the "parable of the ant" from the book *Sciences of the Artificial* by Herbert Simon[384] I describe situations wherein the apparent complexity or even "weirdness" in some of our PIM practices can actually be understood to be a reflection of the informational environment in which we find ourselves.

That said, there are ways in which we systematically differ from one another. One distinction drawn in Chapter 1 of the *Keeping Found Things Found* book is between *information warriors* and *information worriers*. Information warriors see their information and their information tools as a strategic asset. Information warriors are willing to invest time and money to keep up with the latest in mobile, wearable devices, tablet computers, web service, etc. We might say that for an information warrior, investments in information tools (time, energy, and attention as well as money) and in a Practice of PIM is a "profit center."

On the other hand, comparable investments for the information worriers are a cost center: New tools (devices, apps, services) and "… new developments in the alphabet soup of web-based initiatives—these and other developments in information technology represent more time and money that needs to be spent just to keep up with everyone else. Information worriers may have a nagging feeling they could do better in their choice of supporting tools and strategies. But they don't know where to begin" (p. 13).

Are you an information warrior or an information worrier? If you're like me (again … a little different) then you're a little of each.

Another distinction made commonly is with respect to age group and generation. Much has been written, for example, about digital natives vs. digital immigrants[385] and about millennials as now the largest, most diverse generation in the U.S.[386] Though some of the writing falls into hyperbole even to the point of painting the young as practically a separate species, there are indeed important differences to note. Wobbrock writes, for example, that "mobile is the platform of choice for the millennial generation" and that "interactive technologies, from smartphones to websites to mobile apps to SaaS apps, need to provide the most usable, self-guided, hiccup-free, efficient user experiences in history."[387] Fair enough. Though I have a smartphone, my Practice of PIM is centered

---

[383]   Jones, 2007.
[384]   Simon, 1969.
[385]   https://en.wikipedia.org/wiki/Digital_native.
[386]   https://en.wikipedia.org/wiki/Millennials; https://www.whitehouse.gov/sites/default/files/docs/millennials_report.pdf; http://www.uschamberfoundation.org/millennial-generation-research-review.
[387]   Wobbrock, 2015.

on my laptop computer. If you count yourself as a digital native or a member of the millennial generation or if, for any reason your Practice of PIM is focused primarily around your mobile device, then please make appropriate adjustments/translations for what I write in this chapter.

12.2.3 DO BEGIN TO BRING YOUR INFORMATION TOGETHER

Are you experiencing "information overload"? Too much information? Join the crowd. But take some solace from the knowledge that it is not a new problem. Consider the following:

> *We have reason to fear that the multitude of books which grows every day in a prodigious fashion will make the following centuries fall into a state as barbarous as that of the centuries that followed the fall of the Roman Empire. Unless we try to prevent this danger by separating those books which we must throw out or leave in oblivion from those which one should save and within the latter between what is useful and what is not.*

This was said by one Adrien Baillet in 1685.[388]

We will always face information overload. There will alway be more information than there is time (or attention or energy) to handle it all. Though this reality isn't new, the ways we can be distracted and overloaded increase with our reliance on the Web and on our mobile devices. What can we do? Disengage? Probably not. But as I write in Chapter 15 of the *Keeping Found Things Found* book, our reactions to information overload can vary:

> *In a worst case reaction to an oversupply of information, our efforts to process the information breakdown completely… We say something like "oh, the hell with it, I'll just do/ pick this."*

We can do better. In this sub-section we consider first some simple heuristic alternatives to an impossible, "sequential-exhaustive" processing of information. We then consider ways to avoid further information fragmentation and to begin to bring our information together (for "less many" information).

Alternatives to sequential-exhaustive. We can't read it all. We can't do it all either. We may read a novel from start to finish but for nearly everything else we look for alternatives, for shortcuts, for sections we can skim lightly or skip entirely.

Once upon a time (in graduate school when I seemed to have lots more time than I do now) I actually would attempt to read research articles from start to finish (for the most part). Not anymore. Now I skip around. What are the main points? Read the abstract. Read the conclusion. Interesting? Read more in the introduction. Read the implications drawn in the discussion section. Is this believable? Read the Method section.

What about you?

[388]   As noted by Blair, 1961.

I do something similar for magazine articles, though the structure (e.g., of an article from *Time Magazine* or the *Economist*) is not as consistent as for research articles. Even so, it can be kind of a game. Guess what this article is about. Guess its main points. Read a little more to verify. Am I right? I win! Otherwise, I keep reading. I take some comfort in knowing that for many journals and magazines, content is online and searchable so then the point is not to remember every last detail but rather to understand and remember enough of the article to be able to retrieve it again from the Web should the need arise. Sparrow et al.[389] find that in an age of searchable information on the Web people are more inclined to focus on remembering the gist of an article and the means of its retrieval again rather than to remember the article in detail.

I should also mention that I'm a very slow reader. I've tried the Evelyn Wood readings dynamics course.[390] My reading speed did increase. But I never felt comfortable. It wasn't fun to read that fast. The method I describe above, call it the *skip-sample-guess-verify method*, works fine for me.

Chapter 7 ("Managing privacy and the flow of information") reviewed other alternatives to sequential-exhaustive information processing. These include:

> **Satisfice rather than optimize.** The term "satisfice" was coined by Herbert Simon[391] in reference to a strategy of searching only until an alternative meeting some minimal level or set of criteria is found. Satisficing is in contrast to optimizing which requires an exhaustive consideration of all alternatives.
>
> Example: Finding a "good enough" restaurant nearby with an open table for dinner in 30 minutes. It may be best to go with the first restaurant available and acceptable to everyone in your party. Yes, if you keep looking, you may find another restaurant that your party likes even more. But maybe not. And maybe by then the table at the first restaurant is no longer available…

> **Triage (sort) candidates into "no," "yes," and "maybe" categories.** Triage is especially useful when attempting to find a set of acceptable candidates—the players who will make a team, for example, or the papers to be accepted at conference. More concentrated focus can then be given to the "maybe" pile.

---

[389]   Sparrow et al., 2011.

[390]   Long ago back while in 1978 while in graduate school. For a more recent description of the Evelyn Wood Seven-Day Speed Reading and Learning Program and its decidedly mixed reviews, see http://www.amazon. com/Evelyn-Seven-Day-Reading-Learning-Program/dp/1566194024, and also http://mt.artofmemory. com/forums/does-speed-reading-work-1886.html and http://worldsstrongestlibrarian.com/8315/my-experi-ence-with-speed-reading/ or simply search using search phrase like "Does speed reading work?"

[391]   Simon, 1957.

> ➤ **Sample and then optimize within this sample.** Sometimes the criteria aren't known ahead of time. Set a limit on the amount of information that is collected or the number of alternatives or candidates that are accepted for consideration. A job review process, for example, may specify that only the first n job applications will be considered. The sampling approach is especially useful in cases where: (1) Criteria for selection are not well understood ahead of time (and only become apparent through a comparison of candidates); and (2) There is reason to believe that the sample is unbiased and representative of the population as a whole.

Toward "less many" information, there are then the personal, everyday counterparts to the tool design guidelines on information fragmentation of the previous chapter:

> ➤ **Do be careful before signing up for yet another way of organizing information.** Sometimes the extra overhead of another organizational scheme is worth it. I have friends who consider applications like Microsoft OneNote or Evernote to be a life-saver—essential to their way of keeping track, especially of meeting notes. But I've also talked to people who embraced a new application with great enthusiasm only to gradually abandon it as not worth the overhead. Using new apps frequently means using new, different ways to organize. Evernote has its "notebooks" and "tags." Microsoft OneNote has its "sections" (tabs) and "pages." Bookmarking facilities of browsers provide essentially a secondary file structure. Most of us must already maintain "Too many hierarchies!" as Boardman et al. wrote.[392] Avoid adding still more.

> ➤ **Do leverage existing organizational structures.** In particular, leverage your file system structures. But as one of a top "recommended" practice[393] also subscribe to a cloud service (e.g., Dropbox, Google Drive, Microsoft OneDrive) and share your folder structures through this service so that your structures and their contents can be saved, synced, and shared with others.

> ➤ **Do avoid still more "places" to monitor.** LinkedIn, Facebook, Reddit, Twitter, multiple email accounts, multiple calendars, multiple websites for viewing bank and financial information, tax information, utility bills, etc. Enough! We have too many places to monitor. Our financial and banking services are encouraging us to "go paperless" which can be a good thing but currently does not offer digital accessibility and persistence comparable to the paper statements. A tool that might be worth some additional overhead would crawl and consolidate financial and banking state-

---

[392] Boardman et al., 2003.
[393] Jones et al., 2015; see also http://pimworkshop.org/delphi_report.pdf.

ments, as previously discussed in Chapter 6's "Technologies to save our information" of Part 2 in this series, *Transforming Technologies to Manage Our Information.*[394]

> ➤ **Do leverage existing places and existing habits.** Consider your current attentional surfaces—the places you routinely visit, unprompted, on a regular (daily) basis. These likely include your email inbox (or do you have more than one?) and your digital calendar (or do you have more than one?) People commonly send emails to themselves as reminders of tasks and to-dos.[395] This isn't "weird." It's just making good practical use of an attentional space. Likewise, people often use their digital calendar as a place to put "self-appointments" for a particular task or to-do. Sometimes the intention is actually to set aside the designated time represented on the calendar for completion of the task. Other times, the entry is simply a reminder. The drawback of course is that if these appointments are not completed they may need to be moved again to remain visible. But the benefit is a good leverage of an attentional surface.

Other ways to begin to bring your information together come as recommended practices from the "Blue Ribbon Panel Consensus Report on Better Practices of Personal Information Management."[396] These include "organize information by project (one folder per project)" and "store files in the cloud ...". (See subsection 12.2.5 for a complete listing of recommended practices from the report).

12.2.4   COVER CHECKLISTS AS THESE MAKE SENSE FOR YOUR PRACTICE

As you consider the adoption of a new tool or a new practice of PIM, you might, informally, do a quick pass through the checklists reviewed in the previous chapter (Section 11.2.4) or additional checklists you find or create. For example, the six senses in which information can be personal—already used in Table 12.1 to guide and structure the results of an inventory of personal information—can also provide a checklist of questions to ask for any new tool or practice (see Table 12.2).

---

[394]   Jones, 2013.
[395]   See Jones et al. (2003, 2002).
[396]   http://pimworkshop.org/delphi_report.pdf; see also Jones et al., 2015.

Table 12.2: The six senses in which information can be personal can form the basis for a checklist of questions to ask when considering a new tool or practice of PIM

	Relation to "me"	Questions to consider
1	Controlled by, owned by me	How much new information do I "own" or must I manage if I use this tool or practice?
2	About me	What information does the tool keep about me? (Esp. important to ask for web services).
3	Directed toward me	Have I been sure to opt out of notifications I don't want? (e.g., email notifications)
4	Sent (posted, shared) by me	What information do other people see about me? What impression do I make? (This is especially important for services like LinkedIn and Facebook).
5	(Already) experienced by me	Does the tool or practice (i.e., as a by-product) create a log of my activities that could be useful to me later? What does the tool do with this information? (P2). Can other people see this information too? (P4)
6	Relevant (useful) to me	Does the tool or practice increase the likelihood that I'll run across useful information "by chance" that I wouldn't otherwise think to look for?

Similarly, a checklist can be devised from the six activities of PIM. The checklist has relevance for example, when considering a tool such as Evernote (Table 12.3).

Table 12.3: Checklist questions, based on the six activities of PIM, to ask for a tool such as Evernote

PIM activity	Questions to consider
Keeping	How easy is capture and keeping? Is a link preserved to source? Can excerpted information be highlighted in the source? Can I capture from desktop apps (e.g., Microsoft Outlook or Word) as well as from web pages? What about voice?
Finding	Can searchable text be generated from images? From voice? Are notes indexed? Can search handle misspellings?
Maintaining and Organizing	How much do I need to invest in a tagging in order to get benefit?
Managing privacy and information flow	Are my notes private and secure? But then can I selectively share notes with others? With the world? What's the basis for sharing? ("Notebooks"?)
Measuring and evaluating	Does the tool provide any statistics (e.g., based on the notes that I take) that might be useful to me or help me to reflect and reach insights I might not otherwise have?
Making sense of and using	What happens after I take a hundred notes? A thousand? Ten thousand? Do these just become a jumble or are there ways of sorting and grouping these to make sense of "the forest for the trees"?

With reference to Section 11.2.4 of the previous chapter, checklists might also be based on principles of the user-subjective approach (Bergman et al., 2008b).

Or consider the factors determining whether a new tool (or practice) will be successfully adopted in a person's Practice of PIM (Jones et al., 2008):

1. **Visibility**—will you notice and remember to use it?

2. **Integration**—does it connect and work well with your other tools, practices, and overall Practice?

3. **Co-adoption**—is it necessary for others to use the tool or practice as well?

4. **Scalability**—does the tool or practice still work over time and especially as the amount of information continues to increase?

5. **Return on investment (ROI)**—does the tool or practice "pay for itself" over the long run, i.e., do the benefits compensate for cost as measured in your resources (money, energy, attention, but, most especially, time)?

There is often a "honeymoon period" associated with the trial use of any tool or practice. But by the time signs of incompatibility emerge it may already be too late, i.e., your information may be stuck in an unhappy marriage with the tool or practice (e.g., system of organization) only to be extracted through a messy, time-consuming "divorce" (i.e., complicated export that may leave much of the metadata behind). The factors of *co-adoption*, *scalability*, and *ROI* are especially important in determining whether a tool or practice will work out in the longer run.

Conversely, you may dismiss, prematurely, a tool or practice that might actually provide real value to your Practice of PIM. The factors of *visibility* and *integration* are especially important in determining whether a new tool or practice will "take old" in your Practice of PIM. A tool that's out of sight, for example, is frequently out of mind and may be quickly forgotten.

12.2.5 CONSIDER ADOPTING SOME OF THE "RECOMMENDED" PRACTICES OF PIM (IF YOU HAVEN'T DONE SO ALREADY)

From the "Blue Ribbon Panel Consensus Report on Better Practices of Personal Information Management."[397]

1. Take a picture with smartphone (e.g., of paper notes or whiteboard);

2. Email yourself notes, thoughts, tasks/to-dos;

3. Keep a notes or "thoughts" file (e.g., as .txt or Word doc) for each project or topic;

4. Organize information by project (one folder per project);

5. Use standardized file and/or folder names (also do this across devices);

6. Use calendar events to represent the future and to remind of tasks and aid in completion;

7. Use email inbox as to-do list (including use of flags and unread status as reminders, or maintaining a single "to-do" email);

8. Maintain a single, "master" list of all tasks/to-dos;

9. Keep windows and tabs open as a reminder to do something (i.e., they require attention before being closed);

10. Use leading characters in file and folder names to bring important information to the top or to send old/inactive information to the bottom (e.g., "aaa-," "zzz-");

---

[397] http://pimworkshop.org/delphi_report.pdf; see also Jones et al., 2015.

11. Store files in the cloud (e.g., Dropbox, Microsoft OneDrive, Google Drive);

12. Add characters or words to file names—usually trailing—to represent the "who," "when," or recency of a document (e.g., "v1" or "final" at the end of a file name); and

13. Archive old/inactive information into designated subfolder (e.g. "archive").

12.3   METHODS YOU MIGHT USE AS YOU DESIGN YOUR OWN PRACTICE OF PIM

Become a student of your own Practice of PIM. Become an observant participant. Ask basic questions. Where do your resources go? Your money, energy, attention and, most especially, your time? Where do you encounter problems and frustrations? What methods seem to be workarounds? Which techniques seem to "bend" tools for unusual, undesigned use? Are there better ways, better tools, for accomplishing your purpose? You can begin to address these questions using adaptations of methods described in Chapter 11:

1. **Guided tour**—give a friend a guided tour; or do a self-guided "safari" into lesser known regions of your PSI. You may be surprised at what you find.

2. **Setup/test of a cued re-finding task.** Test yourself. Or have a friend test you.

3. **Prompted, in-situ completion of a real information task.** As with #2, you might test yourself as you complete a task—especially one that you've been putting off.

4. **Think aloud.** Thinking aloud can calm the nerves. And it's much more constructive than cursing at the computer.

5. **Life-change timing.** Re-assess your Practice of PIM in the face of major changes in your life—marriage, divorce, children, or a move from one city to another.

Even as I list these methods and their possible use in a program of self-study, I must admit I myself would likely never find the time to try them. I might do better in the use of two other methods knowing as I do that each has had good use by others in their own programs of self-study.

A modified version of *experience sampling* (mentioned in Chapter 11) was used by my graduate school advisor, John R. Anderson. He charted his productivity at half hour intervals through his working day as marked by a recurring buzzer on his watch. I contacted him in 2007 as I worked to include his example in the *Keeping Found Things Found* book. He kindly responded in email:

> *It did occupy at least a 5 year period of my life.*[398] *I think the measure I was trying to get was number of hours of actual productivity. I do remember I never liked the overhead and*

[398]   Roughly from 1977 to 1982.

interruption but I often found myself not being particularly productive when the buzzer rang. One of the reasons I quit was that the behavior I was trying to produce had finally become automated and when the buzzer rang I always found myself at a pretty high level of productivity. I would like to think I have maintained my good ways but maybe I am kidding myself.[399]

And then here is a variation of diary keeping by none other than Benjamin Franklin, a founding father of the United States of America. Here is his method, in his own words:

I made a little book, in which I allotted a page for each of the virtues. I rul'd each page with red ink, so as to have seven columns, one for each day of the week, marking each column with a letter for the day. I cross'd these columns with thirteen red lines, marking the beginning of each line with the first letter of one of the virtues, on which line, and in its proper column, I might mark, by a little black spot, every fault I found upon examination to have been committed respecting that virtue upon that day.

Franklin's daily self-tracking made use of our friend, the table (Figure 12.1). If Benjamin Franklin could track the thirteen virtues surely I (you too?) can do something comparable for the "virtues" of PIM. Your challenge, mine too, would be to determine what these virtues are. I doubt that our lists, when done, would agree.

To each of us, our own.

---

[399]   Email communication with Professor Anderson, April 10th, 2007. Over the past 25 years (as of this communication), Professor Anderson had published 9 books (several in multiple editions) and is first or supporting author of more than 250 articles.

TEMPERANCE.						
EAT NOT TO DULNESS;						
DRINK NOT TO ELEVATION.						

	S.	M.	T.	W.	T.	F.	S.
T.							
S.	*	*		*		*	
O.	**	*	*		*	*	*
R.		*				*	
F.		*			*		
I.			*				
S.							
J.							
M.							
C.							
T.							
C.							
H							

Figure 12.1: A example of the table that Benjamin Franklin used to track the times in a week that he failed with respect to each of the thirteen virtues.

12.4 SOME WAYS TO CHALLENGE YOURSELF IN YOUR PRACTICE OF PIM

So far in this chapter we've considered "dos" and "don'ts" that might apply (or might not) to your Practice of PIM. We've considered methods you might use (or not). In this section then are some longer-range challenges of PIM:

➢ Put more "meta" into your Practice of PIM.

➢ Tell your story to weave your information together.

➢ Look for ways to multi-goal, not multi-task.

➤ Establish your home on the Web.

➤ Manage for a lifetime and for legacy.

We consider a few of these challenges in greater depth before reaching some conclusions for this chapter, this book, and the series.

Put More "Meta" into Your Practice of PIM

One good investment at the meta-level (with respect to maintaining and organizing) is to create your own Personal Unifying Taxonomy or PUT.[400] Mine is realized in folders. I now keep nearly all of these (except for some containing financial information) on Dropbox. I highly recommend a cloud service such as Dropbox (or Google Drive or Microsoft OneDrive...) as a means of saving, syncing, and sharing your information.

A PUT is (a):

➤ **Personal.** People own their PUTs. The "P" might also stand for "Persistent." A PUT grows and develops over a person's lifetime according to their needs rather than the demands of a current tool set.

➤ **Unifying.** All information that relates to a person in one way or another can be classified and organized into the PUT no matter what its form (email, file, or any of several kinds of web information). In some cases the information item itself may reside as a snippet of text in the PUT (e.g., frequently re-used "how to find my office" directions or a hard-to-remember budget number). In many other cases, the information item (file, email, web page) stays where it is (to be managed by its supporting application) and only a reference to this item is stored within the PUT.

➤ **Taxonomy.** As a basis for a classification of personal information, the structure of the taxonomy is better described as a directed graph than a strict hierarchy.

My own folder hierarchy, my PUT, has become ever "flatter" over the years so that now I have one structure of "projects" folders organized by year with each project named first with a relevant date (e.g., range of duration or expected date of completion) in international format (so that projects sorted by name will also sort by relevant date). Everything I'm working on or planning is a project, including holidays, birthdays, family vacations, and, of course, work-related projects. I'm considering calling these "stories" instead (told first in future tense as expressions of intention, then in extended present tense, as I work to fulfill my intentions, finally in past tense as as I reflect, reminisce, and organize project-related information—especially photos).

---

[400] Jones, 2007.

In a separate top-level folder named "persons, places, things, topics" I organize "reference information"[401] relating to the people, places, and things that matter to me (and for which I keep information) and then also topics of general interest to me. Some folders have subfolders (e.g., a "school" subfolder for my son). But the overall structure is quite flat. Even so, with search, a given folder can be found and opened very quickly.

Tell Your Story to Weave Your Information Together

Tool support to do this is still quite limited (see Chapter 11). But you can do things on your own. A simple email conversation with a friend or colleague, for example, can be a way of getting "unstuck" in the articulation of thoughts (e.g., for an article, proposal, or essay). The conversation flows and, later, provides an excellent starting point for what is to be written.

Look for Ways to Multi-Goal, Not Multi-Task

Observe yourself and your performance as you complete tasks. Look for real synergies among the things to be done. Consider a biological metaphor. Tasks frequently compete with one another for your time, energy, and attention. But in cases of "task commensalism," the performance of one task does little to impact the performance of another. In the previous section, we considered cases where the work of one task was sufficiently automated so as to be, so to speak, in the hands and feet, thus freeing our mind to engage in thinking related to another task. We walk or drive a familiar route while thinking of an upcoming meeting for example.

Even better are situations of "task mutualism" where two tasks are performed with mutual benefit to each or, alternatively, where one activity serves two or more ends. There is often a strong social element in such activities. We post a photo to Facebook or Flickr together with an explanatory caption to share with our friends and family. But pictures are there later for us to look at as well (as long as Facebook and Flickr don't go away). And the captions may prove invaluable to us as our memories for the circumstances around taking the picture have faded.

Consider the several ends served by the simple act of emailing a web link to an interested colleague. A relationship is strengthened. He or she may return the favor. Moreover, a useful exchange may ensue. Similarly, some people blog as a way of "thinking out loud" as they grapple with complicated issues about which they must write an article or a term paper. In the course of exchanging email messages or posting to a blog, a person may discover that the material generated puts them well on their way to the completion of the article or term paper.

Or consider the classic case of golfing with a friend or business associate. The experience of golfing is likely more pleasurable for the companionship. Moreover, issues may be discussed and resolved during the golf game that would not be so easily discussed in a more formal meeting

---

[401] Jones, 2007.

explicitly scheduled for this purpose. Some tasks, such as dining, combine well with a number of other tasks, while other tasks such as reading or playing video games, and do not combine well with other activities.

Or consider the following email from a colleague who responded to my request for literature on the human perception of time: "I was happy to do it. I will be writing a mini-lit review on subjective time perception this summer and it gave me an opportunity to get back into the literature without the writing pressure" (email from Anita M. Crescenzi, June 3rd, 2015). This has an element of multi-goaling (helping me and starting her literature review) and also has a storytelling element (email to me represented a less formal way to get started without "the writing pressure").

And then what about the other two challenges/opportunities: **Establish your home on the Web** and **Manage for a lifetime and for legacy**? I'm still trying to figure these out for myself so I have little advice to give. Moreover, my solutions might not work for you.

To each of us, our own.

12.5   CONCLUSIONS: BUILDING A BETTER WORLD

Information is what we extract from the data of our senses. But information is also for imagining worlds we cannot experience directly. Information is what's in documents, emails, web pages tweets and also in the new "online statement ready to view."

We consume information. Information consumes us and our resources—our money, energy, time, and attention.

We also make information. Information is to represent our wishes, whether for a table for two at 7PM or a window seat on the 7AM flight to Seattle. Information is to communicate and coordinate with others and to persuade others to act on our behalf. Information is to know.

Information is made personal as a thing we own and control (P1) in the form, for example, of photos on a smartphone, digital files on a laptop, or paper files in a home office. But information can be "personal" in several other senses: (P2) As a representation of us—our health, our creditworthiness, our "value" to prospective employers. (P3) As a thing directed towards us in the form of distracting advertisements, unsolicited phone calls, and life-saving fire alarms. (P4) As a thing we send to or share with others in the form of emails, tweets, "Snaps," blog posts, and "lectures." (P5) As a thing to support the recollection, reflection, and reminiscence of our life experiences in the form of photographs, diary entries, old emails, and credit card statements. And finally, (P6) as a thing that might be relevant to us as it relates to an interest or a project we're trying to complete.

Each of these six senses of the personal gives us a distinct reason for better managing our information. We manage through minute-by-minute acts of finding and keeping. We manage also through meta-level activities to maintain and organize, to manage privacy and the flow of information, to measure and evaluate, and, overriding other activities, to makes sense of and use information.

Personal information management (PIM) is the art of getting things done in our lives through information.

Shift now from regard for ourselves as individuals to regard for ourselves as a species—Homo sapiens (or Homo sapiens sapiens).

It is the Information—as the representation of our collective scientific and technical know-how, as the thing of knowledge transfer—that has enabled, even driven, the enormous changes we have wrought—for good and ill—to our human condition and to the world about us. In a few hundred thousand years—a cosmic eye blink—we have emerged from a coterie of primate species on the African savanna to build pyramids, a Great Wall, skyscrapers, airplanes, cities with glowing, nighttime skies visible from outer space, bombs with the power of the sun, and a global, light-speed network interconnecting vast amounts computing power and digital storage. In the same period of time the ecological footprint and circumstances of our close relative the chimpanzee have changed nary a bit, other than to be negatively impacted by us.

Our abilities to learn from each other and our circumstances have never been better. And so too our need to do so to keep from destroying the Garden of Eden we call Planet Earth.

It is about the information and our abilities to manage it.

References

Ackerman, M. S., and Cranor, L. (1999). Privacy critics: UI components to safeguard users' privacy. In *CHI '99 Extended Abstracts on Human Factors in Computing Systems* (pp. 258–259). Pittsburgh, Pennsylvania: ACM Press. DOI: 10.1145/632716.632875. 117

Adamczyk, P. D., and Bailey, B. P. (2004). If not now, when?: the effects of interruption at different moments within task execution. In *Proceedings of the SIGCHI Conference on Human Factors in Computing Systems* (pp. 271–278). Vienna, Austria: ACM. DOI: 10.1145/985692.985727. 35

Allan, L. G. (1979). The perception of time. *Perception and Psychophysics*, 26(5), 340–354. DOI:10.3758/BF03204158. 74

Al-Shakhouri, N. S., and Mahmood, A. (2009). Privacy in the digital world: Toward international legislation [legislation, data protection, consumer privacy, ethics]. Retrieved from http://firstmonday.org/htbin/cgiwrap/bin/ojs/index.php/fm/article/view/2146/2153. 117

Ames, M. G., Go, J., Kaye, J. "Jofish," and Spasojevic, M. (2011). Understanding Technology Choices and Values Through Social Class. In *Proceedings of the ACM 2011 Conference on Computer Supported Cooperative Work* (pp. 55–64). New York, NY, USA: ACM. DOI: 10.1145/1958824.1958834. 24

Anderson, C. J., Glassman, M., McAfee, R. B., and Pinelli, T. (2001). An investigation of factors affecting how engineers and scientists seek information. *J. Eng. Technol. Manage.*, 18(2), 131–155. DOI: 10.1016/S0923-4748(01)00032-7. 32

Anderson, J. R. (1990). *The Adaptive Character of Thought*. Hillsdale, NJ: Lawrence Erlbaum Associates. 107

Anderson, J. R., and Skwarecki, E. (1986). The Automated Tutoring of Introductory Computer Programming. *Commun. ACM*, 29(9), 842–849. DOI: 10.1145/6592.6593. 28

Arazy, O., Ortega, F., Nov, O., Yeo, L., and Balila, A. (2015). Functional Roles and Career Paths in Wikipedia. In *Proceedings of the 18th ACM Conference on Computer Supported Cooperative Work and Social Computing* (pp. 1092–1105). New York, NY, USA: ACM. DOI: 10.1145/2675133.2675257. 45

Archambault, A., and Grudin, J. (2012). A longitudinal study of facebook, linkedin, and twitter use. In *Proceedings of the SIGCHI Conference on Human Factors in Computing Systems* (pp. 2741–2750). ACM. Retrieved from http://dl.acm.org/citation.cfm?id=2208671. 33, 34

Auster, E., and Choo, C. W. (1994). How senior managers acquire and use information in environmental scanning. *Inf. Process. Manage.*, 30(5), 607–618. DOI: 10.1016/0306-4573(94)90073-6. 2

Baron-Cohen, S., Leslie, A. M., and Frith, U. (1985). Does the autistic child have a "theory of mind"? *Cognition*, 21(1), 37–46. DOI: 10.1016/0010-0277(85)90022-8. 13

Barreau, D., and Nardi, B. A. (1995). Finding and reminding: file organization from the desktop. *SIGCHI Bull.*, 27(3), 39–43. DOI: 10.1145/221296.221307. 5, 17

Barsalou, L. W. (1983). Ad hoc categories. *Memory and Cognition*, 11(3), 211–227. DOI: 10.3758/BF03196968. 119

Barsalou, L. W. (1991). Deriving categories to achieve goals. In *The Psychology of Learning and Motivation: Advances in Research and Theory*. New York: Academic Press. 119

Bauer, L., Cranor, L. F., Reeder, R. W., Reiter, M. K., and Vaniea, K. (2009). Real life challenges in access-control management. In *Proceedings of the 27th International Conference on Human Factors in Computing Systems* (pp. 899–908). Boston, MA, USA: ACM. 117

Bederson, B. B. (2004). Interfaces for staying in the flow. *Ubiquity*, 5(27), 1–1. DOI: 10.1145/1029383.1074069. 73

Bellotti, V., Ambard, A., Turner, D., Gossmann, C., Demkova, K., and Carroll, J. M. (2015). A Muddle of Models of Motivation for Using Peer-to-Peer Economy Systems. In *Proceedings of the 33rd Annual ACM Conference on Human Factors in Computing Systems* (pp. 1085–1094). New York, NY, USA: ACM. DOI: 10.1145/2702123.2702272. 45

Bellotti, V., Dalal, B., Good, N., Flynn, P., Bobrow, D. G., and Ducheneaut, N. (2004). What a to-do: studies of task management towards the design of a personal task list manager. In *Proceedings of the SIGCHI Conference on Human Factors in Ccomputing Systems* (pp. 735–742). Vienna, Austria: ACM. DOI: 10.1145/985692.985785. 35

Bellotti, V., Ducheneaut, N., Howard, M., and Smith, I. (2003). Taking email to task: The design and evaluation of a task management centered email tool. In *ACM SIGCHI Conference on Human Factors in Computing Systems (CHI 2003)* (pp. 345–352). Ft. Lauderdale, FL: ACM Press. DOI: 10.1145/642611.642672. 35, 71

Bellotti, V., Ducheneaut, N., Howard, M., Smith, I., and Grinter, R. (2005). Quality vs. quantity: Email-centric task-management and its relationship with overload. *Human–Computer Interaction*, 20(1-2), 89–138. DOI: 10.1207/s15327051hci2001&2_4. 4

Bellotti, V., Thornton, J., Chin, A., Schiano, D., and Good, N. (2007). TV-ACTA: embedding an activity-centered interface for task management in email. *Work*, 5, 11, 35

Bellotti, V., and Thornton, J. (2006). Managing Activities with TV-Acta: TaskVista and Activity-Centered Task Assistant. In *PIM 2006, The Second Workshop on Personal Information Management (PIM)*, sponsored by SIGIR. Seattle, WA, USA. Retrieved from http://pim.ischool.washington.edu/pim06/index.htm. 35

Bentley, F. R., and Chowdhury, S. K. (2010). Serendipitous Family Stories: Using Findings from a Study on Family Communication to Share Family History. In *Proceedings of the 12th ACM International Conference Adjunct Papers on Ubiquitous Computing - Adjunct* (pp. 359–360). New York, NY, USA: ACM. DOI: 10.1145/1864431.1864435. 24

Bergman, O., Beyth-Marom, R., and Nachmias, R. (2006). The project fragmentation problem in personal information management. In *Proceedings of the SIGCHI Conference on Human Factors in Computing Systems* (pp. 271–274). Montreal, Quebec, Canada: ACM. DOI: 10.1145/1124772.1124813. 67, 89

Bergman, O., Beyth-Marom, R., Nachmias, R., Gradovitch, N., and Whittaker, S. (2008a). Improved search engines and navigation preference in personal information management. *ACM Trans. Inf. Syst.*, 26(4), 1–24. DOI: 10.1145/1402256.1402259. 89

Bergman, O., Beyth-Marom, R., Nachmias, R., and Whittaker, S. (2008b). The User-Subjective Approach: A New Direction for PIM Systems Design. In *PIM 2008, the Third International Workshop on Personal Information Management*. Florence, Italy. DOI: 10.1007/978-3-642-25691-2_3. 76, 102

Bergman, O., Gradovitch, N., Bar-Ilan, J., and Beyth-Marom, R. (2013). Folder versus tag preference in personal information management. *J. of the Ameri. Soc. for Inf. Sci. and Tech.*, n/a–n/a. DOI: 10.1002/asi.22906. 94, 101

Bergman, O., Whittaker, S., and Falk, N. (2014). Shared files: The retrieval perspective. *J. of the Assoc. for Inf. Sci. and Tech.*, n/a–n/a. DOI: 10.1002/asi.23147. 4

Bergman, O., Whittaker, S., Sanderson, M., Nachmias, R., and Ramamoorthy, A. (2012). How do we find personal files?: the effect of OS, presentation & depth on file navigation. In *Proceedings of the 2012 ACM annual conference on Human Factors in Computing Systems* (pp. 2977–2980). New York, NY, USA: ACM. DOI: 10.1145/2208636.2208707. 89

Bergman, O., Whittaker, S., Sanderson, M., Nachmias, R., and Ramamoorthy, A. (2010). The effect of folder structure on personal file navigation. *J. Am. Soc. Inf. Sci. Technol.*, 61(12), 2426–2441. DOI: 10.1002/asi.21415. 107

Berlin, L. M., Jeffries, R., O'Day, V. L., Paepcke, A., and Wharton, C. (1993). Where did you put it? : issues in the design and use of group memory. In *Conference on Human Factors and Computing Systems, INTERACT '93 AND CHI '93* (pp. 23–30). Amsterdam: ACM. Retrieved from http://portal.acm.org/citation.cfm?doid=169059.169063. 3

Bernstein, M., van Kleek, M., Karger, D., and Schraefel, M. C. (2008). Information scraps: How and why information eludes our personal information management tools. *ACM Trans. Inf. Syst.*, 26(4), 1–46. DOI: 10.1145/1402256.1402263. 72

Bjørn, P., Esbensen, M., Jensen, R. E., and Matthiesen, S. (2014). Does Distance Still Matter? Revisiting the CSCW Fundamentals on Distributed Collaboration. *ACM Trans. Comput.-Hum. Interact.*, 21(5), 27:1–27:26. DOI: 10.1145/2670534. 33

Blair, A. (2003). "Reading Strategies for Coping With Information Overload ca.1550-1700." *Journal of the History of Ideas* - Volume 64, Number 1, January 2003, pp. 11–28, Univ. Pennsylvannia Press. 137

Bloom, B. S. (1984). The 2 Sigma Problem: The search for methods of group instruction as effective as one-to-one tutoring. *Educational Researcher*, 13, 3–15. DOI: 10.3102/0013189X013006004. 28

Boardman, R., and Sasse, M. A. (2004). "Stuff goes into the computer and doesn't come out" A cross-tool study of personal information management. In *ACM SIGCHI Conference on Human Factors in Computing Systems (CHI 2004)*. Vienna, Austria. DOI: 10.1145/985692.985766. 64, 67, 82, 88, 100, 115

Boardman, R., Spence, R., and Sasse, M. A. (2003). Too many hierarchies? : the daily struggle for control of the workspace. In *HCI International 2003 : 10th International Conference on Human-Computer Interaction* (pp. p. 616–620). Crete, Greece. 139

Bolger, N., Davis, A., and Rafaeli, E. (2003). Diary methods: Capturing life as it is lived. *Annual Review of Psychology*, 54(1), 579–616. DOI: 10.1146/annurev.psych.54.101601.145030. 88

Bos, N., Karahalios, K., Musgrove-Chavez, M., Poole, E. S., Thomas, J. C., and Yardi, S. (2009). Research ethics in the facebook era: privacy, anonymity, and oversight. In *Proceedings of the 27th International Conference Extended Abstracts on Human Factors in Computing Systems* (pp. 2767–2770). Boston, MA, USA: ACM. 117

Boyd, D., and Hargittai, E. (2010). Facebook privacy settings: Who cares? First Monday, 15(8). Retrieved from http://www.uic.edu/htbin/cgiwrap/bin/ojs/index.php/fm/article/view/3086/2589. 117

Brown, B. A. T., Sellen, A. J., and O'Hara, K. P. (2000). A diary study of information capture in working life. In *Proceedings of the SIGCHI Conference on Human Factors in Computing Sys-*

tems (pp. 438–445). The Hague, The Netherlands: ACM. DOI: 10.1145/332040.332472. 88

Bruce, H. (2005). Personal, anticipated information need. Information Research, 10(3). Retrieved from http://informationr.net/ir/10-3/paper232.html. 101

Bruce, H., Wenning, A., Jones, E., Vinson, J., and Jones, W. (2010). Seeking an ideal solution to the management of personal information collections. In *Information Seeking in Context Conference -(ISIC) 2010.* Murcia, Spain. 64, 71, 89, 127

Bruns, A., and Humphreys, S. (2007). Building Collaborative Capacities in Learners: The M/Cyclopedia Project Revisited. In *Proceedings of the 2007 International Symposium on Wikis* (pp. 1–10). New York, NY, USA: ACM. DOI: 10.1145/1296951.1296952. 30

Brush, A. J. B., Lee, B., Mahajan, R., Agarwal, S., Saroiu, S., and Dixon, C. (2011). Home Automation in the Wild: Challenges and Opportunities. In *Proceedings of the SIGCHI Conference on Human Factors in Computing Systems* (pp. 2115–2124). New York, NY, USA: ACM. DOI: 10.1145/1978942.1979249. 24

Brynjolfsson, E., and Hitt, L. M. (2000). Beyond computation: Information technology, organizational transformation and business performance. *J. of Econ. Perspect.*, 23–48. DOI: 10.1257/jep.14.4.23. 1

Buckland, M. K. (1991). Information as thing. *J. of the Amer. Soc. for Inf. Sci.*, 42, 351–360. DOI: 10.1002/(SICI)1097-4571(199106)42:5<351::AID-ASI5>3.0.CO;2-3. 14

Burke, M., and Settles, B. (2011). Plugged in to the Community: Social Motivators in Online Goal-setting Groups. In *Proceedings of the 5th International Conference on Communities and Technologies* (pp. 1–10). New York, NY, USA: ACM. DOI: 10.1145/2103354.2103356. 43

Burns, P. J., Lueg, C., and Berkovsky, S. (2012). Using personal informatics to motivate physical activity: could we be doing it wrong? In *Chi 2012 Workshop* (pp. 1–4). Retrieved from http://ecite.utas.edu.au/81716. 118

Bush, V. (1945). As We May Think. *The Atlantic Monthly*, 176(1), 641–649. 5, 123

Capra, R. and Pérez-Quiñones, M. A. (2005). Mobile refinding of web information using a voice interface: an exploratory study. In *Proceedings of the 2005 Latin American conference on Human-computer interaction* (pp. 88–99). New York, NY, USA: ACM. DOI: 10.1145/1111360.1111369. 91, 101

Capra, R., Marchionini, G., Velasco-Martin, J., and Muller, K. (2010). Tools-at-hand and learning in multi-session, collaborative search. In *Proceedings of the SIGCHI Conference on*

Human Factors in Computing Systems (pp. 951–960). New York, NY, USA: ACM. DOI: 10.1145/1753326.1753468. 4

Capra, R., and Teevan, J. (2012). Personal Information Management in a Socially Networked World. In *Proceedings of the ACM 2012 Conference on Computer Supported Cooperative Work Companion* (pp. 1–2). New York, NY, USA: ACM. DOI: 10.1145/2141512.2141514. 1

Capra, R., Vardell, E., and Brennan, K. (2014). File Synchronization and Sharing: User Practices and Challenges. In *77th ASIS&T Annual Meeting*, October 31- November 5, 2014. Seattle, WA, USA. Retrieved from https://www.asis.org/asist2014/proceedings/submissions/papers/161paper.pdf. 3

Card, S. K., Moran, T. P., and Newell, A. (1983). *The Psychology of Human-Computer Interaction*. Hillsdale, NJ: Lawrence Erlbaum Associates. 6, 105

Cheng, P. C.-H. (2002). Electrifying diagrams for learning: principles for complex representational systems. *Cognitive Science*, 26(6), 685–736. 119

Choe, E. K., Lee, N. B., Lee, B., Pratt, W., and Kientz, J. A. (2014). Understanding Quantified-selfers' Practices in Collecting and Exploring Personal Data. In *Proceedings of the SIGCHI Conference on Human Factors in Computing Systems* (pp. 1143–1152). New York, NY, USA: ACM. DOI: 10.1145/2556288.2557372. 118

Christensen, C. M., Johnson, C. W., and Horn, M. B. (2008). *Disrupting Class: How Disruptive Innovation Will Change the Way the World Learns* (1st ed.). Mcgraw-Hill. 29

Christopher, A., and Faden, M. (2005). Tiger tweaks could kill folders. *Wired News*. Retrieved from http://www.wired.com/news/mac/0,2125,67774,00.html. 70

Civan, A., Jones, W., Klasnja, P., and Bruce, H. (2008). Better to Organize Personal Information by Folders Or by Tags?: The Devil Is in the Details. In *68th Annual Meeting of the American Society for Information Science and Technology (ASIST 2008)*. Columbus, OH. DOI: 10.1002/meet.2008.1450450214. 92, 101

Cline, H. F. (2014). *Information Communication Technology and Social Transformation* (1 edition). New York: Routledge. DOI: 10.1080/1369118X.2014.979219. 1

Colineau, N., and Paris, C. (2011). Motivating Reflection About Health Within the Family: The Use of Goal Setting and Tailored Feedback. *User Modeling and User-Adapted Interaction*, 21(4-5), 341–376. DOI: 10.1007/s11257-010-9089-x. 22

Corbett, A. (2001). Cognitive Computer Tutors: Solving the Two-Sigma Problem. In M. Bauer, P. J. Gmytrasiewicz, and J. Vassileva (Eds.), *User Modeling 2001* (pp. 137–147). Springer Berlin Heidelberg. Retrieved from http://link.springer.com/chapter/10.1007/3-540-44566-8_14. DOI: 10.1007/3-540-44566-8_14. 28

Costello, K. L. (2014). Similarity as a credibility cue in online support groups for chronic kidney disease. Retrieved from https://www.asis.org/asist2014/proceedings/submissions/posters/251poster.pdf. DOI: 10.1002/meet.2014.14505101105. 62

Csikszentmihalyi, M. (1991). *Flow: The Psychology of Optimal Experience.* HarperCollins. 73

Csikszentmihalyi, M., and Larson, R. (1987). Validity and reliability of the Experience-Sampling Method. *The Journal of Nervous and Mental Disease,* 175(9), 526–536. DOI: 10.1097/00005053-198709000-00004. 87

Czerwinski, M., Horvitz, E., and Wilhite, S. (2004). A Diary Study of Task Switching and Interruptions. In *Proceedings of the SIGCHI Conference on Human Factors in Computing Systems* (pp. 175–182). New York, NY, USA: ACM. DOI: 10.1145/985692.985715. 35, 68, 88, 101

Dabbish, L. A., and Kraut, R. E. (2006). Email overload at work: an analysis of factors associated with email strain. In *Proceedings of the 2006 20th anniversary conference on Computer supported cooperative work* (pp. 431–440). Banff, Alberta, Canada: ACM. DOI: 10.1145/1180875.1180941. 4

Danis, C., Kellogg, W. A., Lau, T., Dredze, M., Stylos, J., and Kushmerick, N. (2005). Managers' email: beyond tasks and to-dos. In *CHI '05 extended abstracts on Human factors in computing systems* (pp. 1324–1327). Portland, OR, USA: ACM. DOI: 10.1145/1056808.1056907. 2, 35

Davenport, T. H., and Prusak, L. (1997). *Information Ecology: Mastering the Information and Knowledge Environment.* Oxford University Press. Retrieved from http://dl.acm.org/citation.cfm?id=549584. 16

Day, R. S. (1988). Alternative representations. *Psychology of Learning and Motivation,* 22, 261–305. DOI: 10.1016/S0079-7421(08)60043-2. 7, 86

Denning, T., Kohno, T., and Levy, H. M. (2013). Computer Security and the Modern Home. *Commun. ACM,* 56(1), 94–103. DOI: 10.1145/2398356.2398377. 24

Dervin, B. (1992). From the mind's eye of the user: The sense-making qualitative-quantitative methodology. In *Qualitative Research in Information Management* (pp. 61–84). Englewood, CO: Libraries Unlimited. 119

Diekema, A. R., and Olsen, M. W. (2014). Teacher Personal information management (PIM) practices: Finding, keeping, and Re-Finding information. *J. of the Assoc. for Inf. Sci. and Tech.,* 65(11), 2261–2277. DOI: 10.1002/asi.23117. 27, 116, 119

Dillon, A., McKnight, C., and Richardson, J. (1993). Space - the final chapter or why physical representations are not semantic intentions. In *Hypertext: A Psychological Perspective* (pp.

169–192). New York: Ellis Horwood. Retrieved from http://telecaster.lboro.ac.uk/HaPP/chapter8.htmlhttp://www.ischool.utexas.edu/~adillon/BookChapters/space.html. 40

Dix, A., Finlay, J., Abowd, G. D., and Beal, R. (2004). Interaction design basics. Ch. 5 in *Human Computer Interaction*, 189–224. 56

Dourish, P., Lamping, J., and Rodden, T. (1999). Building bridges: customisation and mutual intelligibility in shared category management. In *Proceedings of the international ACM SIG-GROUP conference on Supporting group work* (pp. 11–20). ACM. Retrieved from http://dl.acm.org/citation.cfm?id=320299. DOI: 10.1145/320297.320299. 4

Economist, T. (2005). Death to folders! *The Economist Technology Quarterly*, 30–33. 70

Egelman, S., Tsai, J., Cranor, L. F., and Acquisti, A. (2009). Timing is everything?: the effects of timing and placement of online privacy indicators. In *Proceedings of the 27th International Conference on Human Factors in Computing Systems* (pp. 319–328). Boston, MA, USA: ACM. DOI: 10.1145/1518701.1518752. 117

Eisenberg, M., Lowe, C. A., and Spitzer, K. L. (2004). *Information Literacy : Essential Skills for the Information Age* (Vol. 2nd). Westport, CT.: Libraries Unlimited. 12

Elsden, C., and Kirk, D. S. (2014). A Quantified Past: Remembering with Personal Informatics. In *Proceedings of the 2014 Companion Publication on Designing Interactive Systems* (pp. 45–48). New York, NY, USA: ACM. DOI: 10.1145/2598784.2602778. 118

Engelbart, D. C. (1961). Special considerations of the individual as a user, generator and retriever of information. *American Documentation*, 12(2), 121–125. DOI: /10.1002/asi.5090120207. 123

Engelbart, D. C. (1963). A conceptual framework for the augmentation of man's intellect. In *Vistas inInformation Handling*. London: VI Spartan Books. 123

Engelbart, D. C., and English, W. K. (1968). A Research Center for Augmenting Human Intellect. In *Proceedings of the December 9-11, 1968, Fall Joint Computer Conference, Part I* (pp. 395–410). New York, NY, USA: ACM. DOI: 10.1145/1476589.1476645. 123

Erickson, T. (2006). From PIM to GIM: Personal Information Management in Group Contexts. *Commun. ACM*, 49(1), 74–75. DOI: 10.1145/1107458.1107495. 2

Ericsson, K. A., and Simon, H. A. (1980). Verbal reports as data. *Psychological Review*, 87(3), 215. DOI: 10.1037/0033-295X.87.3.215. 83

Ericsson, K. A., and Simon, H. A. (1998). How to study thinking in everyday life: Contrasting think-aloud protocols with descriptions and explanations of thinking. *Mind, Culture, and Activity*, 5(3), 178–186. DOI: 10.1207/s15327884mca0503_3. 83

Ersner-Hershfield, H. and Bailenson, J. (2008). A Vivid Future Self: Immersive Virtual Reality Enhances Retirement Saving Stanford University Jeremy Bailenson Stanford University. Presented at the Association for Psychological Science, Chicago, IL. Copyright (c) 2008 Association for Psychological Science. Used with permission. 63

Farhoomand, A. F., and Drury, D. H. (2002). Managerial information overload. *Communications of the ACM*, 45(10), 127–131. DOI: 10.1145/570907.570909. 2

Ferro, T. (2012). The rat city rollergirls and the potential of social networking sites to support work. In *Proceedings of the 30th ACM international conference on Design of communication* (pp. 157–166). New York, NY, USA: ACM. DOI: 10.1145/2379057.2379089. 33

Fisher, D., Brush, A. J., Gleave, E., and Smith, M. A. (2006). Revisiting Whittaker \& Sidner's "email overload" ten years later. In *Proceedings of the 2006 20th anniversary conference on Computer supported cooperative work* (pp. 309–312). Banff, Alberta, Canada: ACM. DOI: 10.1145/1180875.1180922. 4

Fourie, I. (2012). Collaboration and personal information management (PIM). *Library Hi Tech*, 30(1), 186–193. DOI: 10.1108/07378831211213292. 3

Froehlich, J. E., Kay, M., Larsen, J. E., and Thomaz, E. (2014). Disasters in Personal Informatics: The Unpublished Stories of Failure and Lessons Learned. In Proceedings of the 2014 ACM International Joint Conference on Pervasive and Ubiquitous Computing: Adjunct Publication (pp. 673–678). New York, NY, USA: ACM. DOI: 10.1145/2638728.2641315. 118

Furnas, G. W., Landauer, T. K., Gomez, L. M., and Dumais, S. T. (1987). The vocabulary problem in human-system communication. *Commun. ACM*, 30(11). DOI: 10.1145/32206.32212. 4

Garvey, W. D. (1979). *Communication, the Essence of Science: Facilitating Information Exchange among Librarians, Scientists, Engineers, and Students*. Oxford ; Pergamon Press. 1

Gleick, J. (2012). *The Information: A History, A Theory, A Flood* (2.5.2012 edition). New York: Vintage. 11, 61

Gollwitzer, P. M., and Sheeran, P. (2006). Implementation Intentions and Goal Achievement: A Meta-analysis of Effects and Processes. In *Advances in Experimental Social Psychology* (Vol. Volume 38, pp. 69–119). Academic Press. Retrieved from http://www.sciencedirect.com/science/article/pii/S0065260106380021. 121

González, V. M., and Mark, G. (2004). "Constant, Constant, Multi-tasking Craziness": Managing Multiple Working Spheres. In *Proceedings of the SIGCHI Conference on Human Factors in Computing Systems* (pp. 113–120). New York, NY, USA: ACM. DOI: 10.1145/985692.985707. 35, 121

Gould, J. D., and Lewis, C. (1985). Designing for usability: key principles and what designers think. *Commun. ACM*, 28(3), 300–311. DOI: 10.1145/3166.3170. 57

Graham, R. (2013, May 21). Knowledge Engines: James Gleick's The Information: A Summary. Retrieved from http://richardnvgraham.blogspot.com/2013/05/james-gleicks-information-summary.html. 11

Gray, W. D. (2008). Cognitive architectures: Choreographing the dance of mental operations with the task environment. *Human Factors: The Journal of the Human Factors and Ergonomics Society*, 50(3), 497–505. 105

Gray, W. D., and Fu, W.-T. (2001). Ignoring Perfect Knowledge In-the-world for Imperfect Knowledge In-the-head. In *Proceedings of the SIGCHI Conference on Human Factors in Computing Systems* (pp. 112–119). New York, NY, USA: ACM. DOI: 10.1145/365024.365061. 107

Gray, W. D., and Hills, T. (2014). Does cognition deteriorate with age or is it enhanced by experience? *Topics in Cognitive Science*, 6(1), 2–4. 107

Grondin, S. (2010). Timing and time perception: A review of recent behavioral and neuroscience findings and theoretical directions. *Attention, Perception, and Psychophysics*, 72(3), 561–582. http://doi.org/10.3758/APP.72.3.561. 74

Grudin, J. (1988). Why CSCW applications fail: problems in the design and evaluation of organization of organizational interfaces. DOI: 10.1145/62266.62273. 2, 76

Grudin, J. (1994). Computer-supported cooperative work: History and focus. *Computer*, 27(5), 19–26. DOI: 10.1109/2.291294. 2

Grudin, J. (2004). Managerial use and emerging norms: effects of activity patterns on software design and deployment. In *Proceedings of the 37th Annual Hawaii International Conference on System Sciences*, 2004 (p. 10 pp.–). DOI: 10.1109/HICSS.2004.1265111. 31

Grudin, J. (2011). Kai: how media affects learning. *Interactions*, 18(5), 70–73. DOI: 10.1145/2008176.2008192. 47

Grudin, J., and Poole, E. S. (2010). Wikis at Work: Success Factors and Challenges for Sustainability of Enterprise Wikis. In *Proceedings of the 6th International Symposium on Wikis and Open Collaboration* (pp. 5:1–5:8). New York, NY, USA: ACM. DOI: 10.1145/1832772.1832780. 35

Gulotta, R., Odom, W., Faste, H., and Forlizzi, J. (2014). Legacy in the Age of the Internet: Reflections on How Interactive Systems Shape How We Are Remembered. In *Proceedings of the 2014 Conference on Designing Interactive Systems* (pp. 975–984). New York, NY, USA: ACM. DOI: 10.1145/2598510.2598579. 23

Gulotta, R., Odom, W., Forlizzi, J., and Faste, H. (2013). Digital Artifacts As Legacy: Exploring the Lifespan and Value of Digital Data. In *Proceedings of the SIGCHI Conference on Human Factors in Computing Systems* (pp. 1813–1822). New York, NY, USA: ACM. DOI: 10.1145/2470654.2466240. 23

Guo, Y., Jones, M., Cowan, B., and Beale, R. (2013). Take It Personally: Personal Accountability and Energy Consumption in Domestic Households. In *CHI '13 Extended Abstracts on Human Factors in Computing Systems* (pp. 1467–1472). New York, NY, USA: ACM. DOI: 10.1145/2468356.2468618. 23

Gurak, L. J. (1991). Evaluating the use of metaphor in software interface design: a rhetorical approach. In *Professional Communication Conference, 1991. IPCC '91. Proceedings. The Engineered Communication., International* (Vol. 1 and 2, pp. 267–271 vol.2). DOI: 10.1109/IPCC.1991.172784. 59

Gurrin, C., Smeaton, A. F., and Doherty, A. R. (2014). LifeLogging: Personal Big Data. Found. Trends Inf. Retr., 8(1), 1–125. DOI: 10.1561/1500000033. 118

Halasz, F., and Moran, T. P. (1982). Analogy Considered Harmful. In *Proceedings of the 1982 Conference on Human Factors in Computing Systems* (pp. 383–386). New York, NY, USA: ACM. DOI: 10.1145/800049.801816. 59

Hanrahan, B. V. (2015). Getting Lost in Email: How and Why Users Spend More Time in Email than Intended. Retrieved from https://vtechworks.lib.vt.edu/handle/10919/51204. 115

Hanrahan, B. V., Pérez-Quiñones, M. A., and Martin, D. (2014). Attending to Email. *Interacting with Computers*, iwu048. 115

Hanrahan, W., and Pérez-Quiñones, M. (2015). Lost in Email: Pulling Users Down a Path of Interaction. In *CHI 2015* (p. in press). Seoul, Korea: ACM. 115

Hardof-Jaffe, S., and Aladjem, R. (2014). Collaborative evaluation of Personal Information Management (PIM) tools for learning contexts. In *World Conference on Educational Multimedia, Hypermedia and Telecommunications* (Vol. 2014, pp. 2441–2443). Retrieved from http://www.editlib.org/p/147817/. 26

Hardof-Jaffe, S., and Nachmias, R. (2011). Students' Goals and Strategies in Personal Information Management (Vol. 2011, pp. 1530–1536). Presented at the World Conference on Educational Media and Technology. Retrieved from http://www.editlib.org/p/38066/. 26

Hicks, B. J., Dong, A., Palmer, R., and Mcalpine, H. C. (2008). Organizing and managing personal electronic files: A mechanical engineer's perspective. *ACM Trans. Inf. Syst.*, 26(4), 1–40. 2, 31

Hollan, J., Hutchins, E., and Kirsh, D. (2000). Distributed Cognition: Toward a New Foundation for Human-computer Interaction Research. *ACM Trans. Comput.-Hum. Interact.*, 7(2), 174–196. DOI: 10.1145/353485.353487. 15

Hoofnagle, C. J. (2009). Beyond Google and evil: How policy makers, journalists and consumers should talk differently about Google and privacy [information privacy; privacy enhancing technologies; self-regulation]. Retrieved from http://firstmonday.org/htbin/cgiwrap/bin/ojs/index.php/fm/article/view/2326/2156. 117

Høyrup, S. (2004). Reflection as a core process in organisational learning. *Journal of Workplace Learning*, 16(8), 442–454. DOI: 10.1108/13665620410566414. 35

Hsu, J. (2008, September 18). The Secrets of Storytelling: Why We Love a Good Yarn: Scientific American. Retrieved January 22, 2012, from http://www.scientificamerican.com/article.cfm?id=the-secrets-of-storytelling#comments. 121

Hutchins, E. (1994). *Cognition in the Wild*. Cambridge, MA: MIT Press. 15, 119

Hutchins, E. (1995). How a Cockpit Remembers Its Speeds. *Cognitive Science*, 19(3), 265–288. DOI: 10.1207/s15516709cog1903_1. 15

Iachello, G., and Hong, J. (2007). End-user privacy in human-computer interaction. *Found. Trends Hum.-Comput. Interact.*, 1(1), 1–137. DOI: 10.1561/1100000004. 117

Irwin, T., Fine, G., and others. (1995). *Aristotle: Selections*. Hackett Publishing. Retrieved from https://books.google.com/books?hl=en&lr=&id=hrJDQ2MZ7LQC&oi=fnd&pg=PR9&dq=Terence+Irwin+and+Gail+Fine,+Cornell+University,+Aristotle:+Introductory+Readings.&ots=GLP2hor4Kf&sig=wC6i85lL4DWuJXVnzxfWxjHy1ng or http://tinyurl.com/nvvkgen, or http://tinyurl.com/q45tzql. 47

Jacques, J., and Fastrez, P. (2014). Personal Information Management Competences: A Case Study of Future College Students. In *Human Interface and the Management of Information. Information and Knowledge Design and Evaluation* (pp. 320–331). Springer. Retrieved from DOI: 10.1007/978-3-319-07731-4_33. 26

Janssen, J. H., Bailenson, J. N., IJsselsteijn, W. A., and Westerink, J. H. D. M. (2010). Intimate Heartbeats: Opportunities for Affective Communication Technology. *IEEE Trans. Affect. Comput.*, 1(2), 72–80. DOI: 10.1109/T-AFFC.2010.13. 37

Janssen, J. H., Ijsselsteijn, W. A., and Westerink, J. H. D. M. (2014). How Affective Technologies Can Influence Intimate Interactions and Improve Social Connectedness. *Int. J. Hum.-Comput. Stud.*, 72(1), 33–43. DOI: 10.1016/j.ijhcs.2013.09.007. 38

Jarusriboonchai, P., and Väänänen-Vainio-Mattila, K. (2012). Using Mobile Technology to Bring Families Together: The Design of a Family History Concept to Motivate Face-to-

Face Communication. *Int. J. Mob. Hum. Comput. Interact.*, 4(2), 1–17. DOI: 10.4018/jmhci.2012040101. 24

Jedrzejowski, A. M. (2009). *Photographs On A Refrigerator: A Display Of Visual Culture.* Ryerson University and George Eastman House. Retrieved from http://digitalcommons.ryerson.ca/download_ds/RULA%3A1708/OBJ/Photographs%20On%20A%20Refrigerator%20%3A%20A%20Display%20Of%20Visual%20Culture or http://tinyurl.com/nky56w7, or http://tinyurl.com/oteneur. 21

John, B. E., and Kieras, D. E. (1996). The GOMS family of user interface analysis techniques: Comparison and contrast. *ACM Transactions on Computer-Human Interaction*, 3, 320–351. DOI: 10.1145/235833.236054. 105

John, B. E., and Suzuki, S. (2009). Toward Cognitive Modeling for Predicting Usability. In J. A. Jacko (Ed.), Human-Computer Interaction. New Trends (pp. 267–276). Springer Berlin Heidelberg. Retrieved from http://link.springer.com/chapter/10.1007/978-3-642-02574-7_30. DOI: 10.1007/978-3-642-02574-7_30. 105

Johnson, M. L., Bellovin, S. M., Reeder, R. W., and Schechter, S. E. (2009). Laissez-faire file sharing: access control designed for individuals at the endpoints. In *Proceedings of the 2009 workshop on New security paradigms workshop* (pp. 1–10). ACM. DOI: 10.1145/1719030.1719032. 4

Johnson, R. D., Hornik, S., and Salas, E. (2008). An empirical examination of factors contributing to the creation of successful e-learning environments. *Int. J. of Hum.-Comp. Studies*, 66(5), 356–369. DOI: 10.1016/j.ijhcs.2007.11.003. 29

Jones, E., Bruce, H., Klasnja, P., and Jones, W. (2008). "I Give Up!" Five Factors that Contribute to the Abandonment of Information Management Strategies. Presented at the 68th Annual Meeting of the American Society for Information Science and Technology (ASIST 2008), Columbus, OH. DOI: 10.1002/meet.2008.14504503115. 76

Jones, S. R., and Thomas, P. J. (1997). Understanding interaction between office-based professionals for the development of advanced communication and information technologies. *J. Inf. Sci.*, 23(5), 353–364. DOI: 10.1177/0165551974231902. 2

Jones, W. (1988). "As we may think"?: Psychological considerations in the design of a personal filing system. In *Cognitive Science and Its Application for Human/Computer Interaction*. Hillsdale, NJ: Lawrence Erlbaum. 55, 107

Jones, W. (2004). Finders, keepers? The present and future perfect in support of personal information management. *First Monday*, 9(3). DOI: 10.5210/fm.v9i3.1123. 66

Jones, W. (2007). *Keeping Found Things Found: The Study and Practice of Personal Information Management*. San Francisco, CA: Morgan Kaufmann Publishers. 4, 6, 21, 36, 55, 67, 71, 75, 86, 136, 147, 148

Jones, W. (2010). No knowledge but through information. *First Monday*, 15(9). DOI, 67: 10.5210/fm.v15i9.3062. 11, 14, 101

Jones, W. (2012). *The Future of Personal Information Management, Part I: Our Information, Always and Forever* (Vol. 4). Morgan and Claypool Publishers. Retrieved from DOI: 10.2200/S00411ED1V01Y201203ICR021. 2, 5, 16, 26, 43, 51, 56, 60, 68, 75, 77, 79. 129

Jones, W. (2013). *Transforming Technologies to Manage Our Information: The Future of Personal Information Management, Part 2*. Synthesis Lectures on Information Concepts, Retrieval, and Services, 5(4), 1–179. DOI: 10.2200/S00532ED1V01Y201308ICR028. 9, 42, 54, 55, 56, 140

Jones, W., and Anderson, J. R. (1987). Short vs. long term memory retrieval: A comparison of the effects of information load and relatedness. *Journal of Experimental Psychology: General*, 116, 137–153. DOI: 10.1037/0096-3445.116.2.137. 74

Jones, W., and Bruce, H. (2005). A Report on the NSF-Sponsored Workshop on Personal Information Management, Seattle, WA, 2005. In *Personal Information Management 2005: A Special Workshop Sponsored by the National Science Foundation*. Seattle, WA, USA. Retrieved from http://pim.ischool.washington.edu/report%20NSF%20PIM%20workshop%20Seattle%202005%20draft.pdf. 66

Jones, W., Bruce, H., and Dumais, S. (2003). How do people get back to information on the web? How can they do it better? In *9th IFIP TC13 International Conference on Human-Computer Interaction (INTERACT 2003)*. Zurich, Switzerland. 77, 86, 87, 140

Jones, W., Bruce, H., Foxley, A., and Munat, C. (2006a). Planning personal projects and organizing personal information. In *69th Annual Meeting of the American Society for Information Science and Technology (ASIST 2006)* (Vol. 43). Austin, TX: American Society for Information Science and Technology. DOI: 10.1002/meet.14504301159. 67

Jones, W., Bruce, H., Jones, E., and Vinson, J. (2009). Providing for paper, place and people in personal projects. *Personal Information Intersections: What Happens When PIM Spaces Overlap*. Retrieved from http://pimworkshop.org/2009/papers/jones-pim2009.pdf. 89

Jones, W., Capra, R., Diekema, A., Teevan, J., Pérez-Quiñones, M., Dinneen, J. D., and Hemminger, B. (2015). "For Telling" the Present: Using the Delphi Method to Understand Personal Information Management Practices. In *Proceedings of the 33rd Annual ACM Conference on*

Human Factors in Computing Systems (pp. 3513–3522). New York, NY, USA: ACM. DOI: 10.1145/2702123.2702523. 71, 102, 108, 139, 140, 143

Jones, W., Dumais, S., and Bruce, H. (2002). Once found, what then? : A study of "keeping" behaviors in the personal use of web information. Presented at the *65th Annual Meeting of the American Society for Information Science and Technology (ASIST 2002)*, Philadelphia, PA. DOI: 10.1002/meet.1450390143. 2, 32, 82, 85, 99, 100, 116, 140

Jones, W., Hou, D., Sethanandha, B. D., Bi, S., and Gemmell, J. (2010). Planz to put our digital information in its place. In *Proceedings of the 28th of the International Conference Extended Abstracts on Human Factors in Computing Systems* (pp. 2803–2812). Atlanta, Georgia, USA: ACM. DOI: 10.1145/1753846.1753866. 120

Jones, W., and Maier, D. (2003). Personal information management group report. In *National Science Foundation (NSF) Information and Data Management (IDM) 2003 Workshop*. Retrieved from http://kftf.ischool.washington.edu/docs/Summary_of_PIM2003.pdf. 65

Jones, W., Munat, C., and Bruce, H. (2005a). The Universal Labeler: Plan the project and let your information follow. In *68th Annual Meeting of the American Society for Information Science and Technology (ASIST 2005)* (p. TBD.). Charlotte, NC: American Society for Information Science and Technology. Retrieved from http://kftf.ischool.washington.edu/UL_ASIST05.pdf. 66, 100, 119

Jones, W. (1986a). On the applied use of human memory models: the memory extender personal filing system. *International Journal of Man-Machine Studies*, 25(2), 191–228. DOI: 10.1016/S0020-7373(86)80076-1. 16, 55

Jones, W. (1986b). The Memory Extender Personal Filing System. In *Proceedings of the SIGCHI Conference on Human Factors in Computing Systems* (pp. 298–305). New York, NY, USA: ACM. DOI: 10.1145/22627.22387. 16, 55

Jones, W., Phuwanartnurak, A. J., Gill, R., and Bruce, H. (2005b). Don't take my folders away! Organizing personal information to get things done. In *ACM SIGCHI Conference on Human Factors in Computing Systems (CHI 2005)* (Vol. 2005, pp. 1505–1508). Portland, OR: ACM Press. 3, 65, 90, 115

Jones, W., Pirolli, P., Card, S. K., Fidel, R., Gershon, N., Morville, P., ... Russell, D. M. (2006b). "It's About the Information Stupid!": Why We Need a Separate Field of Human-information Interaction. In *CHI '06 Extended Abstracts on Human Factors in Computing Systems* (pp. 65–68). New York, NY, USA: ACM. DOI: 10.1145/1125451.1125469. 6, 16

Jones, W., Spool, J., Grudin, J., Bellotti, V., and Czerwinski, M. (2007). "Get Real!": What's Wrong with Hci Prototyping and How Can We Fix It? In *CHI '07 Extended Abstracts on Human*

Factors in Computing Systems (pp. 1913–1916). New York, NY, USA: ACM. DOI: /10.1145/1240866.1240922. 124

Jones, W., and Teevan, J. (2007). *Personal Information Management*. Seattle, WA: University of Washington Press. DOI: 10.1002/9780470713181.ch18. 55

Jones, W., Wenning, A., and Bruce, H. (2014). How Do People Re-find Files, Emails and Web Pages? In *iConference 2014 Proceedings*. Berlin, Germany. Retrieved from http://hdl.handle.net/2142/47300. 89, 94, 101

Jorgensen, D. L. (1989). *Participant Observation: A Methodology for Human Studies*. SAGE. 110

Juristo, N., Moreno, A. M., and Sanchez-Segura, M.-I. (2007). Analysing the impact of usability on software design. *Journal of Systems and Software*, 80(9), 1506–1516. DOI: 10.1016/j.jss.2007.01.006. 124

Kalnikaité, V., and Whittaker, S. (2007). Software or wetware?: discovering when and why people use digital prosthetic memory. In *Proceedings of the SIGCHI Conference on Human Factors in Computing Systems* (pp. 71–80). New York, NY, USA: ACM. DOI: 10.1145/1240624.1240635. 17

Karat, C.-M., Brodie, C., and Karat, J. (2007). Management of Personal Information Disclosure: The Interdependence of Privacy, Security and Trust. In *Personal Information Management*. Seattle: University of Washington Press. 117

Karger, D. R. (2007). Unify Everything: It's All the Same to Me. In *Personal Information Management*. (William Jones and Jaime Teevan). Seattle, WA: University of Washington Press. 71

Katzer, J., and Fletcher, P. T. (1992). The information environment of managers. *Annu. Rev. Inform. Sci. Technol.*, 27, 227–263. 2

Kelley, J. F. (1984). An Iterative Design Methodology for User-friendly Natural Language Office Information Applications. *ACM Trans. Inf. Syst.*, 2(1), 26–41. DOI: 10.1145/357417.357420. 91

Kelly, D., and Teevan, J. (2007). Understanding What Works:: Evaluating PIM Tools. In P*ersonal Information Management*. Seattle: University of Washington Press. 77

Khanipour Roshan, P., Jacobs, M., Dye, M., and DiSalvo, B. (2014). Exploring How Parents in Economically Depressed Communities Access Learning Resources. In *Proceedings of the 18th International Conference on Supporting Group Work* (pp. 131–141). New York, NY, USA: ACM. DOI: 10.1145/2660398.2660415.

Khovanskaya, V., Baumer, E. P., Cosley, D., Voida, S., and Gay, G. (2013). Everybody knows what you're doing: a critical design approach to personal informatics. In Proceedings of the SIGCHI Conference on Human Factors in Computing Systems (pp. 3403–3412). ACM. DOI: 10.1145/2470654.2466467. 118

Kidd, A. (1994). The marks are on the knowledge worker. In *ACM SIGCHI Conference on Human Factors in Computing Systems (CHI '94)* (pp. 186–191). Boston, MA: ACM. DOI: 10.1145/191666.191740. 16

Kirk, D. S., and Sellen, A. (2010). On Human Remains: Values and Practice in the Home Archiving of Cherished Objects. *ACM Trans. Comput.-Hum. Interact.*, 17(3), 10:1–10:43. DOI: 10.1145/1806923.1806924. 20, 22

Kirsh, D. (1995). The Intelligent use of space. *Artif. Intell.*, 73(1-2), 31–68. DOI: 10.1016/0004-3702(94)00017-U. 55

Kirsh, D. (2000). A few thoughts in cognitive overload. *Intellectica*, 30(1), 19–51. 119

Konnikova, M. (2015). Why MOOCs are Failing the People They're Supposed to Help. Retrieved April 6, 2015, from http://www.newyorker.com/science/maria-konnikova/moocs-failure-solutions. 28

Kotovsky, K., Hayes, J. R., and Simon, H. A. (1985). Why are some problems hard? Evidence from Tower of Hanoi. *Cognitive Psychology*, 17(2), 248–294. DOI: 10.1016/0010-0285(85)90009-X. 119

Kriplean, T., Beschastnikh, I., and McDonald, D. W. (2008). Articulations of Wikiwork: Uncovering Valued Work in Wikipedia Through Barnstars. In *Proceedings of the 2008 ACM Conference on Computer Supported Cooperative Work* (pp. 47–56). New York, NY, USA: ACM. DOI: 10.1145/1460563.1460573. 45

Kuutti, K. (2009). *HCI and Design: Uncomfortable Bedfellows.* Binder, Löwgren and Malmborg (eds.), 43–59. 124

Kwasnik, B. H. (1989). How a personal document's intended use or purpose affects its classification in an office. In *12th Annual ACM SIGIR Conference on Research and Development in Information Retrieval (SIGIR 1989)* (Vol. 23, pp. 207–210). Cambridge, MA: ACM SIGIR. Retrieved from DOI: 10.1145/75334.75356. 5, 83, 100

Lamanauskas, V., Šlekienė, V., and Ragulienė, L. (n.d.). Educational Facebook Usage Context: University Teachers and Students Position. Retrieved from http://oaji.net/articles/2014/514-1415817560.pdf. 29

Lamming, M., Brown, P., Carter, K., Eldridge, M., Flynn, M., Louie, G., ... Sellen, A. (1994). The design of a human memory prosthesis. *The Computer Journal*, 37(3), 153–163. DOI: 10.1093/comjnl/37.3.153. 16

Landauer, T. K. (1991). Let's get real: A position paper on the role of cognitive psychology in the design of humanly useful and usable systems. *Carroll* [101], 60–73. 106

Lansdale, M. (1988). The psychology of personal information management. *Appl. Ergon.*, 19(1), 55–66. DOI: 10.1016/0003-6870(88)90199-8. 4, 5, 82

Larkin, J. H., and Simon, H. A. (1987). Why a diagram is (sometimes) worth ten thousand words. *Cognitive Science*, 11(1), 65–100. DOI: 10.1111/j.1551-6708.1987.tb00863.x. 7, 119

Larson, R., and Csikszentmihalyi, M. (2014). The Experience Sampling Method. In *Flow and the Foundations of Positive Psychology* (pp. 21–34). Springer Netherlands. Retrieved from DOI: 10.1007/978-94-017-9088-8_2. 87

Lee, Y. L., and Ik, Y. H. (2014). Expanding the Uses of Blogs in the Classroom: How blogs support self-directed learning and personal information management. *eLearn*, 2014(12), 5. 29

Leftheriotis, I., and Giannakos, M. N. (2014). Using social media for work: Losing your time or improving your work? *Computers in Human Behavior*, 31, 134–142. DOI: 10.1016/j.chb.2013.10.016. 32

Li, I., Dey, A., and Forlizzi, J. (2010). A Stage-based Model of Personal Informatics Systems. In *Proceedings of the SIGCHI Conference on Human Factors in Computing Systems* (pp. 557–566). New York, NY, USA: ACM. DOI: 10.1145/1753326.1753409. 118

Li, I., Dey, A. K., and Forlizzi, J. (2011). Understanding my data, myself: supporting self-reflection with ubicomp technologies. In *Proceedings of the 13th International Conference on Ubiquitous Computing* (pp. 405–414). ACM. DOI: 10.1145/2030112.2030166. 118

Li, I., Medynskiy, Y., Froehlich, J., and Larsen, J. (2012). Personal informatics in practice: improving quality of life through data. In *CHI'12 Extended Abstracts on Human Factors in Computing Systems* (pp. 2799–2802). ACM. DOI: 10.1145/2212776.2212724. 118

Licklider, J. C. R. (1960). Man-computer symbiosis. *IRE Transactions on Human Factors in Electronics*, HFE-1, 4–11. DOI: 10.1109/THFE2.1960.4503259. 123

Licklider, J. C. R. (1965). *Libraries of the Future*. Cambridge, MA: The MIT Press. 123

Lindley, S. E. (2012). Before I Forget: From Personal Memory to Family History. *Human–Computer Interaction*, 27(1-2), 13–36. DOI: 10.1080/07370024.2012.656065. 24

Lutters, W. G., Ackerman, M. S., and Zhou, X. (2007). Group Information Management. In *Personal Information Management: Challenges and Opportunities*. Seattle, WA: University of Washington Press. 2, 3

Malone, T. W. (1983). How do people organize their desks: implications for the design of office information-systems. *ACM Transactions on Office Information Systems*, 1(1), 99–112. DOI: 10.1145/357423.357430. 5, 82, 99, 108

Marchionini, G. (1995). *Information Seeking in Electronic Environments*. Cambridge, UK: Cambridge University Press. DOI: 10.1017/CBO9780511626388. 5

Marchionini, G. (1999). Augmenting library services: Toward the sharium. In *Proceedings of International Symposium on Digital Libraries* (pp. 40–47). Retrieved from http://ils.unc.edu/~march/sharium/ISDL.pdf. 43

Marchionini, G. (2008). Human–information interaction research and development. *Library and Information Science Research*, 30(3), 165–174. DOI: 10.1016/j.lisr.2008.07.001. 16

Marchionini, G., Wildemuth, B. M., and Geisler, G. (2006). The Open Video Digital Library: A Möbius strip of research and practice. *J. of the Ameri. Soc. for Inf. Sci. and Tech.*, 57(12), 1629–1643. DOI: 10.1002/asi.20336. 43

Marcu, G., Dey, A. K., and Kiesler, S. (2014). Designing for Collaborative Reflection. In *Proceedings of the 8th International Conference on Pervasive Computing Technologies for Healthcare* (pp. 9–16). ICST, Brussels, Belgium, Belgium: ICST (Institute for Computer Sciences, Social-Informatics and Telecommunications Engineering). DOI: 10.4108/icst.pervasivehealth.2014.254987. 35

Mark, G. (2015). *Multitasking in the Digital Age*. Synthesis Lectures On Human-Centered Informatics, Morgan and Claypool Publishers. 8(3), 1–113. DOI: 10.2200/S00635ED1V01Y-201503HCI029. 69

Mark, G., Gonzalez, V. M., and Harris, J. (2005). No task left behind?: examining the nature of fragmented work. In *CHI 2005* (pp. 321–330). Portland, OR. DOI: 10.1145/1054972.1055017. 35

Mark, G., Gudith, D., and Klocke, U. (2008). The cost of interrupted work: more speed and stress. In *Proceeding of the Twenty-Sixth Annual SIGCHI Conference on Human Factors in Computing Systems* (pp. 107–110). Florence, Italy: ACM. DOI: 10.1145/1357054.1357072. 35

Mark, G., Iqbal, S., Czerwinski, M., and Johns, P. (2014). Capturing the Mood: Facebook and Face-to-face Encounters in the Workplace. In *Proceedings of the 17th ACM Conference* on *Computer Supported Cooperative Work & Social Computing* (pp. 1082–1094). New York, NY, USA: ACM. DOI: 10.1145/2531602.2531673. 34

Mark, G., and Prinz, W. (1997). What happened to our document in the shared workspace? The need for Groupware conventions. In *Human-Computer Interaction INTERACT'97* (pp. 413–420). Springer. Retrieved from DOI: 10.1007/978-0-387-35175-9_65. 3

Marlow, J., and Dabbish, L. (2011). Photo Sharing in Diverse Distributed Teams. In *Proceedings of the ACM 2011 Conference on Computer Supported Cooperative Work* (pp. 317–320). New York, NY, USA: ACM. DOI: 10.1145/1958824.1958872. 36

Marlow, J., and Dabbish, L. (2012). Designing Interventions to Reduce Psychological Distance in Globally Distributed Teams. In *Proceedings of the ACM 2012 Conference on Computer Supported Cooperative Work Companion* (pp. 163–166). New York, NY, USA: ACM. DOI: 10.1145/2141512.2141568. 36

Marshall, C. C. (2009). No Bull, No Spin: A Comparison of Tags with Other Forms of User Metadata. In *Proceedings of the 9th ACM/IEEE-CS Joint Conference on Digital Libraries* (pp. 241–250). New York, NY, USA: ACM. DOI: 10.1145/1555400.1555438. 121

Marshall, C. C., Bly, S., and Brun-Cottan, F. (2006). The Long Term Fate of Our Digital Belongings: Toward a Service Model for Personal Archives. *Archiving Conference*, 2006(1), 25–30. 116

Marshall, C. C., McCown, F., and Nelson, M. L. (2007). Evaluating personal archiving strategies for Internet-based information. In *Archiving Conference* (Vol. 2007, pp. 151–156). Society for Imaging Science and Technology. Retrieved from http://www.ingentaconnect.com/content/ist/ac/2007/00002007/00000001/art00036. 116

Marshall, C., and Tang, J. C. (2012). That Syncing Feeling: Early User Experiences with the Cloud. In *Proceedings of the Designing Interactive Systems Conference* (pp. 544–553). New York, NY, USA: ACM. DOI: 10.1145/2317956.2318038. 4

Mazurek, M. L., Arsenault, J. P., Bresee, J., Gupta, N., Ion, I., Johns, C., … Reiter, M. K. (2010). Access Control for Home Data Sharing: Attitudes, Needs and Practices. In *Proceedings of the SIGCHI Conference on Human Factors in Computing Systems* (pp. 645–654). New York, NY, USA: ACM. DOI: 10.1145/1753326.1753421. 24

Mézard, M., and Montanari, A. (2009). *Information, Physics, and Computation* (1 edition). Oxford ; New York: Oxford University Press. 11

Miller, A. (2014). *4 Lessons We Can Learn from the "Failure" of MOOCs*. Retrieved April 6, 2015, from http://www.edutopia.org/blog/4-lessons-from-failure-of-moocs-andrew-miller. 28

Miller, C. C., and Rampell, C. (2013, February 25). Yahoo Orders Home Workers Back to the Office. *The New York Times*. Retrieved from http://www.nytimes.com/2013/02/26/technology/yahoo-orders-home-workers-back-to-the-office.html. 34

Mintzberg, H. (1971). Managerial work: analysis from observation. *Management Science*, 18(2), B–97. DOI: 10.1287/mnsc.18.2.B97. 68

Mintzberg, H. (1973). *The Nature of Managerial Work*. New York, N.Y.: Harper and Row. 2

Mizrachi, D. (2013). Individuality and Diversity among Undergraduates' Academic Information Behaviors. *Int. J. of Knowl.Cont. Dev.t and Tech.*, 3(2), 29–42. DOI: 10.5865/IJKCT.2013.3.2.029. 5

Mizrachi, D., and Bates, M. J. (2013). Undergraduates' personal academic information management and the consideration of time and task-urgency. *J. of the Ameri. Soc. for Inf. Sci. and Tech.*, 64(8), 1590–1607. DOI: 10.1002/asi.22849. 5, 26, 64

Moggridge, B., and Atkinson, B. (2007). *Designing Interactions* (Vol. 17). MIT press Cambridge. Retrieved from http://ellieharmon.com/wp-content/uploads/01-21-Moggridge-People.pdf.pdf. 56

Mohammadyari, S., and Singh, H. (2015). Understanding the effect of e-learning on individual performance: The role of digital literacy. *Computers and Education*, 82, 11–25. DOI: /10.1016/j.compedu.2014.10.025. 29

Moore, A. D. (2010). *Privacy Rights: Moral and Legal Foundations*. Penn State Press. Retrieved from https://books.google.com/books?hl=en&lr=&id=ed-TtcfYE-MC&oi=fnd&pg=PR9&dq=Adam+D.+Moore,+2010,+%22Privacy+Rights:+Moral+and+Legal+Foundations,%22+Penn+State+University+Press.&ots=6BpOkOnT3h&sig=8G-PSsQEmsMFxg3cX-ahjb8ifnRI or http://tinyurl.com/oaguw89. 117

Moore, A. D. (2011). Privacy, security, and government surveillance: WikiLeaks and the new accountability. *Public Affairs Quarterly*, 141–156. 117

Morgan, J. T., Gilbert, M., McDonald, D. W., and Zachry, M. (2014). Editing Beyond Articles: Diversity and Dynamics of Teamwork in Open Collaborations. In *Proceedings of the 17th ACM Conference on Computer Supported Cooperative Work and Social Computing* (pp. 550–563). New York, NY, USA: ACM. DOI: 10.1145/2531602.2531654. 45

Morris, M. R., Teevan, J., and Panovich, K. (2010). A Comparison of Information Seeking Using Search Engines and Social Networks. *ICWSM*, 10, 23–26. 34

Muller, M. J. (2003). Participatory Design: The Third Space in HCI. *Human-Computer Interaction: Development Process*, 4235. Retrieved from https://books.google.com/books?hl=en&l-

r=&id=clMsHX-JfyMC&oi=fnd&pg=PA165&dq=participatory+design&ots=7r9P-5pgAIz&sig=5mfUwl_JNQ3hsL4xUipahJxwyqA or http://tinyurl.com/porkhjq. 110

Nelson, T. H. (1982). *Literary Machines*. Sausalito, CA: Mindful Press. 123

Nelson, T. H. (1999). Xanalogical structure, needed now more than ever: parallel documents, deep links to content, deep versioning, and deep re-use. *ACM Computing Surveys (CSUR)*, 31(4es), 33. DOI: 10.1145/345966.346033. 123

Neustaedter, C., Bartram, L., and Mah, A. (2013). Everyday activities and energy consumption: how families understand the relationship. In *Proceedings of the SIGCHI Conference on Human Factors in Computing Systems* (pp. 1183–1192). ACM. DOI: 10.1145/2470654.2466153. 22

Neustaedter, C., Brush, A. J. B., and Greenberg, S. (2009). The calendar is crucial: Coordination and awareness through the family calendar. *ACM Trans. Comput.-Hum. Interact.*, 16(1), 1–48. DOI: 10.1145/1502800.1502806. 22

Neustaedter, C., and Greenberg, S. (2012). Intimacy in long-distance relationships over video chat. In *Proceedings of the SIGCHI Conference on Human Factors in Computing Systems* (pp. 753–762). New York, NY, USA: ACM. DOI: 10.1145/2207676.2207785. 37

Nielsen, J. (1994). *Usability Engineering*. Elsevier. Retrieved from https://books.google.com/books?hl=en&lr=&id=DBOowF7LqIQC&oi=fnd&pg=PP1&dq=Nielsen,+J.+(1993)+The+usability+engineering+lifecycle&ots=Bk34QONUxR&sig=aLix-Ghl6ecE6DDl0oG6L-SfSQoA or http://tinyurl.com/oma7l82. 56

Norman, D. A. (1986). Cognitive engineering. *User Centered System Design: New Perspectives on Human-Computer Interaction, 3161*. Retrieved from http://itu.dk/~miguel/DesignReadings/Readings/Lecture%205%20-%20Where%20ideas%20come%20from/CognitiveEngineering.pdf. 104

Norman, D. A. (1993). *Things that Make Us Smart: Defending Human Attributes in the Age of the Machine*. Reading, MA: Addison-Wesley. 7

Novick, L. R. (1990). Representational transfer in problem solving. *Psychological Science*, 1(2), 128–132. DOI: 10.1111/j.1467-9280.1990.tb00081.x. 119

Novick, L. R., Hurley, S. M., and Francis, M. (1999). Evidence for abstract, schematic knowledge of three spatial diagram representations. *Memory and Cognition*, 27(2), 288–308. DOI: 10.3758/BF03211413. 119

O'Dell, C. S., and Essaides, N. (1998). *If Only We Knew What We Know: The Transfer of Internal Knowledge and Best Practice*. Simon and Schuster. Retrieved from https://books.google.com/books?hl=en&lr=&id=KTaVQdUfMIoC&oi=fnd&pg=PR9&dq=%22If+on-

ly+we+knew+what+we+know%22&ots=66OWgnMd1U&sig=-EEKUxFnM2489IM-bvjVHU0Emp2Y or http://tinyurl.com/p5fd2nb. 11, 14

Odlyzko, A. (1999). The visible problems of the invisible computer: A skeptical look at information appliances. *First Monday*. Retrieved from http://firstmonday.org/htbin/cgiwrap/bin/ojs/index.php/fm/article/view/688/598. DOI: 10.5210/fm.v4i9.688. 21

Odom, W., Banks, R., Durrant, A., Kirk, D., and Pierce, J. (2012). Slow Technology: Critical Reflection and Future Directions. In *Proceedings of the Designing Interactive Systems Conference* (pp. 816–817). New York, NY, USA: ACM. DOI: 10.1145/2317956.2318088. 35

Odom, W. T., Sellen, A. J., Banks, R., Kirk, D. S., Regan, T., Selby, M., ... Zimmerman, J. (2014). Designing for Slowness, Anticipation and Re-visitation: A Long Term Field Study of the Photobox. In *Proceedings of the 32Nd Annual ACM Conference on Human Factors in Computing Systems* (pp. 1961–1970). New York, NY, USA: ACM. DOI: 10.1145/2556288.2557178. 35

Olson, J. S., and Olson, G. M. (2014). How to Make Distance Work Work. *Interactions*, 21(2), 28–35. DOI: 10.1145/2567788. 33

Ong, W. J. (2007). *Orality and Literacy: The Technologizing of the Word* (2nd ed.). Taylor and Francis. 61

Orlikowski, W. (1992). Learning from Notes: organizational issues in groupware implementation. In *CSCW '92: Conference on Computer-Supported Cooperative Work* (pp. 362–369). Toronto, Canada. DOI: 10.1145/143457.143549. 3

Otopah, F. O. and Perpetua, D. (2013). Personal information management practices of students and its implications for library services. *Aslib Proceedings*, 65(2), 143–160. DOI: 10.1108/00012531311313970. 29

Pasek, J., more, eian, and Hargittai, E. (2009). Facebook and academic performance: Reconciling a media sensation with data. *First Monday*. Retrieved from http://firstmonday.org/htbin/cgiwrap/bin/ojs/index.php/fm/article/view/2498/2181. DOI: 10.5210/fm.v14i5.2498. 29

Peebles, D., and Cooper, R. P. (2015). Thirty years after Marr's Vision: Levels of analysis in Cognitive Science. *Topics in Cognitive Science*. Retrieved from http://eprints.hud.ac.uk/22188. 107

Perner, J. (1991). *Understanding the Representational Mind*. The MIT Press. Retrieved from http://psycnet.apa.org/psycinfo/1991-97901-000. 13

Petrelli, D. and Light, A. (2014). Family Rituals and the Potential for Interaction Design: A Study of Christmas. *ACM Trans. Comput.-Hum. Interact.*, 21(3), 16:1–16:29. DOI: 10.1145/2617571. 24

Petrelli, D., Bowen, S., Dulake, N., and Light, A. (2012). Digital Christmas: An Exploration of Festive Technology. In *Proceedings of the Designing Interactive Systems Conference* (pp. 348–357). New York, NY, USA: ACM. DOI: 10.1145/2317956.2318009. 24

Petrelli, D., Bowen, S., and Whittaker, S. (2014). Photo mementos: Designing digital media to represent ourselves at home. *International Journal of Human-Computer Studies*, 72(3), 320–336. DOI: 10.1016/j.ijhcs.2013.09.009. 20

Petrelli, D., Hoven, E. van den, and Whittaker, S. (2009). Making history: intentional capture of future memories. In *Proceedings of the 27th international conference on Human factors in computing systems* (pp. 1723–1732). Boston, MA, USA: ACM. DOI: 10.1145/1518701.1518966. 23

Pirolli, P. (2006). Cognitive models of human-information interaction. In *Handbook of Applied Cognition* (Vol. 2nd). West Sussex, England: John Wiley & Sons. 104, 105

Planet of the phones. (2015, February 28). The Economist. Retrieved from http://www.economist.com/news/leaders/21645180-smartphone-ubiquitous-addictive-and-transformative-planet-phones. 61

Polson, M. C., and Richardson, J. J. (2013). *Foundations of Intelligent Tutoring Systems*. Psychology Press. 28

Poore, M. (2012). *Using Social Media in the Classroom: A Best Practice Guide*. SAGE. 30

Porges, Z., Yang, X., Desai, A., Ho, C., Pallegedara, R., Razzaque, R., and Cosley, D. (2014). Achieve: Evaluating the Impact of Progress Logging and Social Feedback on Goal Achievement. In *Proceedings of the Companion Publication of the 17th ACM Conference on Computer Supported Cooperative Work & Social Computing* (pp. 221–224). New York, NY, USA: ACM. DOI: 10.1145/2556420.2556498. 44

Premack, D., and Woodruff, G. (1978). Does the chimpanzee have a theory of mind? *Behavioral and Brain Sciences*, 1(04), 515–526. DOI: 10.1017/S0140525X00076512. 13

Prensky, M. (2001). Digital natives, digital immigrants part 1. *On the Horizon*, 9(5), 1–6. DOI: 10.1108/10748120110424816. 26

Prilla, M., Degeling, M., and Herrmann, T. (2012). Collaborative Reflection at Work: Supporting Informal Learning at a Healthcare Workplace. In *Proceedings of the 17th ACM International Conference on Supporting Group Work* (pp. 55–64). New York, NY, USA: ACM. DOI: 10.1145/2389176.2389185. 35

Prilla, M., and Renner, B. (2014). Supporting Collaborative Reflection at Work: A Comparative Case Analysis. In *Proceedings of the 18th International Conference on Supporting Group Work* (pp. 182–193). New York, NY, USA: ACM. DOI: 10.1145/2660398.2660400. 35

Rapp, A., and Cena, F. (2014). Self-monitoring and Technology: Challenges and Open Issues in Personal Informatics. In *Universal Access in Human-Computer Interaction. Design for All and Accessibility Practice* (pp. 613–622). Springer. Retrieved from http://link.springer.com/chapter/10.1007/978-3-319-07509-9_58. DOI: 10.1007/978-3-319-07509-9_58. 118

Ravasio, P., Schär, S. G., and Krueger, H. (2004). In pursuit of desktop evolution: User problems and practices with modern desktop systems. *ACM Trans. Comput.-Hum. Interact.*, 11(2), 156–180. 115

Rick, J., and Guzdial, M. (2006). Situating CoWeb: a scholarship of application. *International Journal of Computer-Supported Collaborative Learning*, 1(1), 89–115. DOI: 10.1007/s11412-006-6842-6. 30

Rooksby, J., Rost, M., Morrison, A., and Chalmers, M. C. (2014). Personal Tracking As Lived Informatics. In Proceedings of the 32Nd Annual ACM Conference on Human Factors in Computing Systems (pp. 1163–1172). New York, NY, USA: ACM. DOI: 10.1145/2556288.2557039. 118

Roshan, K. P., Jacobs, M., Dye, M., and DiSalvo, B. (2014). Exploring How Parents in Economically Depressed Communities Access Learning Resources. In *Proceedings of the 18th International Conference on Supporting Group Work* (pp. 131–141). New York, NY, USA: ACM. DOI: 10.1145/2660398.2660415. 28

Rothensee, M. (2008). User Acceptance of the Intelligent Fridge: Empirical Results from a Simulation. In C. Floerkemeier, M. Langheinrich, E. Fleisch, F. Mattern, and S. E. Sarma (Eds.), *The Internet of Things* (pp. 123–139). Springer Berlin Heidelberg. Retrieved from DOI: 10.1007/978-3-540-78731-0_8. 21

Rowley, J. (2007). The wisdom hierarchy: representations of the DIKW hierarchy. *Journal of Information Science*, 33(2), 163–180. DOI: 10.1177/0165551506070706. 18

Rundus, D. (1971). Analysis of rehearsal processes in free recall. *Journal of Experimental Psychology*, 89(63-77). DOI: 10.1037/h0031185. 67

Russell, D. M., Stefik, M. J., Pirolli, P., and Card, S. K. (1993). The cost structure of sensemaking. In *Proceedings of the INTERACT'93 and CHI'93 Conference on Human Factors in Computing Systems*. New York, NY, USA: ACM. DOI: 10.1145/169059.169209. 119

Samson, T. (2012, August 8). Malware infects 30 percent of computers in U.S. Retrieved March 6, 2015, from http://www.infoworld.com/article/2618043/cyber-crime/malware-infects-30-percent-of-computers-in-u-s-.html. 116

Sas, C., and Whittaker, S. (2013). Design for Forgetting: Disposing of Digital Possessions After a Breakup. In *Proceedings of the SIGCHI Conference on Human Factors in Computing Systems* (pp. 1823–1832). New York, NY, USA: ACM. DOI: 10.1145/2470654.2466241. 38

Schmidt, K., and Simonee, C. (1996). Coordination mechanisms: Toward a conceptual foundation of CSCW systems design. *Computer Supported Cooperative Work (CSCW)*, 5(2-3), 155–200. DOI: 10.1007/BF00133655. 2

Schon, D. A. (1984). *The Reflective Practitioner: How Professionals Think In Action*. Basic Books. 35

Schuler, D., and Namioka, A. (1993). *Participatory Design: Principles and Practices*. L. Erlbaum Associates Inc. Retrieved from http://dl.acm.org/citation.cfm?id=563076. 110

Scissors, L. E., Roloff, M. E., and Gergle, D. (2014). Room for Interpretation: The Role of Self-esteem and CMC in Romantic Couple Conflict. In *Proceedings of the 32Nd Annual ACM Conference on Human Factors in Computing Systems* (pp. 3953–3962). New York, NY, USA: ACM. DOI: 10.1145/2556288.2557177. 38

Seffah, A., Gulliksen, J., and Desmarais, M. C. (2005). *Human-Centered Software Engineering-Integrating Usability in the Software Development Lifecycle* (Vol. 8). Springer Science and Business Media. Retrieved from https://books.google.com/books?hl=en&lr=&id=Fx-GORyRvm9oC&oi=fnd&pg=PR11&dq=Human-Centered+Software+Engineering%E2%80%94Integrating+Usability+in+the+Development+Process&ots=4H6c4X-mhWc&sig=KnK4Uf9WhZoAS8aKlLhYQCqaAeQ or http://tinyurl.com/pg5kp4v. DOI: 10.1007/1-4020-4113-6. 56

Seifert, C. M., and Patalano, A. L. (2001). Opportunism in memory: Preparing for chance encounters. *Current Directions in Psychological Science*, 10(6), 198–201. DOI: 10.1111/1467-8721.00148. 121

Sellen, A. J., and Whittaker, S. (2010). Beyond total capture: a constructive critique of lifelogging. *Commun. ACM*, 53(5), 70–77. DOI: 10.1145/1735223.1735243. 55

Settles, B., and Dow, S. (2013). Let's Get Together: The Formation and Success of Online Creative Collaborations. In *Proceedings of the SIGCHI Conference on Human Factors in Computing Systems* (pp. 2009–2018). New York, NY, USA: ACM. DOI: 10.1145/2470654.2466266. 43

Shannon, C. E. (1948). A mathematical theory of communication. *The Bell System Technical Journal*, 27, 379–423, 623–656. DOI: 10.1002/j.1538-7305.1948.tb00917.x. 1

Sheeran, P., Webb, T. L., and Gollwitzer, P. M. (2005). The Interplay Between Goal Intentions and Implementation Intentions. *Personality and Social Psychology Bulletin*, 31(1), 87 –98. DOI: 10.1177/0146167204271308. 121

Simon, H. A. (1957). *Models of Man: Social and Rational; Mathematical Essays on Rational Human Behavior in Society Setting.* New York: Wiley. 138

Simon, H. A. (1969). *The Sciences of the Artificial.* Cambridge, MA: MIT Press. DOI: 10.1126/science.165.3896.897. 136

Simon, H. A. (1971). Designing organizations for an information-rich world. In *Computers, Communications and the Public Interest* (pp. 40–41). Baltimore, MD: The Johns Hopkins Press. 1

Skeels, M. M., and Grudin, J. (2009). When Social Networks Cross Boundaries: A Case Study of Workplace Use of Facebook and Linkedin. In *Proceedings of the ACM 2009 International Conference on Supporting Group Work* (pp. 95–104). New York, NY, USA: ACM. DOI: 10.1145/1531674.1531689. 32

Sparrow, B., Liu, J., and Wegner, D. M. (2011). Google effects on memory: Cognitive consequences of having information at our fingertips. *Science*, 333(6043), 776 –778. DOI: 10.1126/science.1207745. 17, 138

Strauss, L. (1972). *Xenophon's Socrates.* Ithaca, New York; London: Cornell University Press, (hardcover, ISBN 0-8014-0712-5); South Bend, Indiana: St. Augustines Press, 2004 (paperback, ISBN 1-58731-966-7). 48

Swan, L. M. (2010). Artful Systems: Investigating everyday practices of family life to inform the. Retrieved from http://core.kmi.open.ac.uk/download/pdf/6113220.pdf. 21

Swan, L., and Taylor, A. S. (2005). Notes on fridge surfaces. In *CHI'05 extended abstracts on Human factors in computing systems* (pp. 1813–1816). ACM. Retrieved from http://dl.acm.org/citation.cfm?id=1057029. DOI: 10.1145/1056808.1057029. 21

Swan, L., Taylor, A. S., and Harper, R. (2008). Making Place for Clutter and Other Ideas of Home. *ACM Trans. Comput.-Hum. Interact.*, 15(2), 9:1–9:24. DOI: 10.1145/1375761.1375764. 22

Taylor, A. S., Swan, L., Eardley, R., Sellen, A., Hodges, S., and Wood, K. (2006). Augmenting refrigerator magnets: why less is sometimes more. In *Proceedings of the 4th Nordic conference on Human-computer interaction: changing roles* (pp. 115–124). ACM. Retrieved from http://dl.acm.org/citation.cfm?id=1182488. DOI: 10.1145/1182475.1182488. 21

Teevan, J., Alvarado, C., Ackerman, M. S., and Karger, D. R. (2004). The perfect search engine Is not enough: A study of orienteering behavior in directed search. In *ACM SIGCHI*

Conference on Human Factors in Computing Systems (CHI 2004) (pp. 415–422). Vienna, Austria. DOI: 10.1145/985692.985745. 87, 101

Terry, W. S. (1988). Everyday forgetting: Data from a diary study. *Psychological Reports*, 62, 299–303. DOI: 10.2466/pr0.1988.62.1.299. 88

Thayer, A., Bietz, M. J., Derthick, K., and Lee, C. P. (2012). I Love You, Let's Share Calendars: Calendar Sharing As Relationship Work. In *Proceedings of the ACM 2012 Conference on Computer Supported Cooperative Work* (pp. 749–758). New York, NY, USA: ACM. DOI: 10.1145/2145204.2145317. 38

Thayer, A., Sirjani, B., and Lee, C. P. (2013). Recalibrating the Ratio: Enacting Accountability in Intimate Relationships Using Shared Calendars. In *Proceedings of the 2013 Conference on Computer Supported Cooperative Work* (pp. 203–214). New York, NY, USA: ACM. DOI: 10.1145/2441776.2441801. 38

The Economist. (2012, From the print edition: Technology Quarterly, Q1). The quantified self: Counting every moment. The Economist. Retrieved from http://www.economist.com/node/21548493. 118

Thom-Santelli, J., and Millen, D. R. (2009). Learning by Seeing: Photo Viewing in the Workplace. In *Proceedings of the SIGCHI Conference on Human Factors in Computing Systems* (pp. 2081–2090). New York, NY, USA: ACM. DOI: 10.1145/1518701.1519017. 36

Thornton, K., and McDonald, D. W. (2012). Tagging Wikipedia: Collaboratively Creating a Category System. In *Proceedings of the 17th ACM International Conference on Supporting Group Work* (pp. 219–228). New York, NY, USA: ACM. DOI: 10.1145/2389176.2389210. 45

To do with the price of fish. (2007, May 10). The Economist. Retrieved from http://www.economist.com/node/9149142. 61

Tunick, M. (2013). Privacy and Punishment. *Social Theory and Practice*, 39(4), 643–668. 117

Vaishnavi, V. K., and Kuechler, W. (2015). Design science research methods and patterns: innovating information and communication technology. Crc Press. Retrieved from https://books.google.com/books?hl=en&lr=&id=a0SdFtH1yYQC&oi=fnd&pg=PR17&dq=Design+Science+Research+Methods+and+Patterns:+Innovating+Information+and+Communication+Technology&ots=jG_gSf7Ke7&sig=Z9inYe6qnDTmFTDJSEEIOp77ByM or http://tinyurl.com/nojgslr. DOI: 10.1201/b18448. 1

Van Alstyne, M., and Brynjolfsson, E. (2005). Global Village or Cyber-Balkans? Modeling and Measuring the Integration of Electronic Communities. Manage. *Science*, 51(6), 851–868. DOI: 10.1287/mnsc.1050.0363. 44

Van Kleek, M. G., Styke, W., and Karger, D. (2011). Finders/keepers: A longitudinal study of people managing information scraps in a micro-note tool. In *Proceedings of the SIGCHI Conference on Human Factors in Computing Systems* (pp. 2907–2916). ACM. Retrieved from http://dl.acm.org/citation.cfm?id=1979374. DOI: 10.1145/1978942.1979374. 72

Venkatesan, H., Biuk-Aghai, R. P., and Notari, M. (2014). Collaborative Learning of Translation: The Case of TransWiki in Macao. In *Proceedings of The International Symposium on Open Collaboration* (pp. 45:1–45:10). New York, NY, USA: ACM. DOI: 10.1145/2641580.2641629. 30

Von Ahn, L. (2006). Games with a purpose. *Computer*, 39(6), 92–94. DOI: 10.1109/MC.2006.196.

Von Ahn, L., Maurer, B., McMillen, C., Abraham, D., and Blum, M. (2008). recaptcha: Human-based character recognition via web security measures. *Science*, 321(5895), 1465–1468. DOI: 10.1126/science.1160379. 44

Wang, R., Scown, P., Urquhart, C., and Hardman, J. (2014). Tapping the educational potential of Facebook: Guidelines for use in higher education. *Education and Information Technologies*, 19(1), 21–39. DOI: 10.1007/s10639-012-9206-z. 29

Wenger, E. (2014). *Artificial Intelligence and Tutoring Systems: Computational and Cognitive Approaches to the Communication of Knowledge*. Morgan Kaufmann. Retrieved from https://books.google.com/books?hl=en&lr=&id=6ymjBQAAQBAJ&oi=fnd&pg=PP1&ots=-ZpEgc-QrUd&sig=HIoE9XgIs0KdUyFH0fgAEQY9Aw4 or http://tinyurl.com/q5kbpkj. 28

Whittaker, S., and Hirschberg, J. (2001). The character, value and management of personal paper archives. *ACM Transactions on Computer-Human Interaction*, 8(2), 150–170. DOI: 10.1145/376929.376932. 82, 83, 100

Whittaker, S., Bergman, O., and Clough, P. (2010). Easy on That Trigger Dad: A Study of Long Term Family Photo Retrieval. *Personal Ubiquitous Comput.*, 14(1), 31–43. DOI: 10.1007/s00779-009-0218-7. 93, 100

Whittaker, S., Matthews, T., Cerruti, J., Badenes, H., and Tang, J. (2011). Am I wasting my time organizing email?: a study of email refinding. In P*ART 5 -------- Proceedings of the 2011 annual conference on Human factors in computing systems* (pp. 3449–3458). Vancouver, BC, Canada: ACM. DOI: 10.1145/1978942.1979457. 89, 101

Whittaker, S., and Sidner, C. (1996). Email overload: exploring personal information management of email. Retrieved from http://www.acm.org/sigchi/chi96/proceedings/papers/Whittaker/sw_txt.htm. DOI: 10.1145/238386.238530. 4

Winter, S. (1964). Economic "Natural Selection" and the Theory of the Firm (LEM Chapters Series) (pp. 225–272). Laboratory of Economics and Management (LEM), Sant'Anna

School of Advanced Studies, Pisa, Italy. Retrieved from http://econpapers.repec.org/bookchap/ssalemchs/winter-1964.htm. 123

Wobbrock, J. O. (2015). How Millennials Require Us to Design the Technologies of Tomorrow. Retrieved June 13, 2015, from http://insights.wired.com/profiles/blogs/how-millennials-require-us-to-design-the-technologies-of-tomorrow. 136

Woelfer, J. P., and Hendry, D. G. (2010). Homeless Young People's Experiences with Information Systems: Life and Work in a Community Technology Center. In *Proceedings of the SIGCHI Conference on Human Factors in Computing Systems* (pp. 1291–1300). New York, NY, USA: ACM. DOI: 10.1145/1753326.1753520. 25

Woelfer, J. P., and Hendry, D. G. (2011). Homeless Young People and Living with Personal Digital Artifacts. In *Proceedings of the SIGCHI Conference on Human Factors in Computing Systems* (pp. 1697–1706). New York, NY, USA: ACM. DOI: 10.1145/1978942.1979190. 25

Wu, M., Birnholtz, J., Richards, B., Baecker, R., and Massimi, M. (2008). Collaborating to Remember: A Distributed Cognition Account of Families Coping with Memory Impairments. In *Proceedings of the SIGCHI Conference on Human Factors in Computing Systems* (pp. 825–834). New York, NY, USA: ACM. DOI: 10.1145/1357054.1357186. 25

Wulf, V. (1997). Storing and retrieving documents in a shared workspace: experiences from the political administration. In *Human-Computer Interaction INTERACT'97* (pp. 469–476). Springer. Retrieved from DOI: 10.1007/978-0-387-35175-9_72. 3

Yardi, S., and Bruckman, A. (2012). Income, Race, and Class: Exploring Socioeconomic Differences in Family Technology Use. In *Proceedings of the SIGCHI Conference on Human Factors in Computing Systems* (pp. 3041–3050). New York, NY, USA: ACM. DOI: 10.1145/2207676.2208716. 23

Ylirisku, S., Lindley, S., Jacucci, G., Banks, R., Stewart, C., Sellen, A., … Regan, T. (2013). Designing Web-connected Physical Artefacts for the "Aesthetic" of the Home. In *Proceedings of the SIGCHI Conference on Human Factors in Computing Systems* (pp. 909–918). New York, NY, USA: ACM. DOI: 10.1145/2470654.2466117. 23

Zalinger, J. M. (2011). Gmail as storyworld: How technology shapes your life narrative (Ph.D.). Rensselaer Polytechnic Institute, United States—New York. Retrieved from http://search.proquest.com/docview/894086292/abstract?accountid=14784. 62

Zhang, H., De Choudhury, M., and Grudin, J. (2014). Creepy but Inevitable?: The Evolution of Social Networking. In *Proceedings of the 17th ACM Conference on Computer Supported Cooperative Work & Social Computing* (pp. 368–378). New York, NY, USA: ACM. DOI: 10.1145/2531602.2531685. 33

Zhang, J., Qu, Y., Cody, J., and Wu, Y. (2010). A case study of micro-blogging in the enterprise: use, value, and related issues. In *Proceedings of the SIGCHI Conference on Human Factors in Computing Systems* (pp. 123–132). New York, NY, USA: ACM. DOI: 10.1145/1753326.1753346. 34, 35

Zhao, D., and Rosson, M. B. (2009). How and why people Twitter: the role that micro-blogging plays in informal communication at work. In *Proceedings of the ACM 2009 international conference on Supporting group work* (pp. 243–252). New York, NY, USA: ACM. DOI: 10.1145/1531674.1531710. 34

Zhao, X., Schwanda Sosik, V., and Cosley, D. (2012). It's Complicated: How Romantic Partners Use Facebook. In *Proceedings of the SIGCHI Conference on Human Factors in Computing Systems* (pp. 771–780). New York, NY, USA: ACM. DOI: 10.1145/2207676.2207788. 38

Zins, C. (2007). Conceptual Approaches for Defining Data, Information, and Knowledge. *J. of the Ameri. Soc. for Inf. Sci. and Tech.*, 58(4), 479–493. DOI: 10.1002/asi.20508. 11

Author Biography

William Jones is a Research Associate Professor in the Information School at the University of Washington where he works on the challenges of "Keeping Found Things Found" (kftf.ischool.washington.edu). He has published in the areas of personal information management (PIM), human-computer interaction, information retrieval, and human cognition. Prof. Jones wrote the book *Keeping Found Things Found: The Study and Practice of Personal Information Management* and, more recently, *The Future of Personal Information, Part 1: Our Information, Always and Forever"* (for which this book is Part 3).

He holds several patents relating to search and PIM from his work as a program manager at Microsoft in Office and then in MSN Search. Prof. Jones received his doctorate from Carnegie-Mellon University for research into human memory.